T0265853

The Apostle and the Empire

THE APOSTLE
AND THE EMPIRE

Paul's Implicit and Explicit Criticism of Rome

CHRISTOPH HEILIG

WILLIAM B. EERDMANS PUBLISHING COMPANY

GRAND RAPIDS, MICHIGAN

Wm. B. Eerdmans Publishing Co.
4035 Park East Court SE, Grand Rapids, Michigan 49546
www.eerdmans.com

28 27 26 25 24 23 22   1 2 3 4 5 6 7

ISBN 978-0-8028-8223-3

Library of Congress Cataloging-in-Publication Data

A catalog record for this book is available from the Library of Congress.

To my fellow early career scholars—
to those who are succeeding,
to those who are still struggling,
and to those who have already given up

CONTENTS

FIGURES

FOREWORD

Over the last two decades, a significant debate has broken out among scholars regarding the relationship between Paul and the political realities of the Roman Empire. What sparked this (new phase of an old) debate was the suggestion that Paul's letters hide a "subtext" that in hidden or "coded" form proves to be far more critical of Rome than might appear on the surface of the text. Christoph Heilig has played a central role in this discussion. His *Hidden Criticism? The Methodology and Plausibility of the Search for a Counter-Imperial Subtext in Paul* (2015; US edition, with new preface, 2017) introduced a methodological rigor into the debate that was sorely lacking before, while his subsequent monograph, *Paul's Triumph: Reassessing 2 Corinthians 2:14 in Its Literary and Historical Context* (2017), offered a superb case study, analyzing a text where Paul evokes the distinctively Roman practice of the "triumph." For good reason, the debate has not gone away, and in this new monograph Heilig takes into account the latest contributions and modifies, sharpens, and develops his previous work in order to offer fresh and provocative proposals for future discussion. Much is here at stake. To what extent and in what way were Paul and his fellow believers in danger in the Roman political environment? With what tools should we read Paul's texts to discern what might lie "between the lines"? How do we determine what is a plausible hypothesis and distinguish it from what is merely possible? And what might we learn from this about the contours and the contextual specificity of Paul's theology? Since the relationship between the church and state authorities is of acute present-day significance, these historical and exegetical questions have a contemporary resonance that makes this book and its subject matter of interest well beyond the confines of New Testament academia.

Among the many strengths of this book is its mastery of historical detail. Building on recent analysis of the Trajan-Pliny correspondence, Heilig here offers a bold thesis that the degree of popular suspicion regarding Paul's message and its social effects meant that to be a Christ believer was, from the very beginning, "'punishable' in practice if not 'prohibited' in theory." This, he rightly insists, was not dependent on official Roman judgments after the fire of Rome (64 CE) or during the reign of Domitian (81–96 CE): it was an ever-present possibility whose realization depended on the strength of local opposition and the arbitrary decisions of local governors. Thus, when considering Paul's discourse, we have to judge what he might consider to be expedient for young and fragile communities, which did not need more trouble than was absolutely necessary. With similar historical acumen, Heilig turns, in the second half of this book, to the "triumph" reference in 2 Cor 2:14. This, he argues, echoes Claudius's bombastic triumph over the Britons in 44 CE, among whose results was a priesthood *in Corinth* dedicated to the Victoria Britannica. Seen in this light, Paul emerges as an "engaged observer" of his contemporary, local political environment, and the detailed argument concerning this one case should make us open to finding reference to specific, local political phenomena elsewhere in Paul's letters.

One of the refreshing features of Heilig's academic style is his refusal to accept the binary "all or nothing" alternatives that have often characterized the debate about "Paul and Rome": either Paul was an opponent of the Roman Empire (while writing about it in coded terms) or he was politically ignorant, quiescent, or naïve. Heilig is always alert to a spectrum of options, to gray areas, and to fuzzy lines (e.g., the much-discussed line between "hidden" and "public" transcripts). There could be some things on the surface of Paul's texts, and some things deliberately not said; some points where Paul is openly subversive, and some points where he is ambiguous; some texts where the object of critique is highly specific, and others where Paul's statements, or their implications, are general. Written with such nuance, this book does not close down debate but opens it up for further discussion. There is a healthy mixture here of caution and robust argument, of modesty (even self-criticism) and boldness. Those scholars who have contributed to this debate thus far will find themselves at times directly critiqued, but the end result of this book is an invitation to dig deeper, collaborate more effectively, and think harder about how to read Paul well.

Heilig offers many proposals about reading Paul better, but among these I select just three. First, he asks us to consider what Paul might have left unsaid in his letters—neither on the surface, nor hidden in "code"—things that could have been said orally in person or through letter bearers, but that he neither needed nor wanted to put into his carefully focused letters. One reason for that silence could have been a concern not to be more politically provocative than was absolutely necessary for the reception and practice of the "good news." Second, Heilig suggests that we should turn our attention away from the possibility of "coded" criticism—which has been the obsession of much recent debate—and should look more carefully at what is said in plain sight on the surface of the text, in passages like 1 Cor 2:6–8 and 2 Cor 2:14–16. These may be casual or incidental comments, but all the more revealing for that, like tips of icebergs that betray deep structures of thought (whether or not those are "encoded" elsewhere). And third, Heilig suggests that we should add more nuance to claims that Paul was "critical" of the Roman Empire: criticism can be indirect as well as direct, specific as well as general, and sometimes more like wariness or "unease" (German: *Unmut*) than full-blown critique.

Speaking personally, I have received both instruction and correction at many points in this book, and for that I am immensely grateful. But I wonder whether what Paul said mattered as much as what Paul did, and what he encouraged fellow believers to do. In Roman eyes, comparatively insignificant provincials might perhaps say all manner of scurrilous things about the emperor, but what really mattered was if they honored or, alternatively, dishonored (e.g., removed or defaced) an image of the emperor. Actions spoke a lot louder than words, and it is not by accident that Paul encouraged the payment of taxes (Rom 13:6–7), whose refusal would have said something very loud and clear. And, on a larger front, I still wonder how we should understand Paul's politics within the frame of his theology. Anyone familiar with 1 Cor 1–2 knows that Paul is a deeply subversive thinker: in the light of the crucifixion of God's Messiah, *all* human evaluations of power and of wisdom are undercut in the most fundamental way imaginable. With his "apocalyptic" dichotomy between the wisdom of God and the wisdom of "the world," Paul was not likely to be impressed by *any* political ideology, Roman or otherwise, and we can hardly be surprised if his theology is subversive in Roman terms. But was there something special about *Roman* power, religion, and justice that Paul thought particularly ludicrous or impious, or did he categorize that as yet another expression of the stupidity of "the present evil age" (Gal 1:4)? If he had traveled to Parthia, or to Scotland, would he have expected to find something less problematic because it was not Roman? No doubt there are points where his acute sense of local circumstances enabled Paul to find specific examples of the corruption that infected the whole human condition, but it may be only from our perspective that this looks like a specific critique of the *Roman* empire or of *Roman* imperial ideology. Even those who crucified Jesus are labeled by Paul "the rulers of this age" (1 Cor 2:8), as if what matters to him is that they belong to "this age" rather than to the new creation now impinging on all reality since the death and resurrection of Christ. And if this "new creation" is a divinely sourced, apocalyptic reality, is it in principle in *direct competition* with the Roman emperor? Does the triumph of God, the source and completion of all reality, necessarily "push the emperor out of his *quadriga*," as is here suggested in vivid terms? Perhaps the point is that *any* human triumphal procession is of nugatory significance in the larger scheme of things, where the real triumph is the spread of God's grace and life into a decaying world, and the end result is not the replacement of one mortal "Lord" by another, but the defeat of death itself and the accompanying transformation of the whole of creation.

I pose those questions only as a reflection of the enormous stimulus provided by this important book. Heilig has taken the conversation a significant step forward—further than others and further than his own earlier work on this subject. Everyone has something to learn here, and something to ponder, and no one could emerge other than grateful for this fine analysis of a complex and significant topic.

John M. G. Barclay

I wrote my first book on the topic of Paul and Empire—*Hidden Criticism?*—while I was studying for my master's degree at the University of St. Andrews ten years ago. It was the work of someone who was only just discovering the manifold aspects and dynamics of New Testament studies. Still, some of these early observations have stood the test of time and even proven stimulating for further enhancing the debate surrounding this issue. To me, this is not only a personal success, but also a testament to what early career scholars in general have to offer. To be sure, my work lacked, for example, the depth that a senior scholar would have been able to demonstrate with respect to primary sources. But as someone who was coming to this topic without the baggage of a long academic career, I had, among other things, an eye for the places where the scholarly discourse had come to an impasse or diverged into different directions due to unaddressed presuppositions. Now, I am returning to the question of whether or not Paul's letters exhibit a "coded" criticism of Caesar in light of the work of another early career scholar, Laura Robinson, who is currently completing her doctoral degree at Duke University. Her *NTS* article from 2021 on alleged "hidden transcripts" in Paul's letters caught my attention in that she, too, contributed to the issue of a counter-imperial interpretation of Paul in a way that addressed issues at the very basis of this subtext-hypothesis. Since it was her lively argument that prompted me to revisit the question of whether or not we can find an attack against the Roman Empire between the lines in Paul's letters, it seemed very fitting to me to dedicate this book to my fellow early career scholars, emphasizing with this dedication the conviction that we have indeed a lot to contribute to our field—if we are offered opportunities to flourish.

I want to take this opportunity to really underline this last part. After all, it was the carefreeness of my time in St. Andrews that caused me, almost naively, to spend my free time tackling one of the burning issues in Pauline studies. And it was only due to the support of senior scholars who had made the advancement of early career scholars a high priority of their work that it had any impact. This begins with Prof. Jörg Frey, Zurich, who showed an interest in my work and encouraged me to submit it for review for WUNT 2, and it reaches its end, for the moment at least, with Prof. Moisés Mayordomo, Basel, who has likewise supported me in every imaginable way in pursuing my own research interests. And on the way, as a constant companion, there has been Prof. Wayne Coppins, Athens, Georgia, who has once again read the entire manuscript and accompanied the whole process with his friendship. I also want to single out one particular person who made a big difference for me with his support early on, while I was still working on my first book. Prof. John M. G. Barclay, Durham, did not think it beneath him to answer the bold email of a young student who had sent him a draft of an article in which he dared to critique him quite strongly, and on top of that a list of time-consuming questions. The effect of his humble and encouraging response on my further career cannot be overestimated. For this reason, I feel especially honored by the fact that he has now contributed such a kind foreword to the present book. I hope that the reminder of what a difference a single email to a student can make and the choice of this dedication may serve as a nudge for senior scholars to follow this model and to similarly invest or continue to invest in the work of early career scholars.

I write this preface with not only gratefulness in my heart, however. There is also concern for myself and my peers regarding our ability to eventually find a permanent position, and sadness about all those who have already had to drop out of this race. To be sure, I am heartened by seeing that our generation seems by and large to adopt a very supportive attitude toward each other. The interest that I encountered with respect to this project and that kept me going came largely from other early career scholars. I want to mention Emily Gathergood (PhD) representatively for this group of peers who cheered me on with their enthusiasm. Others, like Mike Aubrey (MA), Clint Burnett (PhD), Jacob Cerone (ThM), Chris Fresch (PhD), and Sarah Blake LaRose (DMin), even read through the manuscript or significant parts of it, giving me very valuable feedback. Still, the joy that comes from experiencing this cooperative attitude is clouded by the many stories that early career scholars can tell about the pressures that they experience in academia every day. There is a certain irony to the fact that this book ultimately goes back to an (unsuccessful) job interview (though it gives me some satisfaction that I managed to submit the final manuscript to the publisher before the university could send me their rejection letter). While I seek to remain optimistic about my academic future, it is difficult to know that some of the most talented people I know have already felt the need to drop out of the race for permanent positions. Honoring their contributions with a dedication is poor consolation for the void that they have left. And they will not be the last voices to disappear from our daily discussions. I hope we will soon find solutions that will make academia a kinder, more humane environment that is conductive to the development of early career scholars.

After these rather sorrowful remarks, I am of course expected to close this preface on a lighter note. To this end, I want to share two small pieces of information with you that are almost guaranteed to brighten your day at least a little bit. First, please note that when speaking about the meaning of words I use double quotation marks for glosses and single quotation marks for their corresponding concepts and for definitions that aim at fleshing them out verbally more fully. It is a practice that costs little effort, and if you are not already following a similar convention, I encourage you to adopt it, too. Our lives as biblical scholars will suddenly become much more enjoyable. Second, while the absurdity of the amount of information that I have acquired concerning Roman sarcophagi and spolia in the process of tracking down figure 12 comes in a close second, the actually most useless and still most amusing thing I have learned during the production of this book is that elephant jokes apparently go back to an outburst of creativity among the US population in the 1960s (Ed Cray and Marilyn Eisenberg Herzog, "The Absurd Elephant: A Recent Riddle Fad," *Western Folklore* 26 [1967]: 27–36).

Ulm/Basel
June 24, 2022

ABBREVIATIONS

Primary Sources

BGU	*Ägyptische Urkunden aus den Königlichen Staatlichen Museen zu Berlin, Griechische Urkunden.* 19 vols. Berlin: Weidmann, 1895–
CIL	*Corpus Inscriptionum Latinarum.* 17 vols. Berlin, 1862–
CCSL	Corpus Christianorum: Series Latina
IG XII	*Inscriptiones Graecae,* XII: *Inscriptiones insularum maris Aegaei praeter Delum: 4. Inscriptiones Coi, Calymnae, Insularum Milesiarum.* Edited by Dimitris Bosnakis and Klaus Hallof. Berlin: de Gruyter, 2012
IKosPH	Paton, William R., and Edward L. Hicks, eds. *The Inscriptions of Cos.* Oxford, 1891. Reprint: Hildesheim, 1990
IRhodM	Maiuri, Amedeo, ed. *Nuova silloge epigrafica di Rodi e Cos.* Florence: Le Monnier, 1925
Iscr. di Cos	*Iscrizioni di Cos.* Edited by Mario Segre. Monografie della Scuola Archeologica di Atene e delle Missioni Italiane in Oriente, 6. Rome: L'Erma di Bretschneider, 1993
Kent	Kent, John Harvey. *The Inscriptions: 1926–1950.* Vol. 8.3 of *Corinth: Results of Excavations Conducted by the American School of Classical Studies at Athens.* Princeton: The American School of Classical Studies at Athens, 1966
LCL	Loeb Classical Library
OECT	Oxford Early Christian Texts
TAM II	Kalinka Ernst, ed. *Tituli Lyciae linguis Graeca et Latina conscripti.* Vol. 2 of *Tituli Asiae Minoris.* Vienna: Hölder, 1920–1944
TGV	Η Αγία Γραφή στη Δημοτική (Today's Greek Version). Athens: Hellenic Bible Society, 1997

West	West, Allen Brown. *Latin Inscriptions: 1896–1926.* Vol. 8.2 of *Corinth: Results of Excavations Conducted by the American School of Classical Studies at Athens.* Cambridge: Harvard University Press for the American School of Classical Studies at Athens, 1931

Secondary Sources and Reference Works

AAR	American Academy of Religion
AGG	von Siebenthal, Heinrich. *Ancient Greek Grammar for the Study of the New Testament.* Oxford: Lang, 2019
BABESCH	*Bulletin Antieke Beschaving*
BARIS	BAR (British Archaeological Reports) International Series
BDAG	Danker, Frederick W., Walter Bauer, William F. Arndt, and F. Wilbur Gingrich. *Greek-English Lexicon of the New Testament and Other Early Christian Literature.* 3rd ed. Chicago: University of Chicago Press, 2000. Numbers refer to the entries of the digital version of BibleWorks.
BECNT	Baker Exegetical Commentary on the New Testament
Bib	*Biblica*
BTZ	*Berliner Theologische Zeitschrift*
BZ	*Biblische Zeitschrift*
BZNW	Beihefte zur Zeitschrift für die neutestamentliche Wissenschaft
CBQ	*Catholic Biblical Quarterly*
CBR	*Currents in Biblical Research*
CCSL	Corpus Christianorum: Series Latina. Turnhout: Brepols, 1953–
CGL	Diggle, James, ed. *The Cambridge Greek Lexicon.* Cambridge: Cambridge University Press, 2021
CJ	*Classical Journal*
ClQ	*Classical Quarterly*
ECL	Early Christianity and Its Literature
EKKNT	Evangelisch-katholischer Kommentar zum Neuen Testament
ETL	*Ephemerides Theologicae Lovanienses*
FB	Forschung zur Bibel
GR	*Greece and Rome*
HNT	Handbuch zum Neuen Testament
HTR	*Harvard Theological Review*
JETS	*Journal of the Evangelical Theological Society*
JRS	*Journal of Roman Studies*
JSNT	*Journal for the Study of the New Testament*
JSNTSup	Journal for the Study of the New Testament Supplement Series

JTS	*Journal of Theological Studies*
L&N	Louw, Johannes P., and Eugene A. Nida, eds. *Greek-English Lexicon of the New Testament: Based on Semantic Domains.* 2nd ed. New York: United Bible Societies, 1989
LNTS	The Library of New Testament Studies
LSJM	Liddell, Henry G., and Robert Scott. *A Greek-English Lexicon.* Revised and supplemented by H. S. Jones with the help of von R. McKenzie. 9th ed. with revised supplement. Oxford: Clarendon, 1996. Numbers refer to the entries of the online version: http://stephanus.tlg.uci.edu/lsj/
NAC	New American Commentary
Neot	*Neotestmentica*
NIB	Keck, Leander E., ed. *The New Interpreter's Bible.* 12 vols. Nashville: Abingdon, 1994–2004
NICNT	New International Commentary on the New Testament
NIDNTTE	Silva, Moisés, ed. *New International Dictionary of New Testament Theology and Exegesis.* 5 vols. Grand Rapids: Zondervan, 2014
NovT	*Novum Testamentum*
NovTSup	Supplements to Novum Testamentum
NTS	*New Testament Studies*
RIC	*Roman Imperial Coinage: Volume 1—From 31 BC to AD 69.* Revised ed. Edited by C. H. V. Sutherland and R. A. G. Carson. London: Spink and Son, 1984
RPC	*Roman Provincial Coinage.* Edited by Andrew Burnett et al. London: British Museum Press; Paris: Bibliothèque Nationale, 1992–
RTR	*Reformed Theological Review*
SBL	Society of Biblical Literature
SBLRBS	Society of Biblical Literature Resources for Biblical Studies
SemeiaSt	Semeia Studies
SJT	*Scottish Journal of Theology*
SNTSU	Studien zum Neuen Testament und seiner Umwelt
SSA	Semantic and Structural Analysis Series
SymS	Symposium Series
TAPA	*Transactions of the American Philological Association*
TAPS	Transactions of the American Philosophical Society
TBLNT²	Coenen, Lothar, and Klaus Haacker, eds. *Theologisches Begriffslexikon zum Neuen Testament.* Rev. ed. in one vol. ("3. Sonderauflage"; slightly supplemented version of the revised two-volume edition of 1997/2000). Wuppertal: Brockhaus, 2014
TDNT	Kittel, Gerhard, and Gerhard Friedrich, eds. *Theological Dictio-*

	nary of the New Testament. Translated by Geoffrey W. Bromiley. 10 vols. Grand Rapids: Eerdmans, 1964–1976
TENTS	Texts and Editions for New Testament Study
TLG	*Thesaurus Linguae Graecae: Canon of Greek Authors and Works.* Edited by Luci Berkowitz and Karl A. Squitier. 3rd ed. New York: Oxford University Press, 1990
TLZ	*Theologische Literaturzeitung*
TWNT	Kittel, Gerhard, and Gerhard Friedrich, eds. *Theologische Wörterbuch zum Neuen Testament.* Stuttgart: Kohlhammer, 1932–1979
TynBul	*Tyndale Bulletin*
WUNT	Wissenschaftliche Untersuchungen zum Neuen Testament
YCS	Yale Classical Studies
ZNW	*Zeitschrift für die neutestamentliche Wissenschaft und die Kunde der älteren Kirche*

INTRODUCTION

For a long time in Pauline studies, the default assumption has been that the apostle, for whatever reasons, refrained from making critical remarks about the Roman Empire. It seemed like everything we could say in this regard could be boiled down to his call to be subordinate to the governing authorities and pay taxes in Rom 13. With that apparent profile, the apostle Paul was often misused to legitimate ideological regimes.

Then, in the 1990s, a group of scholars began to criticize this view as naïve. According to them, Paul's attitude toward the Roman Empire was much more critical than previously thought. To explain why Paul seems to remain silent on the injustices of Roman power, they pointed to the apparent danger of criticizing imperial ideology publicly—thus locating Paul's allegedly subversive remarks in the subtext of his letters. Accordingly, they said exegetes today must unearth these hidden treasures—which, after all, constitute new material for political ethics. Reading between the lines and deciphering code are not typical exegetical activities. For many biblical scholars, however, this makes the whole endeavor even more exciting.

It has not escaped critics of this approach that the search for resistance against an oppressive system in antiquity seems to depend on who is in charge in US politics,[1] with the approach having its heyday during what many per-

---

1. Note how Seyoon Kim in his endorsement of the Fortress edition of my *Hidden Criticism?* from 2017 writes: "Counter-imperial interpretation of the NT appears to wax and wane with the flux of imperial hybris in the United States. With the inauguration of a new United States president, making Christoph Heilig's book more widely available through this publication is to be welcomed. It will certainly stimulate scholars to devise better criteria for discerning the counter-imperial intent in Pauline texts than we have seen to date" (https://www.fortresspress.com/store/product/9781506428123/Hidden-Criticism-The-Methodology -and-Plausibility-of-the-Search-for-a-Counter-Imperial-Subtext-in-Paul).

ceived as a kind of "imperialism" under George W. Bush.[2] During the Barack Obama years that followed, these voices became significantly quieter.[3] The four years of the Donald Trump administration witnessed an increasing awareness of the problem of specifically Christian nationalism in the United States[4] and also led to attempts to interact critically with these ideas from a theological perspective.[5] However, in such discussions "an entire paradigm shift for how we see the origins of Christianity in its proper historical context as specifically an anti-imperial movement" is not infrequently already presupposed as a fact.[6]

If one looks at the scholarly literature on the subject, things are a bit more complicated. The hypothesis of an anti-imperial subtext has received a good deal of pushback. And postcolonial perspectives have sensitized scholars to the power dynamics within early Christianity and cautioned us against whitewashing the legacy of pioneering figures in the Jesus movement. At the very least, we must admit that the way the Bible is actually used in political discourse defies easy categorizations. It was on display as a symbol of "law and order" in Trump's photo op at St. John's Church on June 1, 2020. But Bible verses also featured in the events of the "resistance" from January 6, 2021,[7] which were

2. Joel R. White, "Anti-Imperial Subtexts in Paul: An Attempt at Building a Firmer Foundation," *Bib* 90 (2009): 305, begins his article with the observation that the anti-imperial reading of the apostle seems "to have especially flourished in the political climate of the Bush era."

3. To be sure, some continued to castigate elements in US politics that they saw continued even under the new president. See, for example, N. T. Wright's perspective on the killing of Osama bin Laden in "America's Exceptionalist Justice," *The Guardian*, May 5, 2011, https://www.theguardian.com/commentisfree/belief/2011/may/05/america-lone-ranger.

4. Kristin Kobes Du Mez, *Jesus and John Wayne: How White Evangelicals Corrupted a Faith and Fractured a Nation* (New York: W. W. Norton, 2020).

5. Cf., e.g., Jeffrey W. Robbins and Clayton Crockett, eds., *Doing Theology in the Age of Trump: A Critical Report on Christian Nationalism* (Eugene: Cascade, 2018).

6. Jeffrey W. Robbins and Clayton Crockett, "Introduction," in Robbins and Crockett, *Doing Theology in the Age of Trump*, xvi.

7. Admittedly, quotes from Paul's letters do not seem to have featured prominently as far as I can see. One of the rioters, Michael Sparks, wore a T-shirt from the company Kerusso with the caption "Armor of God," which explicitly cites and references Eph 6:11 (Peter Manseau, "His Pastors Tried to Steer Him Away from Social Media Rage: He Stormed the Capitol Anyway," *The Washington Post*, February 19, 2021, https://www.washingtonpost.com/religion/2021/02/19/michael-sparks-capitol-siege-jan-6-christian/). The same phrase also occurs on patches sewed on military clothing (see, e.g., Gettyimages, "US-POLITICS-ELECTION-TRUMP," https://www.gettyimages.de/detail/nachrichtenfoto/supporters-of-us-president-donald-trump-wear-gas-masks-nachrichtenfoto/1230505388). Interestingly, the relevant passage from Ephesians was also cited in the immediate aftermath by Christians

anything but an expression of religiously motivated political quietism.[8] There is an unintentional, almost breathtaking irony in the fact that those who were storming the Capitol and shouting "Hang Mike Pence!" were also carrying with them wooden crosses—not simply a symbol of the Christian faith but indeed a Roman instrument of execution.

In any case, it is clear that "the Bible and politics" is far from being a settled issue. From a theological perspective, the desire to find more material for constructive political ethics in Paul's letters is certainly understandable. Many Christian laypeople would also like to see their theological and political intuitions brought into alignment with the biblical basis of their faith—in such a way that these foundational documents of Christianity can offer both resources for resistance against truly oppressive forces and guidance against obvious attempts to hijack their religion.

Of course this little book cannot answer this whole complex nexus of questions. However, I do think it contributes to this necessary discussion by revisiting a specific historical question that to me seems very relevant indeed: Is there a "coded" criticism of Roman political power in Paul's letters?

This book is not the first time that I have weighed in on this issue. In a monograph from 2015,[9] I concluded that this paradigm indeed had potential, while pointing to several modifications that I thought would be necessary for it to adequately explain Paul's texts. I both cautioned against the overexcitement of some scholars who found denunciations of Caesar in almost every passage

---

opposed to the storming of the Capitol and the associated violence. See, e.g., the video from January 6th by Bishop Leila Ortiz, Metro D.C. Synod, Evangelical Lutheran Church in America, "From the Bishop's Desk: Addressing the Events of January 6, 2021," *Facebook*, January 6, 2021, https://www.facebook.com/watch/?v=827487214464232.

8. On the latter, see, e.g., Emma Green, "A Christian Insurrection," *The Atlantic*, January 8, 2021, https://www.theatlantic.com/politics/archive/2021/01/evangelicals-catholics-jericho-march-capitol/617591/.

9. Christoph Heilig, *Hidden Criticism? The Methodology and Plausibility of the Search for a Counter-Imperial Subtext in Paul*, WUNT 2/392 (Tübingen: Mohr Siebeck, 2015), 160. (In what follows, I will cite the Fortress edition from 2017, which, however, contains only minor corrections.) In fact, during the copy-editing process a negation was dropped from the very last paragraph that was meant to encourage continued research on the topic. It was only in 2017 that the late Larry Hurtado, an excellent reader, notified me about this embarrassing mistake. It is rectified in the Fortress edition that was published later that year (Minneapolis: Fortress, 2017), 160: "Despite the associated problems, we should not, therefore, avoid this complex of questions but tackle it in the most methodologically sound way possible. If this book is judged to have contributed to this endeavour, it has fulfilled its purpose."

and pushed back against those who declared the whole approach to be dead on the basis of historical arguments.

In the last couple of years, research on the topic had plodded along in a rather unspectacular way. It seemed like everybody had said his or her foundational piece and now simply continued in one of the two established interpretive tracks. A 2021 *New Testament Studies* article by Laura Robinson, however, was different in several ways.[10] Her essay clearly aims at putting the final nail in the coffin of the anti-imperial subtext hypothesis by questioning "the thesis that Paul disguised anti-imperial sentiments in his letters specifically because speaking out against imperial authorities was too dangerous," which is, according to Robinson, "the basic assumption behind the search in Paul's letters for 'hidden' or 'coded' transcripts."[11] Moreover, what makes Robinson's piece so intriguing is that she does not simply reiterate earlier assessments but rather seeks to introduce new evidence where assertions have reigned up to now, contributing to a necessary "deep dive into the historical evidence about treason law and evidence-gathering in antiquity," something she thinks has largely remained undone so far.[12]

In what follows, I will first sketch the background of the debate that Robinson is entering, including my own earlier thoughts on the matter (chapter 1). Then I want to respond to some of her criticism that seems unconvincing to me, before turning to other observations in her article that I find very stimulating and that call for further differentiations. Having established this refined theoretical basis in chapter 2, I will then discuss a specific textual example in chapters 3 and 4, before closing with some indications for how research might continue in the future in chapter 5. The conclusion will then recapitulate the main points of my argument.

---

10. Laura Robinson, "Hidden Transcripts? The Supposedly Self-Censoring Paul and Rome as Surveillance State in Modern Pauline Scholarship," *NTS* 67 (2021): 55–72.

11. Robinson, "Hidden Transcripts?," 55.

12. Robinson, "Hidden Transcripts?," 57.

1 | THE CLASSICAL SUBTEXT-HYPOTHESIS

The Wright-Barclay Debate

N. T. Wright—former bishop of Durham, then research professor at the University of St. Andrews, and now senior research fellow at Wycliff Hall, Oxford University—is undoubtedly one of the most prominent proponents of the aforementioned anti-imperial subtext-hypothesis. His article from 2000, "Paul's Gospel and Caesar's Empire," remains an important text for those interested in this approach.[1] In his 2005 book *Paul: In Fresh Perspective*, he then sketched a fuller picture, drawing this time on Richard B. Hays's criteria for identifying weak intertextual allusions—"echoes"—to Scripture[2] and applying them to the realm of Roman ideology in order to offer a theoretical ("What are we looking for?") and methodological ("How can we find it?") basis for his approach.[3]

The very same move also appears in works by Neil Elliott that were published in 2008.[4] It is this use of Hays's criteria that originally drew my attention. I am convinced that a careful analysis from the perspective of Bayesian confirmation

---

1. N. T. Wright, "Paul's Gospel and Caesar's Empire," in *Paul and Politics: Ekklesia, Israel, Imperium, Interpretation: Essays in Honor of Krister Stendahl*, ed. Richard A. Horsley (Harrisburg: Trinity Press International, 2000), 160–83.

2. Richard B. Hays, *Echoes of Scripture in the Letters of Paul* (New Haven: Yale University Press: 1989).

3. N. T. Wright, *Paul: In Fresh Perspective* (Minneapolis: Fortress, 2005), 59–79.

4. Neil Elliott, *The Arrogance of Nations: Reading Romans in the Shadow of Empire* (Minneapolis: Fortress, 2008) and Neil Elliott, "'Blasphemed among the Nations': Pursuing an Anti-Imperial 'Intertextuality' in Romans," in *As It Is Written: Studying Paul's Use of Scripture*, ed. Stanley E. Porter and Christopher D. Stanley, SymS 50 (Atlanta: Scholars Press, 2008), 213–33.

theory demonstrates that this set of criteria is not suitable for the task of identifying either scriptural or Roman echoes.[5] This sounds more complicated than it is. The basic idea behind this judgment is that it can be deduced from probability theory that whenever we make claims about how "probable" a hypothesis is we need to take into account two parameters for the competing hypotheses:

1. Assuming that the hypothesis is true, how well does it explain the evidence in question? (The "likelihood" or simply "explanatory potential.")
2. How plausible is the hypothesis against the background of the rest of our knowledge, regardless of the new evidence that is to be integrated? (The "prior-probability" of the hypothesis, or, in less technical language, its "background plausibility.")

If viewed against this backdrop, it becomes clear that while Hays's theses on the elaborate dynamics behind the production of Paul's letters remain relevant,[6] the use of his specific set of criteria cannot be encouraged. It is prone to the misunderstanding that counting the number of fulfilled criteria might be a valid procedure for verifying the existence of an intertextual echo, which is an unreliable procedure. One main reason is the fact that the criteria do not carry equal argumentative weight.[7] In other words, when working with these criteria one can very easily overemphasize one of the two above-mentioned "meta-criteria"—which need to be applied with *even* measure in order for the inference to be correct.

In search of a method for evaluating the hypothesis by Wright, Elliott, and others, I then encountered a convincing attempt by John M. G. Barclay (Durham). His essay "Why the Roman Empire Was Insignificant to Paul" was published in 2011.[8] It goes back to an interaction with Wright at the annual SBL meeting in San

5. I first made this argument in Christoph Heilig, "Methodological Considerations for the Search of Counter-Imperial 'Echoes' in Pauline Literature," in *Reactions to Empire: Proceedings of Sacred Texts in Their Socio-Political Contexts*, ed. John A. Dunne and Dan Batovici, WUNT 2/372 (Tübingen: Mohr Siebeck, 2014), 73–92. It is then repeated with more detail in Christoph Heilig, *Hidden Criticism? The Methodology and Plausibility of the Search for a Counter-Imperial Subtext in Paul* (Minneapolis: Fortress, 2017), chapter 2.

6. See the detailed discussion in Christoph Heilig, *Paulus als Erzähler? Eine narratologische Perspektive auf die Paulusbriefe*, BZNW 237 (Berlin: de Gruyter, 2020), chapter 16.

7. It is unfortunately still employed by Joseph R. Dodson, "The Convict's Gibbet and the Victor's Car: The Triumphal Death of Marcus Atilius Regulus and the Background of Col 2:15," *HTR* 114 (2021): 201–2.

8. John M. G. Barclay, "Why the Roman Empire Was Insignificant to Paul," in *Pauline*

Diego in 2007.[9] Prior to this encounter, Wright had spoken on the topic in the research seminar in Durham.[10] For the SBL event, they then changed the order of the speakers at the last minute and had Barclay's critique precede Wright's paper, which aimed at establishing the validity of the subtext-hypothesis. The impression of Barclay's paper as a "takedown" of the anti-imperial approach to Paul, held by many of those present at the event, is probably in part to be explained as a result of this change to the order of their papers.

However, the experience I have with students mimics this dynamic regularly. While they are quite convinced of the paradigm after having read Wright on the subject, Barclay's essay gives them the sudden impression that it has been disproven on several levels at once. This certainly is the hallmark of a good scholarly paper, and the question of how Barclay achieves this remarkable effect deserves further attention. First, we can observe that his critique is very fundamental. However, he does not seem to have a problem with Hays's criteria themselves, only with Wright's application to Roman ideology.[11] What makes his piece so effective is that he identifies a series of *necessary conditions* of Wright's hypothesis and adduces actual evidence from primary sources in his argument that several of these conditions are not fulfilled. I reproduce these necessary conditions in what follows:[12]

1. Are the Pauline letters affected by the rules of public discourse at all?
2. Do these rules forbid open criticism of aspects of the Roman Empire?
3. Did Paul have an exposure to these elements, and did he perceive them as specifically Roman?
4. Can we expect him to have had a critical stance toward those elements?
5. Is it reasonable in light of Paul's personality to assume that he expressed this critical stance in the subtext of his letters?

Churches and Diaspora Jews, ed. John M. G. Barclay, WUNT 275 (Tübingen: Mohr Siebeck, 2011), 363–87.

9. The original audio files can be found toward the end of Andy Rowell, "Tony Jones, N. T. Wright, Richard Bauckham, Scot McKnight, James K. A. Smith, Robert Bella and John Milbank: Audio from SBL and AAR," *Church Leadership Conversations*, November 21, 2007, andy rowell.net/andy_rowell/2007/11/audio-from-a-fe.html. A transcript of Barclay's lecture also exists (http://robbdavis.pbworks.com/f/Barclay+Why+Rome+Insignificant+to+Paul.pdf).

10. John M. G. Barclay in personal communication, email from May 10, 2021.

11. Barclay, "Roman Empire," 370 and 380.

12. Cf. Theresa Heilig and Christoph Heilig, "Historical Methodology," in *God and the Faithfulness of Paul: A Critical Examination of the Pauline Theology of N. T. Wright*, ed. Christoph Heilig, J. Thomas Hewitt, and Michael F. Bird, WUNT 2/413 (Tübingen: Mohr Siebeck, 2016; Minneapolis: Fortress, 2017), 146.

Each of these questions and follow-up questions needs to be answered affirmatively for Wright's hypothesis to be at least theoretically viable. It has to be noted that the necessary conditions together are not a sufficient condition for the hypothesis to be true. If they were all judged to be fulfilled this would not yet imply that the hypothesis should be regarded as the most probable explanation for specific Pauline passages. It would just mean that the hypothesis has not yet been falsified and that—to use Bayesian terminology—the prior-probability is not zero.

Assigning a precise number to this hypothetical assessment of the background plausibility is both impossible and unnecessary.[13] But it seems fair to say that the idea that Paul used the subtext of his letters to communicate criticism that would have been too dangerous as open statements would be considered much more favorably by many exegetes in their analysis of individual passages if all these conditions were indeed fulfilled. To determine whether the hypothesis is "likely" with respect to any of these concrete text-parts, we must also consider the second crucial parameter demanded by Bayes's theorem: the way it explains or fails to explain the passages in question. Barclay also addresses this second meta-criterion, arguing that in many cases overlap in vocabulary does not need to be explained with subversive intentions but is simply due to "common language"[14] that can, at least initially, be regarded as neutral. In my opinion, however, his achievement of identifying and addressing not one but several crucial aspects for assessing the background plausibility of Wright's subtext-hypothesis is mainly what makes his piece so convincing.

Let us go through each of these conditions quickly. First, in order for Wright's hypothesis to be taken seriously, we need to clarify whether Paul's letters would have been affected by the rules of public discourse in the first place. Barclay ar-

13. See again Christoph Heilig, "What Bayesian Reasoning Can and Can't Do for Biblical Research," *Zürich New Testament Blog*, March 27, 2019, https://www.uzh.ch/blog/theologie-nt/2019/03/27/what-bayesian-reasoning-can-and-cant-do-for-biblical-research/. In my view, Eckart David Schmidt, review of *Hidden Criticism? The Methodology and Plausibility of the Search for a Counter-Imperial Subtext in Paul*, by Christoph Heilig, *SNTSU* 42 (2017): 230–31, misses the essence of the value of Bayes's theorem for biblical studies. Of course, background "knowledge" is itself derived through the updating of other priors and is not completely certain. And this certainly contributes to the rightly made observation that (mathematical!) "precision" cannot be achieved. However, this situation is not different in a variety of other fields, in which Bayesian confirmation theory has become well-established. See the inter- and transdisciplinary project "Bayes and Bible," funded by the cogito foundation: https://theologie.unibas.ch/en/departments/new-testament/bayes-and-bible/.

14. Barclay, "Roman Empire," 376–79.

gues that this is not the case and that what we find in Paul's letters is indeed the "hidden transcript" of the Pauline churches in its purest form. This terminology comes from the sociologist James C. Scott, who differentiates between a "public transcript," which comprises the roles of both the elites and the suppressed in their public interaction, and two separate "hidden transcripts," which refer to the behavior and discourse in each of these groups in private.[15] According to Barclay, applying this concept to Paul's letters—something explicitly done by proponents of the anti-imperial reading of Paul like Neil Elliott and Richard A. Horsley[16]—shows that here we have a perfectly clear insight into what Paul actually thought and said in private. This, in turn, removes any need—as is likewise the case for diaries—to use code to express criticism that might have been controversial in the public sphere. If these assumptions were right, Wright's whole edifice of ideas would already collapse at this point in the analysis.

Second, even if one disagrees with Barclay's assessment of the first necessary condition, one would further have to demonstrate that it would have been dangerous to voice criticism of the Roman Empire publicly. Barclay adduces several historical examples of ancient figures—Tacitus, Philo, and Josephus—to show that this danger has been overstated by people like Wright. In the end, Paul's own appeal to Caesar might be taken as evidence that there was room *within* the "public transcript" of the Roman Empire for a critique of Roman actions.

Third, assuming again that the second question can be answered affirmatively, we would then have to demonstrate that Paul had been exposed to the elements of Roman ideology that he is said to have criticized. While Barclay is careful not to overstate his case here and argues only that Paul's epistemology seems to have led him to lump emperor worship together with other manifestations of paganism in general,[17] other critics have put forth the argument

---

15. James C. Scott, *Domination and the Arts of Resistance: Hidden Transcripts* (New Haven: Yale University Press, 1990).

16. Richard A. Horsley, "Introduction: Jesus, Paul, and the 'Arts of Resistance': Leaves from the Notebook of James C. Scott," in *Hidden Transcripts and the Arts of Resistance: Applying the Work of James C. Scott to Jesus and Paul*, ed. Richard A. Horsley, SemeiaSt 48 (Atlanta: Scholars Press, 2004), 1–26.

17. See also John M. G. Barclay, "Paul, Roman Religion and the Emperor: Mapping the Point of Conflict," in *Pauline Churches and Diaspora Jews*, ed. John M. G. Barclay, WUNT 275 (Tübingen: Mohr Siebeck, 2011), 355: "He recognizes that there are 'many gods' and 'many lords' (1 Cor 8.5), but he shows no interest in their differing identities, lumping them together into a single category."

that imperial cults were indeed insignificant in the East of the Roman Empire and thus not a plausible object of criticism in the first place.[18]

Fourth, assuming that Paul did in fact know about these things, we still need to address the question of whether it is plausible to assume that he would have found them objectionable. Perhaps he was well aware of these Roman concepts but was fine with them? While some have argued in this direction,[19] Barclay himself remains cautious, stressing merely that Paul might have disliked many aspects of Roman culture but apparently chose to ignore them instead of addressing them explicitly.

Fifth, we are left with the question of whether the idea that Paul chose the subtext for his criticism in order to avoid persecution is compatible with our assumptions concerning his personality. Again, Barclay is not convinced. Such an assessment would "underrat[e] Paul's courage."[20]

In my own analysis of these necessary conditions, I found reason to defend in particular the first two necessary conditions against Barclay's critique.[21] Conditions 3 and 4 also seemed to hold up against the variegated challenges directed against them by various parties.[22] The fifth and last condition, however, finally convinced me that the hypothesis by Wright/Elliott was in serious trouble.

Barclay points in particular to the fact that Paul does not shy away from criticizing idol worship in very stark terms—even though it was such a fundamental aspect of Greco-Roman society, and his attack was thus potentially a quite dangerous move. Even more convincing is the related fact that in at least one instance we *do* seem to have a very blunt criticism of Roman action. In 1 Cor 2:6 Paul says that the wisdom he is teaching is "not a wisdom of this age nor of the rulers of this age" (σοφίαν δὲ οὐ τοῦ αἰῶνος τούτου οὐδὲ τῶν ἀρχόντων τοῦ

18. Colin Miller, "The Imperial Cult in the Pauline Cities of Asia Minor and Greece," *CBQ* 72 (2010): 314–32.

19. A more nuanced example would be J. Albert Harrill, *Paul the Apostle: His Life and Legacy in Their Roman Context* (Cambridge: Cambridge University Press, 2012).

20. Barclay, "Roman Empire," 380.

21. Heilig, *Hidden Criticism?*, chapters 3 and 4.

22. I was surprised to see how uncritically the (at points bizarre) claims by Miller, "Imperial Cult," were accepted in the scholarly literature. In my response (Heilig, *Hidden Criticism?*, chapter 4, section 2) I had unfortunately missed the earlier contribution by Apostolos F. Kralidis, "Evidence for the Imperial Cult in Thessalonica in the First Century C.E.," *ΚΟΣΜΟΣ/COSMOS* 2 (2013): 87–102. I have made a habit of criticizing our discipline for not sufficiently considering the modern phase of the Greek language and scholarship produced by its speakers. This failure of mine is unfortunately symptomatic of just that attitude.

αἰῶνος τούτου).[23] His point so far seems to be pretty clear already, but he then continues ". . . who are in the process of perishing" (τῶν καταργουμένων). Here Paul seems to go out on a limb—in an entirely unnecessary manner. Adding this participle is a provocation that he could just as well have avoided if keeping a low profile had been especially high on his agenda. After all, even *implying* what he says out loud here may have been the reason for some serious legal trouble just a couple of years earlier in Thessalonika![24]

One can of course argue that Paul is thinking about demonic forces here, but the mention of the Roman method of execution—crucifixion—in v. 8 seems to make such an interpretation rather unlikely. To me at least, this passage settled the issue in my initial analysis. I could not see why a writer who is fearless—or at least careless—like that should feel the need to use elaborate coding in other instances. Wright's hypothesis seemed to have met an unsurmountable obstacle with this necessary condition. Thus, I argued that for the subtext-hypothesis to remain an option in some form, it would be necessary to modify the claimed *motivation* behind the alleged decision to communicate criticism only in such a subtle manner.[25]

---

23. Unless otherwise noted, quotations of Scripture are my own translation.

24. This would assume that Edwin A. Judge, "The Decrees of Caesar at Thessalonica," *RTR* 30 (1971): 71–78 (reprinted in Edwin A. Judge, *The First Christians in the Roman World: Augustan and New Testament Essays*, WUNT 229 [Tübingen: Mohr Siebeck, 2008], 456–62), is right when he proposes that the prohibition of prophesying the death of others, including the emperor, constitutes the legal backdrop for this conflict. Cf. critically Justin K. Hardin, "Decrees and Drachmas at Thessalonica: An Illegal Assembly in Jason's House (Acts 17.1–10a)," *NTS* 52 (2006): 29–49. Cf. already Heilig, *Hidden Criticism?*, 63 and 81 on Acts 17:1–9. Most recently, D. Clint Burnett, *Studying the New Testament through Inscriptions: An Introduction* (Peabody: Hendrickson, 2020), chapter 4, has argued that the epigraphical evidence has been misused in attempts to equate "Caesar's decrees" with imperial loyalty oaths. According to Burnett, a more nuanced assessment of the epigraphical evidence suggests that the Thessalonians might have been concerned with the status of their city. Its freedom had been assured to them in letters from the emperors, and they did not want to risk this privilege by behavior that might be seen as being inappropriate in a city with such a relationship to Rome. This approach leaves the question open about what precisely in Paul's gospel the inhabitants might have viewed as a potential risk to their good standing with Rome. Perhaps what at first look seems like an "obscure" and "possibly garbled" portrayal of the accusation on Luke's side (A. N. Sherwin-White, *Roman Society and Roman Law in the New Testament* [Oxford: Clarendon, 1963], 96) might actually reflect the rather desperate attempt of the inhabitants to make their accusation sound somehow official, while in the end it was based mostly on an intuitive impression that this message would not "sit well with Rome."

25. Heilig, *Hidden Criticism?*, chapter 5, section 2.2.

Regrettably, the call for such a fundamental restructuring of the subtext-hypothesis has remained largely unanswered in recent years. Wright devotes the entire twelfth chapter of *Paul and the Faithfulness of God* (2013) to a rebuttal of Barclay's critique. Unfortunately, I had only a brief chance to consider this substantial book for my own monograph. As argued elsewhere, however, it does not do so in the most effective way,[26] i.e., by a focused response to the implicated necessary conditions. Barclay himself does not seem too keen on continuing this conversation, mentioning the issue only as an aside[27] in a blistering critique of Wright's magnum opus, focusing mainly on the alleged "stories" in and behind Paul's letters.[28]

There are other indications that scholars have lost some interest in this debate. In my interaction with Bruce Winter's *Divine Honours for the Caesars*[29] from 2015, I maintain that this search for a subtle interaction with Roman ideology—something Winter explicitly does not focus on (he concentrates solely on finding traces of social conflict in light of imperial cults in the New Testament)—still seems to be a viable path.[30] In the new introduction to the 2017 Fortress edition of *Hidden Criticism?* I then admit that "it would probably be wrong to claim that this quite specific paradigm has yielded a significant amount of concrete research over the last two years."[31] In that assessment, I still "continue to believe," however, "that it is indeed the most promising background for addressing the issue of Paul and the Roman Empire."[32]

Where do we stand in 2022? As far as I can see, theoretical advancements have been made more from those who tend toward the critical side of the spectrum.[33] Against this backdrop, I was excited to see Robinson's new piece

---

26. Heilig and Heilig, "Historical Methodology," 145–48.

27. John M. G. Barclay, review of *Paul and the Faithfulness of God*, by N. T. Wright, *SJT* 68 (2015): 236.

28. On this, see Heilig, *Paulus als Erzähler?*

29. Bruce W. Winter, *Divine Honours for the Caesars: The First Christians' Responses* (Grand Rapids: Eerdmans, 2015).

30. Christoph Heilig, "The First Christians' Responses to Emperor Worship," *Reviews of Biblical and Early Christian Studies*, November 30, 2016, https://rbecs.org/2016/11/30/fcrw/, and Christoph Heilig, review of *Divine Honours for the Caesars: The First Christians' Responses*, by Bruce Winter, *JTS* 67 (2016): 754–57.

31. Christoph Heilig, "Introduction," in Heilig, *Hidden Criticism?*, xi.

32. Heilig, "Introduction," xi. See also p. xii with respect to the less text-centered approach by Winter in *Divine Honours*.

33. See Najeeb T. Haddad, *Paul, Politics, and New Creation: Reconsidering Paul and Empire* (Washington, DC: Rowman & Littlefield, 2020), who introduces the "emic" category of figured speech. I have not yet had a chance to take a detailed look at Niko Huttunen,

in *New Testament Studies*, which seems to focus on precisely the debate in which I had been interested. In what follows, we will take a look at what she thinks about the current state of research and then, in chapter 2, formulate a response to her assessment.

On the Alleged Safety of Public Criticism

Robinson does not pull any punches in her article. Here is her conclusion, which is worth being cited in full:

> Here's a joke. Why don't you see elephants hiding in trees? Answer: because they are really good at it. For years in Pauline scholarship, this logic has also answered the question, "Why don't you see Paul criticising the Roman Empire?" Answer: because he is really good at hiding it. What makes the elephant joke funny (or at least a little funny) is that assuming that elephants are present but well concealed in trees is a cumbersome explanation that ignores the obvious truth: there are no elephants in the trees. Perhaps the next step for reading Paul in his world is accepting the disappointing fact that radical denouncements of the Roman Empire are the Pauline equivalent of elephants in trees. Maybe they are well concealed, but they probably are not there at all.[34]

How does Robinson arrive at this forceful rejection of Wright's subtext-hypothesis? Let us take a look at her argument against the backdrop of the five necessary conditions that I identified on the basis of Barclay's work.

As the title "Hidden Transcripts? The Supposedly Self-Censoring Paul and Rome as Surveillance State in Modern Pauline Scholarship" indicates pretty clearly, Robinson focuses on the nexus of questions that are connected with the *first two* necessary conditions. This is confirmed by the layout of her article. After an introduction, she takes a look at the "Hidden Criticism Trope in Modern Pauline Scholarship."[35] She heavily criticizes analogies provided by scholars like Wright for the phenomenon we supposedly find in Paul, arguing that they stem

---

Early Christians Adapting to the Roman Empire: Mutual Recognition, NovTSup 179 (Leiden: Brill, 2020). From what I have seen so far, Justin Winzenburg, *Ephesians and Empire: An Evaluation of the Epistle's Subversion of Roman Imperial Ideology*, WUNT 2/573 (Tübingen: Mohr Siebeck, 2022), might turn out to be an encouraging exception to the noted trend.

34. Laura Robinson, "Hidden Transcripts? The Supposedly Self-Censoring Paul and Rome as Surveillance State in Modern Pauline Scholarship," *NTS* 67 (2021): 72.

35. Robinson, "Hidden Transcripts?," 58–62.

from modern police states and that the evidence does not back up the assumption that the same dynamics can be applied to Paul's Roman context: "When counter-imperial readers of Paul look for hidden resistance in his writing on the grounds that Paul's speech was at risk of being heard and prosecuted by a repressive government, these grounds are usually either assumed without evidence, or supported by appeals to larger theoretical frameworks."[36] It is her intention to fill this gap by introducing relevant historical evidence that falls into two obviously very related issues: "'Controlled Speech' in Antiquity" and "Surveillance."[37] In her concluding remarks ("What Paul Would Say, and What He Did Say"),[38] Robinson also puts forward some other considerations that we will address later (chapter 2). For the moment, however, we can safely conclude that her arguments in the two main sections relate to the necessary conditions number 1 and number 2, respectively. If it is even unclear whether Paul's potential criticism might have been viewed as "seditious"[39] (condition number 2) and it is moreover implausible that his letters would have been subjected to any kind of surveillance (condition number 1), the search seems to be undermined from the outset.

In my analysis, Wright's hypothesis broke down at condition number 5. I would not have cared if that happened already at an earlier point. One goal of providing such a list was, after all, to facilitate the formulation of such fundamental concerns.[40] Moreover, while the kind of "hidden criticism" that I had continued to regard as a potentially fruitful category relates to many of the same passages adduced by Wright and his colleagues, whether Paul's letters might turn out not to have been subject to rules of public discourse—or, alternatively, if these rules were less strict than I had thought—would not be relevant for the analysis of these cases within my own framework. After all, I had become convinced that the motivation for choosing the subtext in these cases could not be the attempt to avoid persecution. In fact, one could even point to the way the above necessary conditions are nested—with each one following from a more fundamental necessary condition—and argue on that basis that *if* Robinson's evidence bears the weight she thinks, there is not even a need to discuss the apparently more ambiguous aspect of "controlled speech," which could lead readers to come away with the impression that there was still some potential wiggle room for the subtext-hypothesis. It would totally suffice

---

36. Robinson, "Hidden Transcripts?," 61.
37. Robinson, "Hidden Transcripts?," 62–67 and 67–71, respectively.
38. Robinson, "Hidden Transcripts?," 71–72.
39. An option not *entirely* ruled out by Robinson, "Hidden Transcripts?," 66.
40. Heilig, *Hidden Criticism?*, 44, and Heilig, "Introduction," xviii.

to point to the more foundational condition number 1, which according to her discussion of "surveillance" does not seem to be met even by a big stretch of the imagination. It is already here—in a discussion that occurs later in the article—that Wright's hypothesis would find its insurmountable obstacle.

And indeed, in at least one respect Robinson is very convincing. She certainly succeeds in her attempt to point out that the Roman Empire was not a "police state." In some sense, this is of course a trivial statement to which no serious student of ancient history would object, and one might ask whether she is not beating a dead horse. However, I think it is indeed justified to reiterate this point,[41] given that a lot of the *perceived strength* of the argument advanced by Wright and others (i.e., regardless of how this should actually feed into the inference) rests upon the analogies they adduce.

It is with great care that Robinson demonstrates that Wright's anonymous playwright, whom Robinson identifies as a person with the name Wu Han, cannot serve as an appropriate analogy for alleged coded criticism by an ancient letter writer like Paul.[42] Critiques like these are indeed valuable. Such analogies are in the end what makes hypotheses plausible for many readers, regardless of the "actual" weight they theoretically carry.[43] It is for the very same reason that I had criticized the reference to Hays's criteria for intertextuality. They had never been actually *used* as a "method" for finding individual echoes. Rather, both Wright and Elliott had referred to them to lend credibility to their search in a very fundamental way, never returning to them again in the analysis of actual Pauline passages. Therefore, it does seem legitimate to me that Robinson focuses on the example of Wu Han. Her critique demonstrates that much of what has been taken for granted in this discussion and much of what might prove persuasive is questionable in many respects.

That being said, I still have a problem with Robinson's larger argument. Unfortunately, she accepts the idea that the question of whether or not the context of the alleged coded criticism can be characterized as a "police state" presents

41. Already made by Barclay, "Roman Empire," 381, and taken up in Heilig, *Hidden Criticism?*, 65.

42. Robinson, "Hidden Transcripts?," 60–61.

43. See Heilig and Heilig, "Historical Methodology" for a discussion of how the plausibility of a hypothesis *should* be determined, even though human intuition regularly ignores these inferential structures. Cf. also Heilig, *Paulus als Erzähler?*, chapter 9, section 3.2, on "narrative probability" and "narrative fidelity" according to the "narrative paradigm" by Walter R. Fisher, "Narration as a Human Communication Paradigm: The Case of Public Moral Argument," *Communication Monographs* 51 (1984): 1–22, and Walter R. Fisher, "The Narrative Paradigm: An Elaboration," *Communication Monographs* 52 (1985): 347–67.

the appropriate standard for the historical analysis concerning anti-imperial subtexts in Paul's letters. In my view, it is, by contrast, entirely sufficient for the fulfillment of the second necessary condition to note that early Christian churches were in a marginalized position basically everywhere in the first century and with respect to a variety of societal fronts. Interestingly, Robinson *herself* mentions the highly controversial nature of Paul's mission—apparently avoiding, however, what I regard as the only natural conclusion:

> If we look at our earliest source for Paul's legal trouble, Acts, it seems that local officials did not need to know much about what Paul taught in order to find him dangerous. Paul's high-conflict relationship with other Christians, his complicated status in non-Christian synagogues and his mission to bring pagans into monolatrous worship of Israel's God made him a troubling figure already. Paul did not need to be found denouncing the emperor to end up in prison. His conflict with virtually every existing social group outside his own churches was a problem already. Paul was a frequent recipient of synagogue discipline. He disturbed the peace enough to earn corporal punishment. He made a habit of convincing pagans to abandon their religion and follow foreign gods. Wherever he went, there were riots. When placed in this context, Paul's eventual execution is not a mystery that needs to be explained with anti-imperial codes. Paul was a habitual, highly visible troublemaker, and his letters would not need to be "decoded" to prove that.[44]

I am not entirely sure how best to enter into a constructive dialogue here. For, in my view, Robinson herself sketches a pretty clear backdrop for why the congregations of Paul should indeed have been very careful not to evoke the impression—be it correct or not—that they might be politically subversive. In other words, it seems to follow in a straightforward way from Robinson's own assessment that we do not need (a) a police state with (b) very specific limitations on free speech in order to come to the conclusion that (a) the Pauline churches would have been under a lot of *scrutiny* and that (b) everything that could even be (mis)construed as being seditious would have been extremely *dangerous* for them.

In fact, concerning the second point, (b), I will make the argument that pretty much everything Robinson—rightfully—says with respect to the lack of precise legal standards that might have been feared by Paul could just as well

---

44. Robinson, "Hidden Transcripts?," 70–71.

be said about later generations—at times when our sources are pretty clear that local events of persecution, including executions, *did* happen.

We know from Pliny's famous letter to Trajan (Pliny, *Ep.* 10.96)—which is noticeably absent from Robinson's discussion—that under the reign of that emperor (perhaps in the winter of 112/113 CE; the precise date is debated) a series of trials took place against Christians, probably in Amastris (today: Amasra).[45] Pliny repeatedly interrogated those who confessed. If they still confessed that they were Christians at the end of that process, they were killed. The "legal" reasoning that Pliny offers in retrospect is that they certainly deserved such a punishment for their "stubbornness" (*pertinacia*) and "inflexible obstinacy" (*inflexibilis obstinatio*), accusations that of course do not feature in Robinson's analysis, who seems to think that anything less than an actual plot to overthrow the regime would have been viewed as harmless.[46] This contrast alone should give us pause in claiming that against the backdrop of Roman law, Paul and his followers would have been safe. Whatever Pliny might have been suspicious about in the first place, his decision to let the Christians be executed has little to do with what he discovered during the trial and much more with making sure no problems would arise in the first place. As Corke-Webster concludes: "Pliny is ignorant about Christianity at this point. Nor does he make any effort to learn more; he dismisses it as irrelevant (*qualecumque*). Christianity in and of itself is quite clearly not his concern. Most important, Pliny initiates no investigation at this stage. He sentences those before him on the basis of his suspicions and sense that they seem troublesome. In such circumstances rapid suppression was the natural response."[47] And "such circumstances" could of course also have arisen in Paul's time. The members of his congregations, with the exception of the few who could have demanded a trial in Rome as citizens, would have been "exposed to harassed governors

---

45. For context, see Roy K. Gibson, *Man of High Empire: The Life of Pliny the Younger* (Oxford: Oxford University Press, 2020), chapter 8, on his time as governor of Pontus-Bithynia.

46. Joachim Molthagen, *Der römische Staat und die Christen im zweiten und dritten Jahrhundert*, 2nd ed., Hypomnemata 28 (Göttingen: Vandenhoeck & Ruprecht, 1975), 15, emphasizes that this most certainly was not the *official* reason given for the verdict but a statement in retrospect, after Pliny had uncovered that the *nomen ipsum* was not, as he probably had assumed, associated with more specific crimes. James Corke-Webster, "Trouble in Pontus: The Pliny-Trajan Correspondence on the Christians Reconsidered," *TAPA* 147 (2017): 385, convincingly argues that the listed reasons are placeholders that encourage "Trajan to read back the Christians' later refusal to sacrifice into his initial interactions with them." And it seems very likely that Pliny would have listed clear crimes if he could have.

47. Corke-Webster, "Trouble," 381. Gibson, *Man of High Empire*, 216–21, follows this assessment.

whose main imperial directive was to maintain order," just like the Christians in Pontus.[48]

But a closer look at what happened subsequently to what has been recounted so far makes Robinson's argument even more problematic. Under Pliny, Roman citizens were spared immediate execution and sent to Rome. Up until this point, Pliny does not seem to have been bothered very much by the events. Soon, however, things get worse when names of alleged Christians are published anonymously. It is only due to the situation taking on much bigger dimensions that Pliny writes to Trajan and we gain some insight into the consequences that Christians could face at that time for their faith. According to the way Robinson presents the issue,[49] *delatores* are greedy persons who would only have risked the dangers associated with an accusation if there was a lot of money to be made. The scenario that in actual fact unfolded just a couple of decades later does not even seem to be considered in Robinson's assessment—while for Pliny it seems to be the most *natural* development in the world (*ut fieri solet*)![50]

But the problems that the Pliny-Trajan exchange create for Robinson's thesis do not stop there. What the interaction ultimately demonstrates is that what Pliny did would need to be feared just as well, at least in principle, by Paul's congregations—precisely because it shows that following the Christian faith had *always* been dangerous because *no* law against it was needed to execute members of the congregations. Let us unpack this observation by paying closer attention to how the events continued to unfold.

Confronted with the multitude of accused persons mentioned, Pliny decides to employ a three-part test: Those who prayed to the Roman gods, offered incense and wine before the image of the emperor, and cursed the name of Christ were let go. By pointing out that "real Christians" would never do that, the test retrospectively offers a more than sufficient rationale for the initial killings that had occurred when it had not yet been clear that the matter would take on such dimensions:

48. Gibson, *Man of High Empire*, 217.

49. Robinson, "Hidden Transcripts?," 68–70.

50. To be sure, when executing the first group of Christians he most certainly had hoped this would end the matter and he would not have to write a letter to Trajan. Cf. Corke-Webster, "Trouble," 384.

Since [the test] discovers that Christians will not swear to the gods or sacrifice to the emperor, it established what Pliny had earlier suspected—that Christians were troublemakers. There was not of course any positive requirement on individuals to sacrifice to either gods or emperor of their own volition. But a refusal to do so when asked was a clearly rebellious gesture that more than justified the quick dispatch of non-citizens, especially if the official in question was already worried about these individuals being part of a mysterious collective. . . . [B]y demonstrating that Christians would not sacrifice, it provided legitimation for the executions Pliny had ordered initially.[51]

But the governor was still left with many people who were willing to take the test but admitted that they had been part of this strange group in the past.[52] Pliny is obviously concerned with the large number of people from all parts of society that are accused. Now, it is important to note that Pliny's primary concern is not with the Christians themselves but with *his* role as a governor. What he wants to avoid is the danger of navigating himself into a situation of excessive brutality, with his draconian rule ultimately resulting in unrest among the population that he governs—and correspondingly negative consequences for his career.[53] If, however, we decide to look at the correspondence specifically through the particular perspective of early Christianity, it is clearly Pliny—ironically as it may sound, given that he is known as a "slayer" of Christians—who takes the side of the Christians. Since he comes to the conclusion that in the end they do not commit any specific crimes, he wants Trajan to commit to a program of rehabilitation instead of punishment.[54] But what had been ignored in previous scholarship is that Pliny primarily becomes active because he fears for his reputation. He found out through interrogation of the former Christians and torture of two female slaves that at least his initial suspicion of specific crimes had been baseless, and this discovery "meant that

51. Corke-Webster, "Trouble," 385.

52. There might have been continuously confessing Christians in this group too. Cf. Corke-Webster, "Trouble," 382n47. Also, though less likely, this last group may have been due to a different informer. Cf. Corke-Webster, "Trouble," 386n62.

53. See the convincing argument in Corke-Webster, "Trouble," 374: "*Ep.* 10.96, I suggest, records just such a case where a governor caught between the ideal and the reality of the job sought imperial affirmation as a shield to guard against any future provincial provocation."

54. Cf. Klaus Thraede, "Noch einmal: Plinius d. J. und die Christen," *ZNW* 95 (2006): 102–28.

the Roman official's authority was undermined," which had the potential of damaging his future career.[55]

In his response, also known as his "rescript" (Pliny, *Ep.* 10.97), Emperor Trajan emphasized that no general decision was possible with regard to this matter. He thus left a lot of room for different kinds of actions by Roman governors for more than a century.[56] Much more importantly for Pliny, Trajan gave him the kind of confirmation that he had been eager to get—the confirmation that he had acted appropriately.[57] Looking at this again from the perspective of early Christianity, it seems to be a slightly positive development that Trajan adds one specific stipulation, namely that anonymous pamphlets should not be considered at all (that one should not actively search for Christians was simply in line with Pliny's own practice).

Even though there has been some debate about this issue in the past, the position that Trajan, with this decision, made things worse for the Christians by allegedly being the first to officially declare Christianity illegal seems untenable to me.[58] This notion is usually combined with the implication that 1 Peter and Revelation would have to be dated quite late.[59] This would also justify Robinson's implicit assumption that Paul's congregations were affected by a different, much more lax, public transcript concerning their faith. To the contrary, upon closer examination and paying attention to the dynamics of governmental practices in the provinces, the exchange indeed seems to show that Trajan only confirmed what Pliny had concluded for himself too, namely that the *nomen ipsum*—the fact of calling oneself a Christian alone—was a punishable crime because it went hand in hand with troublesome behavior (as demonstrated by the test).

Thus, the real question does not seem to be whether Christians might have

55. Cf. Corke-Webster, "Trouble," 387, 389–93.

56. The idea that Trajan's rescript had been perceived as official law that regulated affairs with Christians from that point in time forward is criticized now by Corke-Webster, "Trouble," 375.

57. See Corke-Webster, "Trouble," 375 for a succinct summary of the thesis of the pragmatics of the exchange and 397–404 for more details.

58. The idea that it was only through Trajan that the Christians first got into their precarious situation was forcefully argued for by Angelika Reichert, "Durchdachte Konfusion: Plinius, Trajan und das Christentum," *ZNW* 93 (2002): 227–50.

59. On this, see Angelika Reichert, "Gegensätzliche Wahrnehmungen einer ambivalenten Krisensituation: Das Plinius-Trajan-Konzept, der 1. Petrusbrief und die Johannesapokalypse," in *Bedrängnis und Identität: Studien zu Situation, Kommunikation und Theologie des 1. Petrusbriefes*, ed. David S. du Toit, with the help of Torsten Jantsch, BZNW 200 (Berlin: de Gruyter, 2013), 281–302.

faced persecution "even before" Trajan. It is possible (but not necessary) that Pliny felt encouraged in his decision to have the first group of Christians killed because he had some vague knowledge of similar incidents in the past (despite his admission of ignorance in *Ep.* 10.96.1, which could simply mean his prior lack of personal involvement).[60] Be that as it may, for similar things to have happened earlier, what is needed is simply a similar constellation of prejudices and willing accusers.

This is of course denied by those who assume that Pliny had acted upon *official* legal stipulations from the time of Nero, after 64 CE, or Domitian.[61] This would still shift the *terminus post quem* for writings such as 1 Peter and Revelation,[62] but it would not undermine Robinson's proposal insofar as at least the authentic Pauline epistles would have been written before the official verdict that would have made things so much worse. However, even though the unfortunate idea of a "Christengesetz" is still astonishingly prevalent in New Testament scholarship, "it has long been recognized that there is no good evidence of any legal precedent against Christians before Pliny's actions."[63] We, thus, must conclude that Pliny had simply acted within the realm of his own authority (*extraordinaria cognitio/cognitio extra ordinem*), which allowed him to conduct trials from beginning to end,[64] being encouraged—perhaps but not necessarily—in this particular situation by the knowledge that he would not be the first to do so because there was an established practice of precedential cases.

If the correspondence indeed implies, as it seems to do, that Christians could have been executed just as well before Trajan's rescript and if there never was a legal requirement, e.g., an edict that established this process in the first place, this means that there *never* was a period in the early church when being

---

60. *Cognitionibus de Christianis interfui numquam* in Pliny, *Ep.* 10.96.1 does not necessarily imply that Pliny wants to deny all knowledge about trials against Christians. Cf. Thraede, "Noch einmal," 113–14.

61. Molthagen, *Der römische Staat*, 16 and then 21–27, has influentially argued for this position. See also, more recently, his forceful restatement of that case in Joachim Molthagen, "'Cognitionbus de Christianis interfui numquam': Das Nichtwissen des Plinius und die Anfänge der Christenprozesse," *Zeitschrift für Theologie und Gemeinde* 9 (2004): 112–40.

62. Cf., e.g., Joachim Molthagen, "Die Lage der Christen im römischen Reich nach dem 1. Petrusbrief: Zum Problem einer Domitianischen Verfolgung," *Historia* 44 (1995): 422–58, who thinks that Domitian adopted Nero's more local stipulations and thus prepared the legal basis for trials as witnessed later under Pliny.

63. Corke-Webster, "Trouble," 380.

64. This has been reiterated recently by Wolfram Kinzig, *Christian Persecution in Antiquity*, trans. Markus Bockmuehl (Waco: Baylor University Press, 2021), 31.

a Christian was not potentially dangerous—and this includes the time of Paul's missionary activity. Any attempt to create a dichotomy between this period and later times is thus *deeply* flawed.[65]

65. Joachim Molthagen, "Die ersten Konflikte der Christen in der griechisch-römischen Welt," *Historia* 40 (1991): 42–76, concludes that before the persecution of Christians in Rome in 64 CE there were no conflicts with Roman officials as they would later be common. This assessment is due to mainly three factors. First, Molthagen is pretty pessimistic when it comes to the historical accuracy of Acts. The accusation of Acts 17:6–7, for example, is said to reflect Luke's own time (p. 56), around 90 CE (p. 44). This assessment smacks of circularity. For the idea that the "politischen Verdächtigungen" cannot be part of the original context can only be maintained if one already presupposes that the dimension of a political front would only emerge later. Second, and this time clearly circular, is of course the very selection of documents that are admitted as evidence for this period. Molthagen concludes his article (p. 75) with the assessment that the new situation of a "tödliche Dimension" is reflected in 1 Peter: "Diese neue Situation spiegelt sich im 1. Petrusbrief." And this letter is then dated to the reign of Domitian because it does not reflect an "Alltagssituation," "wie sie für die christlichen Gemeinden seit ihren ersten Anfängen immer bestand," but the new legal status of it being a crime to be a Christian (Molthagen, "Lage," 439). Cf. Molthagen, "Lage," 452–53, where he again describes the dichotomy that he himself has created through the assumption of a "kaiserliche Initiative, die in rechtlich wirksamer Weise das Christsein reichsweit strafbar machte" (p. 455). Third, his assumption of the official criminalization of Christianity under Nero makes it impossible for Molthagen to accept the idea of a gradual (geographically and periodically varying) intensification. Even when the events that are narrated are indeed fixed in time (i.e., unlike in the case of Acts and 1 Peter), they must not be understood as implying serious conflict because such a result is ruled out by the assumption of law-abiding, religiously liberal governors. Cf., for example, Molthagen, "Konflikte," 75: "Von den ersten Konflikten, die Apostelgeschichte bezeugt, führt kein gradliniger Weg zu den späteren Christenprozessen." To be sure, if any accusation after 64 CE inevitably led to execution, then we must note that the Roman governors in Acts behave qualitatively differently. If, however, there was no official stipulation for executing Christians under Nero, this allows for the possibility of later trials at times having a more positive outcome—and earlier trials already ending in death or at least being associated with that danger. It should also be noted that even in later times, when Christians were being sought out and killed, people were sometimes punished lightly. One big obstacle for Molthagen, "Konflikte," 63–65, is of course the potential trial in front of the proconsul of Asia in Ephesus, as implied by Phil 1:13. The real possibility of death (cf. Phil 1:20–22) is also acknowledged by Molthagen, "Konflikte," 64. How then can he conclude (p. 75) that in the time of Paul's mission, the situation looks totally different from the scenario under Pliny? In a strange reading of Phil 1:13 Molthagen claims (p. 64) that Paul wants to say "daß seine nichtchristliche Umgebung am Sitz des Statthalters offenbar erst während seiner Gefangenschaft die Einsicht gewonnen habe, daß er wegen seines Glaubens an Christus—nichtchristlich gesprochen: wegen seiner religiösen Überzeugung—in Haft sei." Then, Molthagen's strict insistence that a Roman governor would not have convicted Christians without legal precedent leads him to the conclusion (p. 65) that if the proconsul would have agreed with the assessment that the

Some seem to be uncomfortable with this conclusion and choose a middle route, which in the end also proves unconvincing. Schnelle, for example, does not seem to assume an *official* decision that would have made being a Christian illegal but still associates the start date of this legal trouble with the persecution of Christians in Rome in 64 CE.[66] However, this seems to stand in tension with his own recognition that the conflict between emerging Christianity and the Roman Empire was "inevitable" due to the Christology at its very basis.[67] Thus I think that even in earlier times being a Christian would come with prejudices concerning anti-social behavior that would have made the safety of Christian communities dependent on the goodwill of individual governors.[68] The *nomen ipsum* might not have been an official crime before Trajan, but it arguably

---

imprisonment was due to Paul's association with Christianity, he would have been *forced* to let him go again.

66. Udo Schnelle, *Die ersten 100 Jahre des Christentums: 30–130 n. Chr.*, 3rd ed. (Göttingen: Vandenhoeck & Ruprecht, 2019), 465: "Gegen Bagatellisierungen und Relativierungen ist daran festzuhalten: Die Christen galten *seit 64 n. Chr.* allein durch ihre Existenz/ihren Namen als potentiell bestrafungswürdig" (emphasis added). On the effect of the persecution in 64 CE, see pp. 451–52. David G. Horrell, *Becoming Christian: Essays on 1 Peter and the Making of Christian Identity*, LNTS 394 (London: Bloomsbury, 2013), chapter 6, section 6.4, offers a similar perspective. Horrell correctly emphasizes—against other views in the secondary literature on 1 Peter—that (a) being a Christian was already dangerous before Trajan's rescript, (b) the dichotomy between public hostility and official sanctions is wrong, and (c) this situation was not due to official legislation. Note, however, how he too treats 64 CE, at least implicitly, as a *terminus post quem* on, e.g., p. 190: "At least from the time of Trajan and probably from that of Nero . . . , profession of Christianity was indeed treated, albeit sporadically, as a crime punishable by death, but one in which trial and punishment depended first and foremost on persons being brought to Roman attention by an accuser and then on the disposition of particular governors, who wielded considerable power and freedom and did not need an imperial edict to act in such matters." Christianity was "effectively illegal from the time of Nero . . . , but this did not mean it was outlawed by edict, nor systematically targeted in some officially organized action. Rather, cases came to court when circumstance and popular hostility led to accusations, and when governors were disposed to hear and judge them." See p. 193 for more details. Later (p. 196) he concludes that "trials like those [Pliny] describes were certainly not unknown; they could well have taken place any time after 64 CE." It is only on p. 194 that he indicates that the persecution in Rome under Nero might not be the start date of Christian trouble with the Romans: "It is notable, however, that many Roman historians believe that Christianity was effectively illegal—regarded as inherently criminal—from the time of Nero (*or even before*), whether or not there was formal legislation to this effect, such that Trajan's rescript largely confirms rather than innovates policy regarding the Christians" (emphasis added).

67. Cf. Schnelle, *Die ersten 100 Jahre*, 444.

68. Cf. Heilig, *Hidden Criticism?*, 88–89.

was not one after his rescript either![69] Later Christian authors who speak of
persecution because of "Christ's name" (cf. Mark 13:13; Luke 21:12) probably
simply picked up rhetoric from the New Testament, without the Pliny-Trajan
correspondence—which they sometimes adduce—constituting the historical
basis.[70] If we—contra Molthagen—do not work within a dichotomous framework in which being Christian became illegal and only with that development
punishable, the entire search for a "starting point" that scholars like Schnelle
and Horrell keep from these earlier discussions becomes obsolete. From a
chronicler's perspective, one governor will have been the first to execute Christians. However, what ultimately mattered for Christian communities, at any
point during Paul's time and throughout later generations, was that being a
Christian came with suspicions of anti-social behavior that could very easily
lead to trials and convictions.[71] Even mundane commands, like the command
to keep a low profile by "calmly" pursuing one's job (cf. 2 Thess 3:12: . . . ἵνα
μετὰ ἡσυχίας ἐργαζόμενοι τὸν ἑαυτῶν ἄρτον ἐσθίωσιν), had life-and-death
consequences, like being left alone by governors (cf. 1 Tim 2:2: ἵνα ἤρεμον καὶ
ἡσύχιον βίον διάγωμεν ἐν πάσῃ εὐσεβείᾳ καὶ σεμνότητι). In talking about the

69. See Corke-Webster, "Trouble," 397–404. There is no evidence to suggest that Trajan's
rescript was a "legally binding response" (Kinzig, *Christian Persecution*, 48). Such readings
fall prey to the rhetorical instrumentalization of the correspondence between Pliny and
Trajan by later Christian authors (Tertullian and Eusebius). This has been convincingly
demonstrated by James Corke-Webster, "The Early Reception of Pliny the Younger in Tertullian of Carthage and Eusebius of Caesarea," *ClQ* 67 (2017): 247–62. Those who assume that
the rescript constituted the legal basis for dealing with Christians for subsequent generations
explain variegated outcomes of the ambiguity of Trajan's advice (so Kinzig, *Christian Persecution*, 48–49) and often assume that the disputed rescript attributed to Hadrian (handed
down to us in Justin, *1 Apol.* 68.6–10; Eusebius, *Hist. eccl.* 4.9.1–3) is authentic and further
complicated attempts to persecute Christians. See Kinzig, *Christian Persecution*, 51: "Such
limits on denunciations appear to explain why there is no evidence of any lawsuits against
Christians during the reign of Hadrian." They are also forced to assume that Justin, who
(in *1 Apol.* 2) presupposes that Christians should not be convicted just for being Christians
and who apparently assumes that Hadrian's rescript (which he adds in an appendix) follows
the same line of reasoning, presupposes an inaccurate legal situation. Kinzig continues:
"Hadrian . . . presupposed the rescript of Trajan, thereby retaining the possibility of a conviction solely for membership of Christianity, *without* proof of any additional crimes. We
do not know if Justin misunderstood the legal position or deliberately interpreted it in a
way that favored the Christians."
70. Corke-Webster, "Trouble," 402–4.
71. On the suspected anti-social behavior of Christians, cf. Corke-Webster, "Trouble,"
383. Molthagen, *Der römische Staat*, 16, is much too optimistic about the restraint of Roman
governors when he writes: "Es ist undenkbar, daß ein Statthalter ganz von sich aus Christen
auf ihr bloßes Bekenntnis hin so selbstverständlich hätte hinrichten lassen."

"anti-imperial" nature of early Christian writings we unfortunately often miss that what might have seemed to fellow citizens—or at least might have been presented to governors by fellow citizens—as "anti-imperial" are day-to-day issues through which Christians might somehow have looked suspicious to their neighbors.[72]

Therefore, we conclude that at the time of Paul being a Christian was "punishable" in practice even though it was not "prohibited" in theory.[73] As Corke-Webster concludes with respect to Pliny's convicts, "These Christians suffered not for anything unique to them as Christians but simply as maligned members of a minority provincial association coming before an overworked governor. No new mechanisms were required to deal with them; they simply experienced the routine brutality of Roman provincial administration."[74]

Exactly this danger loomed over Paul's converts too—whether it ever materialized or not. To be sure, if indeed this fate never met early Christians, acute fears might not have been as high as they might have been in the wake of actual executions of people in the community. But consequential (mis)judgments by Roman governors were hardly an overlooked possibility among the marginalized followers of a Jew who had been executed in Jerusalem under Pontius Pilate! For those involved, the question of whether "being a Christian alone" or the assumed associated anti-social crimes constituted the problem was a rather moot distinction.[75]

72. I am grateful to Prof. Stefan Krauter (Zurich), who is very skeptical about counterimperial subtexts in the letters of Paul, for drawing my attention to this consequence of the reinterpretation of the Pliny-Trajan correspondence.

73. Molthagen, "Lage," 70, fails to make this distinction and thus assumes that a legal watershed event must have taken place prior to the writing of 1 Peter: The letter "verdankt sich offenbar einer für die Christen *neuen* Situation, nämlich daß sie nicht mehr nur allgemein Verleumdungen seitens der Bevölkerung ausgesetzt waren, sondern allein wegen ihres Christseins gerichtlich angeklagt und verurteilt werden konnten" (italics original). Against the backdrop of the research by Corke-Webster, "Trouble," one would rather have to argue that *due* to the general defamation by contemporaries, Christians would *always* have to have reckoned with the possibility of being "accused and convicted." That is all that ever happened under the various emperors that are listed as potential reference points for New Testament writings.

74. Corke-Webster, "Trouble," 406.

75. Biblical scholarship—including nuanced treatments like Horrell, *Becoming Christian*, chapter 6—has focused too much on whether the *nomen ipsum*, the fact of being a Christian alone, was punishable (with or without official criminalization) before and after Trajan's rescript. However, it is precisely Pliny's uncertainty of whether belonging to this movement is punishable in itself, even if the—expected!—associated crimes cannot be confirmed (*nomen ipsum, si flagitiis careat, an flagitia cohaerentia nomini puniantur*; Pliny, *Ep.* 10.96.2),

We can thus conclude that any talk about dating "the beginning of persecution of Christians" to *either* 64 or 113 CE would be misleading on *two* accounts. Neither was it an innocent matter to be a Christian before nor was there much interest in the first two centuries from the side of Roman officials in eradicating this strange new superstition by excessive force.[76] Still, accusations in court by contemporaries were always possible, and whether or not admitting to being a Christian automatically implied or at least suggested that one was guilty of an offense against Roman piety or something else was up to the assessment of the individual Roman official. Ironically, it is precisely the interest in the "persecution of Christianity" as an isolated phenomenon[77] that has led to an unhelpful focus on the question of whether it was "under Trajan" or already "under Domitian" or even already "under Nero" (with disastrous consequences also for claims concerning the *terminus post quem* for the composition of New Testament texts)[78] that Christians had to fear for their lives. From the perspective of the Roman governor, what ultimately mattered was avoiding unrest and that could mean rather drastic measures, especially if it seemed like such measures could nip things in the bud.

To be sure, there were events throughout the first century, such as the persecution of 64 CE, which would have raised the acute risk for Christians in the provinces too. And even before that, the edict of Claudius in 49 CE might have had a similar effect.[79] Last but not least, Jewish-Roman tensions under

---

that is important to appropriately consider here. First, it implies that there was a general assumption about specific crimes that a Christian would be guilty of. Whether or not an accused Christian might escape punishment thus, second, depended to a large extent on the diligence of the individual governor. Also, third, the incidence shows that even if the initial suspicions were not confirmed to the extent that was expected, a governor might still decide to simply execute the small group just to make sure that no further trouble would arise.

76. It should be noted here that there has been some very valid pushback with respect to the notion of a systematic persecution of Christians under Roman rule. See in particular Candida Moss, *The Myth of Persecution: How Early Christians Invented a Story of Martyrdom* (New York: HarperCollins, 2013). At the same time, we must not belittle the real risks associated with being part of a movement that at least during the time of Paul was made up of groups that were marginalized in their societal environments. For a short summary of persecutions of Christians in the Roman Empire see Kinzig, *Christian Persecution*.

77. Corke-Webster, "Trouble," 406: "There is thus a wider methodological point here. Our attempts to uncover Christian experience must start not with early Christian texts but with the experience of non-Christians in similar circumstances. That is, the similarities of Christians with their fellow provincials must come before their differences."

78. See p. 110. James Corke-Webster and I are planning to write an article on this specific issue.

79. See Heilig, *Hidden Criticism?*, 81.

Caligula (see below, p. 31) would certainly also have constituted a reason for heightened alertness by Roman officials that might have affected Christian communities. On this basis, one might argue that the background plausibility for actual instances of excessive force increases significantly with time due to the fact that the Christian faith spreads and governors become more likely to become confronted with it. As a further argument supporting this tendency, one could indeed point to the fact that the less the early Christians appeared to be a part of recognized Judaism and the more their congregations resembled *collegia* the greater this danger would certainly be.[80] At the same time, the Pliny-Trajan correspondence should caution us against relying too heavily on this tendency. After all, it documents that a governor might choose excessive force precisely when he was of the opinion that a troublesome group was still a marginal phenomenon. Also, we know from the book of Acts that it did not take very much to end up before the Roman governor (Gallio hears charges against Paul in Acts 18:12–17, and Felix and Festus in Acts 24:1–25:12 conduct Paul's trial that leads him to Rome; cf. also Phil 1:13 for the potential imprisonment in Ephesus).[81]

This also has consequences for dating New Testament writings that are usually regarded as works that reflect a clearer confrontation between Rome and early Christians than Paul's letters. What is primarily needed in order to bolster the background plausibility of proposed dates is a plausible scenario under a specific Roman governor. This does *not* mean, for example, that Gaius Fonteius Agrippa is likely to be the "second beast" of Rev 13:11–18 and that the conflict behind the text should thus be dated to 68 CE,[82] but it does imply that a later date cannot simply be assumed to be more plausible on the grounds that it would need to be "under Domitian" or "under Trajan." It is the validity of the specific suggested occasion that will be determinative for the background plausibility of the hypothesis, not the decade in which it is situated per se.[83]

Now, when dealing with *Paul's* letters and potential fear of persecution, we

80. For the situation under Trajan, cf. Pliny, *Ep.* 10.33–34. See in particular 10.34.1 for the general suspicion toward associations: *Quodcumque nomen ex quacumque causa dederimus iis, qui in idem contracti fuerint, hetaeriae eaeque brevi fient.* The general dynamic is undisputed. See Kinzig, *Christian Persecution*, 47.

81. And then there is the positive case of the meeting with Sergius Paulus in Acts 13:7–12. On Luke's portrayal of governors, see Joshua Yoder, *Representatives of Roman Rule: Roman Provincial Governors in Luke-Acts*, BZNW 209 (Berlin: de Gruyter, 2014), chapter 5.

82. Winter, *Divine Honours*, chapter 12.

83. On the circularity that is often involved in dating 1 Peter under Domitian, see generally Heilig, *Hidden Criticism?*, 32–33. See also pp. 22–23 n. 65, above, and 110–11, below.

need to look for comparatively small conflicts. We do not need to prove actual draconian measures by a specific governor. For Paul and his congregations to be worried that they might end up in trouble, what is needed is sufficient evidence that their contemporaries might have accused them of anti-social behavior. And indeed, it seems pretty clear to me that the tensions that existed between Christians and their non-Christian neighbors automatically created sparks that from the beginning had the potential to make the tinder box explode in exactly the way that it is attested under Pliny.

The desire to gain possession of the accused person's wealth, put into focus by Robinson, might have indeed been *one* potential danger.[84] And contrary to Robinson's assessment, it seems to me that this might have been a potential "trigger" for avoiding public criticism of the Roman Empire. After all, there would have been enough members with substantial wealth in the early Christian communities to make this an attractive option, at least in some places.[85] Robinson seems to overlook this option by problematically limiting the discussion to the itinerant apostle himself:

> The more prestige an individual had, the more prestige a *delator* stood to gain by bringing him down. This makes Paul an unattractive target. Paul was a day labourer; the only real estate he probably had was at best a couple of tents. Financial and political advancement from bringing down Paul would have been minimal. Besides all this, even if a potential *delator* heard seditious material read from a Pauline letter, at the point at which the *delator* heard it Paul might be hundreds of miles away in another city. Even if a *delator* did covet Paul's tents and wish to bring a charge against him he would have to go and find Paul first.[86]

The almost breathtaking rhetorical ease with which Robinson makes us overlook those members of the congregation who had been and remained part of the local civic communities does not seem ultimately helpful.[87]

More importantly, however, this is far from the only reason why people might

84. Robinson, "Hidden Transcripts?," 68–70. So also Kinzig, *Christian Persecution*, 32.

85. On the variety within the socioeconomic profile of early Christians, see, e.g., Bruce W. Longenecker, "Socio-Economic Profiling of the First Urban Christians," in *After the First Urban Christians: The Social-Scientific Study of Pauline Christianity Twenty-Five Years Later*, ed. Todd D. Still and David G. Horrell (London: T&T Clark, 2009), 36–59.

86. Robinson, "Hidden Transcripts?," 69.

87. Cf. again Longenecker, "Socio-Economic Profiling," on the varying socioeconomic statuses within the congregations.

accuse somebody of belonging to a suspicious new cult. Paul's missionary activity came with real economic consequences (cf. Acts 16:19), which could easily have been a reason for accusations of being "un-Roman" (16:21). These dynamics were not monolithic at all. In Ephesus, where Paul creates a similar effect, it is the chaotic response that is feared (see 19:23–40, especially v. 40) as something that might lead to Roman discipline. In the case of Pliny too, the anonymous accusations might have originated "among local vendors who had suffered financially because of the decline in animal sacrifice."[88] Loss of income can be just as much a financial motivation as the prospect of becoming rich. There might not always have been acute reasons to elevate the conflict to the level that we can see in the correspondence between Pliny and Trajan, but there is no reason to deny that it was simmering just below the surface.

In addition, there is of course the (inner-)Jewish front. Robinson apparently does not think the move "from antagonism with Jewish leaders to treason accusations" is clear at all.[89] This is inexplicable to me. Acts 17:1–9 seems to offer, after all, a pretty clear example in that regard[90] and is fully in line with conflicts between early Christians and established synagogues as a concomitant phenomenon of the "parting of the ways."[91] Justin Hardin has even argued that the conflict in the Galatian churches is to be explained as the result of Jewish Christian attempts to keep non-Jewish members of the churches associated

88. Corke-Webster, "Trouble," 384.

89. Robinson, "Hidden Transcripts?," 59. Robinson is referring here to the argument made by Judith A. Diehl, "Empire and Epistles: Anti-Roman Rhetoric in the New Testament Epistles," *CBR* 10 (2012): 222. To be fair, Diehl does not specify the role of Jewish opposition precisely, but on a charitable reading the passage does make sense to me:

> Though he was Jewish by birth and custom, perhaps it was the "Roman-ness" of Paul that allowed him to travel freely in the Empire, to speak relatively openly, and to write with comprehension to Roman audiences. It is apparent that the combination of Paul's Jewish background and his Roman citizenship helped him advance the gospel message across Asia Minor. Yet, we know that not infrequently, Paul and his message were rejected by the local Jews (Acts 22–23). Surrounded by hostility on all sides, Paul and his associates may have found it necessary to "codify" their words, or use "hidden language" so as not to incite the wrath of the Roman establishment, or of the Jewish leaders. When he wrote to his fellow believers in the Empire, was he cautious with his language so that he did not place his recipients in danger of treason? How did Paul's message about a Jewish messiah figure effectively explain the "kingdom of God and the lordship of Christ" in an environment that recognized only "Caesar as Lord"?

90. Heilig, *Hidden Criticism?*, 62–63. Robinson ("Hidden Transcripts?," 64) does not discuss the incident, even though she relies heavily on Hardin, "Decrees," for primary sources.

91. See Kinzig, *Christian Persecution*, chapter 1, for a succinct summary.

with accepted Judaism by having them get circumcised—so that they would avoid scrutiny for their obvious refusal to participate in imperial cults.[92] It is questionable whether this can actually be inferred from hints like the mention of the desire of the "troublemakers" to avoid persecution (Gal 6:12).[93] But while we cannot know whether said scenario is indeed the constellation behind this particular letter, the general dynamic that Hardin describes is extremely plausible. Facing scrutiny for "asocial" behavior and negotiating relationships with Judaism as a potential haven will most certainly have constituted important parameters of social life in the early stages of many Pauline churches.[94]

In conclusion, we can say that the small insight that we can gain into Christian-Roman relations from the exchange between Pliny and Trajan seems to add important nuances to Robinson's discussion, which focuses too exclusively on the potential accusation of "treason" (*crimen maiestatis*).[95] To be clear, the above considerations do not prove any specifics about concrete sanctions or looming threats for Pauline churches. But I do think that they shift the burden of proof. If the legal situation of Paul and his congregations had been as unproblematic as Robinson thinks it was, the events that are attested under Pliny should never have happened. After all, the Christians executed under his authority did not find themselves in a situation that was significantly different from the one that Paul's converts experienced.[96] They just happened to find themselves confronted with a governor who thought that executions might solve the problem of potential trouble from these suspicious

92. Justin K. Hardin, *Galatians and the Imperial Cult*, WUNT 2/237 (Tübingen: Mohr Siebeck, 2008).

93. The problem seems to me that the alternative explanation—broadly speaking identifying the conflict as occurring between Jews and Jewish Christians—also has good background plausibility and explanatory potential.

94. Cf. also Markus Öhler, "Römisches Vereinsrecht und christliche Gemeinden," in *Zwischen den Reichen: Neues Testament und Römische Herrschaft*, ed. Michael Labahn and Jürgen Zangenberg, Texte und Arbeiten zum neutestamentlichen Zeitalter 36 (Tübingen: A. Francke, 2002), 62.

95. Robinson, "Hidden Transcripts?," 62–65.

96. This, again, assumes that in the meantime there was no official ruling on how to deal with people who identified themselves as Christians. Theoretically, it would of course be possible to still make the case that under Pliny the legal situation of the Christians had changed due to other laws. Note, however, that it will not suffice to point to stricter regulations with respect to the *collegia*. After all, Pliny explicitly acquits the accused of this specific charge. See Öhler, "Römisches Vereinsrecht," 63. For a more nuanced understanding of the role of illegal associations in the Pliny-Trajan correspondence, see Corke-Webster, "Trouble," 381, who thinks it was an "initial suspicion" that was enhanced by more general prejudices (p. 383).

people. The Roman Empire might not have been a "police state" but this does not mean that Christians would have enjoyed unfettered religious liberty, as Robinson seems to imply. To the contrary, it is precisely the lack of clear legal regulations in the background of Pliny's behavior which makes it plausible that similar things could have happened also much earlier.

Analogously, it seems extremely problematic to me when Cohick, in a similar move, emphasizes Roman liberalism by pointing to the fact that Eastern cults (though—and it seems like this would merit much greater emphasis!—"closely watched and condemned if their practices were determined to undermine Roman political or moral convictions") were still "allowed to establish meeting places and to openly identify themselves in Rome."[97] True, this "include[s]" Judaism (not that this relationship would have been without any conflicts, right?), but in many ways this is a particularly bad example because of the special status of Jews[98] and the apparent struggle of Christians (to which we will turn shortly), who were perceived more and more as a separate entity. In any case, Philo's *Embassy to Gaius* can only be called "instructive" in this regard if it is read in the broader context of his interaction with the Roman Empire.[99] When viewed from such a broad perspective, the following characterization seems to be dramatically off target: "[Philo] assumes a delegation could present their case and persuade Emperor Caligula of their cause's rightness; there was no need to hide or write private letters in coded message." It would be more accurate to say that, first, in this particular case the conflict had become so bad in 38 CE that for the Jews of Alexandria there was the need to interact with the emperor in Rome himself. Second and more importantly, Cohick confuses "story and discourse" here. The writing itself ironically demonstrates the opposite of the liberalism that Cohick implies. It is a prime example of a "hidden transcript in veiled form," using the bad example of Caligula to indirectly influence the new emperor, probably Claudius.[100]

In my opinion, this renewed insistence on the alleged safety of public criticism of the Roman Empire by early Christians as put forward by authors like Robinson and Cohick has failed pretty clearly—at least in its generalizing form. To be sure, Phil 4:22 might indeed give us some reason to be cautious

97. Lynn H. Cohick, "Philippians and Empire: Paul's Engagement with Imperialism and the Imperial Cult," in *Jesus Is Lord, Caesar Is Not: Evaluating Empire in New Testament Studies*, ed. Scot McKnight and Joseph B. Monica (Downers Grove: IVP Academic, 2013), 176.

98. See Heilig, *Hidden Criticism?*, chapter 4, section 1.

99. Heilig, *Hidden Criticism?*, chapter 1.

100. Heilig, *Hidden Criticism?*, 79–82.

with respect to assuming that Paul and his followers constantly lived in a situation of acutely perceived danger. Otherwise, we might want to assume, as Barclay points out, that Paul "foolishly blows the cover of Christians (perhaps even in Rome itself!) by sending greetings from believers in the household of Caesar."[101] Admittedly, this argument seems to have some plausibility: either Paul did not think that knowledge of such converts might lead to a crackdown—or he was, as Barclay instead suggests, confident that at least this particular letter would not fall into hostile hands. However, it seems to me that such an analysis might still miss an option. Perhaps Paul did indeed expect his writings to be scrutinized[102] *and* might have been aware of the fact that he was risking some people's safety, but he *nevertheless* regarded this risk as being worth it—either, something usually not considered, because he simply assigned an especially high value to the communication of the greetings or because, by drawing special attention (cf. μάλιστα) to the emperor, he could make an important point about the Rome-critical message of the letter as a whole.[103] And, as I will argue in more detail later (see below, pp. 37–38),

---

101. Barclay, "Roman Empire," 381.

102. Angela Standhartinger, "Die paulinische Theologie im Spannungsfeld römisch-imperialer Machtpolitik: Eine neue Perspektive auf Paulus, kritisch geprüft anhand des Philipperbriefs," in *Religion, Politik und Gewalt*, ed. Friedrich Schweitzer, Veröffentlichungen der Wissenschaftlichen Gesellschaft für Theologie 29 (Gütersloh: Gütersloher Verlagshaus, 2006), 376, concludes: "Besuch und materielle Unterstützung von Gefangenen war jedoch zumindest durch Bezahlen entsprechender Bestechungsgelder möglich, ebenso das Verfassen von Texten und der Austausch von Nachrichten. Allerdings war die Furcht vor einer Selbstgefährdung durch solche Texte durchaus begründet. Es leuchtet schon deshalb ein, dass Paulus die Philipper über Grund und Einzelheiten seiner Haft lieber mündlich informieren möchte. Schriftlich beschränkt er sich im Philipperbrief auf Andeutungen und mehrdeutige Aussagen." Cf. also Angela Standhartinger, "Aus der Welt eines Gefangenen: Die Kommunikationsstruktur des Philipperbriefs im Spiegel seiner Abfassungssituation," *NovT* 55 (2013): 140–67, and Angela Standhartinger, "Letter from Prison as Hidden Transcript: What It Tells Us about the People at Philippi," in *The People beside Paul: The Philippian Assembly and History from Below*, ed. Joseph A. Marchal, ECL 17 (Atlanta: SBL Press, 2015), 107–40.

103. Gordon D. Fee, *Paul's Letter to the Philippians*, NICNT (Grand Rapids: Eerdmans, 1995), 459–60, thinks Paul might emphasize "especially" these greetings because "Paul and the Philippans . . . have a common source of opposition": "While the Philippians suffer at the hands of Roman citizens loyal to Caesar, Paul is an actual prisoner of Caesar." Paul is fully aware of the fact that the implication that the gospel has penetrated Caesar's household is deeply subversive. Fee does not comment on the potential risk in making this statement but obviously thinks that there is a great payoff with it being "a word of encouragement to the Philippians in the midst of their present struggle." Flexsenhar's point that it is by no means clear that the πραιτώριον in Phil 1:13 refers to the emperor's bodyguard in Rome (see

the practice of making the "hidden transcript" clearly visible in the public discourse at select points in time is one of the most overlooked aspects in the application of the work of James C. Scott to the New Testament. The costs of such outbursts are notoriously difficult to calculate in advance—they are usually only evaluated, justified, or regretted in retrospect. A realistic assessment of Paul's situation should thus make us *expect* that for Paul himself it might have been difficult to calculate precisely the extent to which he might have put other Christians in danger with his comment in order to achieve some degree of satisfaction.[104] In fact, it is telling that Standhartinger in a more recent article[105] suggests that the mention of the Καίσαρος οἰκία in Phil 4:22 might have referred to "Paul's believing co-prisoners"—as a "spontaneously coined code, a creative metaphor reflecting the conditions of a prisoner in an imperial prison in Ephesus."[106] Modern scholars cannot even agree on whether the explicit evocation of the emperor might have inevitably (and unnecessarily!) attracted the attention of Roman officials or whether it would have constituted a cover for believing co-prisoners, "conceal[ing] their names behind the creative metaphor 'saints from the house of Caesar' in order to protect them in a highly dangerous moment of life."[107] So, we should reckon with the possibility that for Paul himself writing down this phrase would have been associated with some uncertainty concerning possible effects. In any case, this single verse can

---

most recently Michael Flexsenhar III, "Paul the Trojan Horse: The Legacy of Triumph in Philippians," *JSNT* 43 [2021]: 437–49) is well taken. I think, however, that he overplays his hand. To be sure, the idea of Paul having "infiltrated" the empire has often been integrated in a larger "triumphalist narrative" of Christianity. However, what Flexsenhar seems to miss, in my opinion, is that even if the historically accurate picture "is not as grand as one might imagine" (p. 443), it is still *Paul's language*, and not just the desire of modern exegetes, that evokes this impression. To use another example that is close at hand, Paul might not have portrayed himself as a victorious general in 2 Cor 2:14 as has been assumed for a long time in the history of exegesis (cf. chapters 3 and 4, below). But he is the one who intentionally evoked the figure of the Roman emperor and removed him from his traditional place in the triumphal chariot.

104. The delicacy of this whole matter can be seen from the more general observation that Paul contents himself with vague hints with respect to his imprisonment in general—which is precisely what makes the reconstruction of his circumstances so difficult for us. On this, cf. Standhartinger, "Die paulinische Theologie," 376.

105. Cf. her earlier comments in Standhartinger, "Aus der Welt eines Gefangenen," 160–61, and "Letter from Prison," 129–30.

106. Angela Standhartinger, "Greetings from Prison and Greetings from Caesar's House (Philippians 4.22): A Reconsideration of an Enigmatic Greek Expression in the Light of the Context and Setting of Philippians," *JSNT* 43 (2021): 468.

107. Standhartinger, "Greetings," 480.

hardly justify the assumption that being a Christian was not associated with any risks during Paul's time (and it is not even adduced by Robinson to this end). There are just too many well-established, everyday-life factors that could prompt an intensification of social, and also official, pressure at any moment. What it does emphasize, however, is that this oscillation of circumstances on a micro-level should make us expect a *constant testing of the limits of public discourse.* This can already be taken as a first indication that we need rather nuanced categories when talking about "hidden" criticism of the Roman Empire in Paul's letters. In the next chapter, we will explore this consideration in more detail.

2 | Beyond Hidden Criticism

Reviving Hidden Criticism

As explained in chapter 1, I remain unconvinced that Robinson has succeeded in making Wright's hypothesis collapse right at its foundation. In fact, her insistence on the manifold troubles that Paul faced with respect to a variety of contexts (see above, p. 16) has even caused me to reconsider my own criticism—necessary condition number 5—of the classical subtext-hypothesis, which is based on the assumption that criticism was hidden in order to avoid persecution. Against the backdrop of Robinson's lively portrayal, one might raise the question of whether it would not be plausible after all to assume that Paul would have had a tendency to avoid at least *unnecessary additional* trouble. After all, Robinson's sketch seems to allege that Paul had a kind of all-or-nothing mindset.[1] Robinson apparently wants to convince us that because Paul already encountered problems on many fronts, he would not have cared that much for the potential additional mess of his churches being regarded as politically subversive gatherings by their contemporaries.

---

1. To be sure, "catastrophizing" is a powerful mental dynamic in other areas of life and is, for example, characteristic of so many failed attempts at weight loss: once the daily calorie level is slightly overstepped, all rational constraints are thrown away and binge-eating begins, which is very destructive to the long-term goals. This is impressively demonstrated in an experiment by Paul Aveyard, professor of behavioural medicine at Oxford University, who, in episode three of the BBC show "What's the Right Diet for You? A Horizon Special," BBC, https://www.bbc.co.uk/food/articles/whats_the_right_diet_for_you, demonstrates that people trying to lose weight are prone to binge-eating when they think that they have already broken their calorie limit. The members of the control group—who thought they had been given extremely low-calorie cake and who thus had not "failed" yet—did not participate in such "catastrophic thinking" and its consequences.

Students regularly point out to me that my assessment of necessary condition number 5 seems to be the weakest line of argument in my book.[2] In less than four pages I manage to conclude that the Wright-Elliott hypothesis needs to be discarded due to its inconsistency with Paul's "personality." Admittedly, I have never been particularly shy about using this psychological category in historical arguments and am aware that it is not without problems to not only assign motives for concrete actions but also construct more abstract personality traits behind them.[3] In fact, I remember being quite relieved that I could simply quote Barclay, who had said that the assumption that Paul expressed his criticism only in coded form because he feared persecution "underrates Paul's courage."[4] As he explains: "It is hard to imagine Paul, whose preaching frequently landed himself and his converts in trouble, being afraid to speak his mind in his letters; since he expects believers to face 'persecution' (Phil 1.27–30), he is hardly going to shade the *gospel* to avoid it."[5]

The more I think about this issue now, the more I come to the realization that such a dichotomy in the end does not do justice to the historical realities and that we probably need to think about Paul's behavior as a *constantly negotiated compromise* between what was necessary to remain truthful to the gospel and what was necessary for the proclamation of the gospel to even remain possible. Already in *Hidden Criticism?* I had hinted at Paul's "diplomatic" approach toward pagan elements in his environment.[6] In addition I now think that we should be open toward the possibility that competing interests resulted in a variegated picture with respect to the entirety of Paul's decisions on whether or not he should react to certain Roman elements of his world and how he should do so. In fact, the circumstance that Paul stood before several Roman governors without suffering the fate of those killed under Pliny demonstrates pretty clearly that he could, under certain conditions, tone down his message

2. Christoph Heilig, *Hidden Criticism? The Methodology and Plausibility of the Search for a Counter-Imperial Subtext in Paul* (Minneapolis: Fortress, 2017), 125–29. I am particularly thankful to Annina Völlmy for her critique, which is reflected in what follows.

3. Cf. Christoph Heilig, "The New Perspective (on Paul) on Peter: How the Philosophy of Historiography Can Help in Understanding Earliest Christianity," in *Christian Origins and the Establishment of the Early Jesus Movement*, Christian Origins and Greco-Roman Culture 4, ed. Stanley E. Porter and Andrew W. Pitts (Leiden: Brill, 2018), 482.

4. Heilig, *Hidden Criticism?*, 126; John M. G. Barclay, "Why the Roman Empire Was Insignificant to Paul," in *Pauline Churches and Diaspora Jews*, ed. John M. G. Barclay, WUNT 275 (Tübingen: Mohr Siebeck, 2011), 380.

5. Barclay, "Roman Empire," 381.

6. Heilig, *Hidden Criticism?*, 127.

for strategic reasons[7]—the Paul of the Martyrdom of Paul 3.2[8] as well as the Paul of 1 Cor 2:6, 8 or Phil 2:6–11 would have been sent to Rome in a heartbeat (on a good day, that is).[9]

Note that the constant negotiation I suggest encompasses more than just conscious processes. If the categories of hidden and public transcript are of any use for the present issue, it lies in the fact that they can remind us of how fuzzy their borders can actually be—and how incompetent human beings sometimes are at navigating between these spheres. After all, it regularly occurs that people make wrong assumptions about which transcript even applies in a certain situation.[10] I at least sometimes say things in public that I know, or certainly should know, are not in accordance with the public transcript. Right at the beginning of his book, Scott himself adduces an example "of the hidden transcript storming the stage."[11] And even though he is famous for his focus on the more subtle precursors of such a public manifestation of the hidden transcript, he has nevertheless devoted a whole chapter to "what happens when the frontier between the hidden and the public transcripts is decisively breached," discussing such open revolt also with an eye to what happens in the heat of passion and to the psychological relief it can bring, "despite the actual risks often run."[12] Perhaps, one could argue, Paul simply could not hold back his rather aggressive comment in 1 Cor 2:6, even though he knew it was not the wisest thing to do. We must

7. Cf. Cédric Brélaz, "The Provincial Contexts of Paul's Imprisonments: Law Enforcement and Criminal Procedure in the Roman East," *JSNT* 43 (2021): 494–97, on Paul's situation while writing Philippians. If the charge was indeed comparable to Acts 17—"subversion against Roman rule"—and Paul did not regain freedom through an escape (see below, pp. 107–8 n. 16), we must conclude that the governor let him go (either as a result of the trial or because the governor did not think that there were grounds for a trial, unless we assume Roman imprisonment).

8. In this early Christian text, which circulated both as part of the Acts of Paul and independently and told the story of Paul's execution under Nero, Paul speaks in a very militaristic tone to the emperor, calling Christ a "king" who commands "soldiers."

9. Cf., for example, Pliny *Ep.* 2.11.8 on the case of Marius Priscus, who had accepted bribes in order to even punish a Roman knight.

10. I am reminded, for example, of a recent scandal involving a German governor (Bodo Ramelow) who had apparently miscalculated the public nature of his appearance on the app "clubhouse." His apparently belittling comments on Chancellor Angela Merkel and various other topics sparked serious outrage. See Cathrin Gilbert and Martin Machowecz with Bodo Ramelow, "Ich verstecke mich nicht mehr," DIE ZEIT 5/2021, January 28, 2021, https://www.zeit.de/2021/05/bodo-ramelow-thueringen-ministerpraesident-clubhouse-candy-crush.

11. James C. Scott, *Domination and the Arts of Resistance: Hidden Transcripts* (New Haven: Yale University Press, 1990), 6.

12. See Scott, *Domination*, 208; cf. all of his chapter 8.

not ignore such "explosions" (see also above, pp. 32–33, on Phil 4:22).[13] Lastly, we should expect inconsistencies with respect to the contours of the public transcript just as much as we do with regard to inconsistencies in behavior.[14] Things that Paul might have deemed borderline but ultimately worth the risk in Corinth might have been too controversial for Rome[15] (and, vice versa, fine if Philippians were written from Ephesus but just a little too much if written from the capitol itself).[16]

All these considerations have made me wary of my former assumption

13. See Scott, *Domination*, 9, for this choice of words.

14. I regularly experience this on social media, where the dominance of English as the language of my posts seems to be taken by at least some US Americans as evidence for the idea that their specific set of social norms and conventions are unquestionably accepted around the world.

15. See Heilig, *Hidden Criticism?*, 147 on Rome as the destination of a letter.

16. For the most recent summary of why the traditional assumption of Rome as the place of composition of the Letter to the Philippians is far from obvious, see Michael Flexsenhar III, "Paul the Trojan Horse: The Legacy of Triumph in Philippians," *JSNT* 43 (2021). The general argument is valid. It remains the case that "the most probable place for the apostle to have been 'in chains' is the headquarters of a governor" (Brélaz, "Provincial Contexts," 495), with Ephesus being a very reasonable guess (cf. p. 496). The case for Corinth presented by Douglas A. Campbell, "The Provenance of Philippians: A Response to the Analyses of Michael Flexsenhar, Heike Omerzu, Angela Standhartinger and Cédric Brélaz," *JSNT* 43 (2021): 508–22, does not seem to be complete yet. For example, he notes (p. 517) that the Corinthian congregation would have been in existence "for around eleven years by the time Philippians was written, but an Ephesian congregation for less than two." From this he develops the following argument: "The presence of a household of converted imperial slaves who had migrated from Philippi to Paul's place of writing is therefore more plausible for Corinth than for Ephesus. More than a decade has passed during which this relocation to Corinth could have happened, as against just over one year in Ephesus, heightening the sense of coincidence involved with the latter suggestion." However, this examination of the "prior-probabilities" of the hypotheses (to use Bayesian terminology) seems to be based mostly in rhetorical power, not actual evidence. One could just as well give "intuitive" reasons for the opposite conclusion. Does more time imply more opportunities for migration? Sure. But more elapsed time might also decrease the probability of there still being a motivation to send greetings. Personally, I would be more likely to send such greetings to persons that I had seen only recently. We can fall very quickly into the trap of relying too much on our own experiences (of *both* migration and greetings). In the end, although Flexsenhar has rightly pointed to problems with the assumption of the letter being sent from Rome, I think he overestimates the significance of the question of origin (cf. pp. 438–40). His suggestions are interesting mainly from a perspective of migration (on this, cf. also Heike Omerzu, "Paul, the *Praetorium* and the Saints from Caesar's Household: Philippians Revisited in Light of Migration Theory," *JSNT* 43 [2021]: 450–67). The implications for the interpretation of the letter, however, have been exaggerated. See above, pp. 32–33 n. 103.

that Paul would have surely hazarded the consequences of public criticism because, after all, he did so in at least one instance. Even on a purely theoretical level, it now seems to me that the picture Robinson paints—the idea that Paul would risk persecution of his churches left and right because they were already viewed with suspicion by their contemporaries anyway—is even more dubious than the idea that Paul is quite blunt in 1 Cor 2:6 but might navigate cautiously in other places. Here, Wright's defense from *Paul and the Faithfulness of God* seems appropriate: "Barclay's implied either/or, in which people must always be either blunt or oblique but never both, does not fit Philo, or Josephus; or Paul."[17]

In chapters 3 and 4 I will take a detailed look at one other Pauline passage (2 Cor 2:14) and mention other potential candidates in passing. This process will result in some confirmation for the view that 1 Cor 2:6 does not offer a unique insight into Paul's confrontational personality (with him not having to criticize much in other places, where he remains mute), but rather marks one end of a spectrum that might be attested in Paul's letters in a very differentiated way, moving from open criticism to more ambiguous statements.

From Hidden to Unexpressed Criticism

Toward the end of her article, Robinson considers the option that we might "find a motive other than Roman surveillance and prosecution" for the use of hidden criticism.[18] Unfortunately she then only adduces Wright's theory from *Paul and the Faithfulness of God* (2013) that Paul remained indirect with his anti-imperial attacks so as not to encourage his congregations to an outright revolution.[19] It is thus a fundamental shortcoming of Robinson's article that she does not consider alternative motivations for choosing the subtext for potential criticism besides fear of persecution and the further suggestion by Wright that he might have over-motivated Christians in view. I sketched some options after my rejection of both of these rationales.[20] But what needs to be emphasized is that even within the much more limited framework of revisiting

17. N. T. Wright, *Paul and the Faithfulness of God*, Christian Origins and the Question of God 4 (London: SPCK, 2013), 1316. To be sure, one could argue that Wright himself contributed to this picture by using analogies for the kind of subtext he found in Paul that implied a rather strict limitation to critique staying below the threshold of being punishable.

18. Laura Robinson, "Hidden Transcripts? The Supposedly Self-Censoring Paul and Rome as Surveillance State in Modern Pauline Scholarship," *NTS* 67 (2021): 71.

19. Wright, *Paul and the Faithfulness of God*, 1315.

20. Heilig, *Hidden Criticism?*, 129–38.

the classical hypothesis by Wright/Elliott and ignoring later modifications, Robinson's argument ultimately remains unconvincing.

This does not mean, however, that her contribution has not advanced the debate. On the contrary, I believe that Robinson has made some very enlightening observations that we should take as a stimulus for further refinements of the theoretical gridwork for analyzing Paul's critical interaction with the Roman Empire. One comment that I found especially striking was her assessment that we are "trapped in the cycle of trying to tease out what Paul would have said if his circumstances were different."[21] This hits the nail right on the head! Scholars struggle to conceal their disappointment about Paul, whom they believe to be nothing short of a revolutionary, but who, in an unfortunate coincidence, did not tell us nearly enough about what he really thought (and additionally expressed himself in a rather confusing manner when he did pen Rom 13). Reading Paul's letters through the lens of the Martyrdom of Paul, we can easily imagine the things that might ultimately have cost his life and that he would have been very much in a position to express as a historical figure. The temptation is great to make good for the lack of actual Pauline material by pointing out that Paul "could have written" a snarky statement found in other Jewish or early Christian sources of his time.

To be sure, it is, in fact, of course absolutely appropriate to incorporate material that is truly comparable in order to find out more about Paul's worldview. And Robinson is unfortunately quite unfair to Wright when she claims that "Wright does set up this discussion of coding with two historical examples he considers to be analogous."[22] The problem with Robinson's statement is that in addition to homoerotic codes and the Chinese playwright, Wright adds the following sentence for which he also provides references: "In the first century, exactly the same has been argued in relation to Philo on the one hand and Nero on the other."[23] And indeed, on closer examination Philo's differentiated—and not always that subtle!—critique of Roman power offers fascinating parallels to the letters of the apostle.[24] More generally, we can note that in reconstructing what Paul thought, we are always dependent on deductions made on the basis of extant texts that in other parts exhibit parallels to the letters of the apostle that we possess. However, Robinson's remark points

21. Robinson, "Hidden Transcripts?," 71.
22. Robinson, "Hidden Transcripts?," 60.
23. N. T. Wright, *Paul: In Fresh Perspective* (Minneapolis: Fortress, 2005), 61.
24. See Heilig, *Hidden Criticism?*, chapter 1 on potential subtle criticism of Rome in Philo, *Somn.* 2. See Heilig, *Hidden Criticism?*, chapter 5, section 1 on Paul's attitude toward the Roman Empire.

beyond these facts, which should be manifest to all, to a differentiation that is actually quite simple but nevertheless elusive.

In the end, we must not forget that it is one thing to refer to the prospect of sanctions as an explanation for why we do not find more examples of aggressive criticism of the Roman Empire in Paul's letters.[25] Yet, it is an entirely separate and very different thing to move from this admission to a claim that such attacks that Paul "could have expressed" somehow made their way into his letters in the form of coded criticism, i.e., between the lines. Just because it is reasonable to assign a certain opinion to Paul, it does not follow that he felt compelled to express it, let alone that he did so in the particular medium of his letters. Robinson discusses letter carriers only against the backdrop of them being potential "traitors" to the apostle. She rightly finds it implausible that Paul would have had reasons to mistrust them, given how close they were to him as coworkers.[26] One could also spin this in the other direction. Given how important these letter carriers were for ensuring the successful communicative attempt associated with the written letter,[27] having them convey in person any important information that would have been too sensitive for the medium of the letter would be a very obvious choice.[28]

But even the very assumption that Paul felt a need to communicate what he thought about certain aspects of the Roman Empire is itself far from obvious. It is certain that Paul had more thoughts in his mind than the little testimonies of his intellectual activity that have been handed down to us. There is also no real question that this applies to many aspects of the Roman Empire (which, I believe, he would have recognized as such, i.e., it is not just a modern construct for a variegated reality that he would have conceptualized entirely differently).[29] Yes, of course he would have been able to say things about the Roman emperor—and specific caesars too—that would have been very provocative if not outright unacceptable within the public transcript. If Scott's categories can teach us anything, then it is that as historians we constantly overestimate

25. Contrary to Robinson's assessment and to the caution I have previously expressed in this respect, I now think this is indeed a legitimate explanation.

26. Robinson, "Hidden Transcripts?," 68–69.

27. On Phoebe, see Paula Gooder, *Phoebe: A Story (with Notes): Pauline Christianity in Narrative Form* (London: Hodder & Stoughton, 2018).

28. Cicero regularly omits controversial information and refers to the (trusted!) letter carrier for details. See John Nicholson, "The Delivery and Confidentiality of Cicero's Letters," *CJ* 90 (1994): 41–42. Cf. Col 4:7 for Tychicus being charged with delivering additional information.

29. On this, see Heilig, *Hidden Criticism?*, 98–104. On the idea that Paul moved within a variety of subcultures that made him miss the forest for the trees, see below, pp. 85–86.

our access to hidden transcripts of the past. Some of these thoughts will have remained private, while Paul might have shared others in more intimate circles. The idea that there is just one version of a "Pauline hidden transcript" is naïve. There will have been many different *layers* of willingness to share private thoughts with other individuals.

Therefore, what we need in order to move forward in our assessment of the background plausibility of Wright's hypothesis seems to be an additional necessary condition that was lacking from my initial list:

1. Are the Pauline letters affected by the rules of public discourse at all?
2. Do these rules forbid open criticism of aspects of the Roman Empire?
3. Did Paul have an exposure to these elements and perceive them as specifically Roman?
4. Can we expect him to have had a critical stance toward those elements?
5. **Can we even identify a plausible occasion that might have compelled Paul to express these opinions in a specific situation?**
6. Is it reasonable in light of Paul's personality to assume that he expressed this critical stance in the subtext of his letters?

As I stated already in *Hidden Criticism?*, this list was meant as an attempt to make the assessment of the subtext-hypothesis's prior-probability more transparent—and as an attempt to provide an opportunity for other scholars to locate their disagreement precisely, either by coming to different results with respect to the listed conditions themselves or by pointing out "that important necessary conditions are missing."[30]

Robinson is to be thanked for putting her finger on an underexamined issue. What precisely are the circumstances that might have prompted the apostle Paul to deem it necessary to communicate part of his private thoughts on aspects of the Roman Empire to the recipients of his letters? As already admitted in *Hidden Criticism?*, the explanatory potential of the hypothesis of intended criticism might differ widely for the very same terms, depending on the letter they occur in. It stands to reason that when writing to Rome, Paul would have had to take into account heightened sensitivities among his

---

30. Heilig, *Hidden Criticism?*, 44. For disagreement on the evaluation of individual criteria, cf. Heilig, "Introduction," in Heilig, *Hidden Criticism?*

readers, especially in light of the expulsion of Jews a decade earlier, potentially because of inner-Jewish conflicts over the status of Jesus ("Chrestos").[31]

Analogously, to me it now seems worthwhile to point out that similar dynamics apply to the background plausibility factor as well. It is only natural to suppose that sometimes the emperor(s) would have been more on Paul's mind than in other cases. All too easily we forget that "things happened" around Paul, events that in their detailed nature and their impact on his state of mind go far beyond what we can cobble together in textbooks. In the end, the addition of this necessary condition calls for a detailed and diachronic analysis of the sociopolitical circumstances of Paul's letter-writing activity. There have at least been proposals for individual letters that need to be taken into account. Besides the already mentioned case of the imperial cult in Galatia as a potential cause for efforts to get gentile Christians circumcised, I would like to point to Bruce W. Winter's case for reading 1 Corinthians against the backdrop of the newly established imperial cult of the Achaean League (likely in Corinth, possibly in 54 CE).[32]

It is evidence for proposals like these that we need to demand in light of Robinson's critique. If such circumstances cannot be made plausible for specific letters, we do not have—assuming that the addition of the new criterion to the list of necessary conditions is justified—any substantive reason for assuming that Paul in this text intentionally communicated any detailed criticism of the Roman Empire. In this scenario, my admission that the argument from Paul's courageous personality has some weaknesses would not help Wright's original hypothesis much. After all, the fact that Paul might find the subtext an attractive vehicle for safe criticism becomes irrelevant if he had no interest in communicating such content to the recipients of the letter in the first place.

---

31. See Suetonius, *Claud.* 25.4. Cf. Heilig, *Hidden Criticism?*, 147.

32. On Galatia, see Justin K. Hardin, *Galatians and the Imperial Cult*, WUNT 2/237 (Tübingen: Mohr Siebeck, 2008). On 1 Corinthians, see Bruce W. Winter, *Divine Honours for the Caesars: The First Christians' Responses* (Grand Rapids: Eerdmans, 2015), 196–225, and the classic treatment by Antony J. S. Spawforth, "Corinth, Argos, and the Imperial Cult: Pseudo-Julian, *Letters* 198," *Hesperia* 63 (1994): 211–32. The dating of the letter that Winter uses is currently in question. An up-to-date critical assessment of Winter's thesis will be available in due course, once the relevant research questions have been settled, in D. Clint Burnett, *Imperial Divine Honors and Paul's Churches in Greece* (Grand Rapids: Eerdmans, forthcoming).

From Hidden to Merely Overlooked Criticism

From what we have looked at so far, Wright's original hypothesis emerges as subject to yet another necessary condition—but at the same time, somehow surprisingly, revived. As I have also made clear, more research is needed to evaluate the background plausibility more precisely. And—as always—nothing can be said about the overall probability unless *explanatory potentials* of competing hypotheses are evaluated. A general "feel" that a passage might have been perceived controversially if read before a Roman governor and that it is not "just" an allusion to the Septuagint will no longer be satisfying.[33] We will have to be very careful in laying out what kinds of textual phenomena we expect on the basis of the precise shape of our subtext-hypotheses and in demonstrating that the actual formulations in the text correspond better to these expectations than to the predictions from alternative hypotheses.

It needs to be noted (and is, as we have seen, admitted by Robinson toward the end of her analysis) that it was Wright himself who had transformed the monolithic subtext-hypothesis—based on the avoidance of persecution due to external examination of the letters—into a nexus of variegated considerations regarding the internal dynamics of Paul's churches. Perhaps Paul "is anxious, as a pastor writing or speaking to his flock might well be anxious, about people getting the wrong end of the stick, and either seizing too enthusiastically upon, or taking fright at, what to the wrong ears might sound like a literal call to arms."[34] These two options constitute *two rather different explanations* for why Paul's critique of the Roman Empire might be coded. The concern about someone perhaps "reporting to the authorities that Paul and his communities believed that there was 'another king, namely Jesus'" seems to call for an entirely *different kind of code talk* than the idea that if these things were only said out loud, they might cause people to take up arms immediately. I do not say that the two options are exclusive. They might explain different sets of phenomena in Paul's letters. But they certainly evoke different expectations with respect to how Paul would formulate his critique, and they will thus come with widely differing explanatory potentials for the text that we are actually faced with.[35]

The same can be said with even greater force if we also take into account the kinds of "resonances" that I suggested in *Hidden Criticism?* as a category in an attempt to modify the classical subtext-hypothesis so that it would not

33. Heilig, *Hidden Criticism?*, chapter 6.
34. Wright, *Paul and the Faithfulness of God*, 1315.
35. Cf. Heilig, *Hidden Criticism?*, 130–31, and Robinson, "Hidden Transcripts?," 71–72.

run into the problem of necessary condition number 5—nor number 1 and number 2, by the way, which is why it is a bit disappointing that Robinson does not address this possibility at all.[36] First, the idea behind this suggestion is that it should not be taken for granted that making use of the subtext is *ineffective* in influencing people's attitudes.[37] If the subtext is not a second-rate option, the whole attempt to justify why the criticism is not stated publicly—and why a courageous person like Paul might have committed such acts of apparent cowardice—becomes irrelevant. Second, I pointed to the fact that the notion of criticism is itself a variegated one and that there are options besides the obvious idea of full-fledged anti-imperial "attacks." Sometimes, I suggested, early Christian writers use language—and are not infrequently almost even forced to do so due to their rootedness in Jewish traditions—that would seem inevitably provocative from a Roman perspective, with the Christian authors being at least aware of it and not bothered enough to change their wording.

Originally, I had used the acoustic metaphor of "resonances" to distinguish such cases of more or less *accidental conceptual clash* with Roman ideology from "echoes" that pick up language from that realm directly.[38] Later, in my monograph *Paul's Triumph*, I modified the terminology a little bit because my focus shifted to the pragmatic effect of the Pauline text and I was less interested in differentiating with respect to its possible sources. Criticism might not be the primary objective of Paul, but, I argued, his wording often evokes, as a kind of by-product to the main message, *resonances* "that might occur with a view to Roman 'texts' in the broadest sense in light of the primary text of the letter."[39] With "resonances" I thus now refer to the two phenomena that I had previously separated into "echoes" and "resonances" based on their source. It is of course still possible to make this distinction within the broad concept of resonances. Readers might be reminded of Roman concepts due to actual echoes in the sense of direct borrowing but also due to language that is not derived from the Roman realm itself. I will leave it to someone else to find a fitting term for this counterpart to the "echo." What is important to me here is to emphasize that sometimes—but by no means always!—the "resulting conceptual comparison" enabled by both kinds of resonances might be "full

---

36. See Heilig, *Hidden Criticism?*, 129–38.

37. My considerations from *Hidden Criticism?* need to be supplemented with a much more robust account of communicative intentions. See Heilig, *Paulus als Erzähler? Eine narratologische Perspektive auf die Paulusbriefe*, BZNW 237 (Berlin: de Gruyter, 2020), section 4.

38. Heilig, *Hidden Criticism?*, 148.

39. Christoph Heilig, *Paul's Triumph: Reassessing 2 Corinthians 2:14 in Its Literary and Historical Context* (Leuven: Peeters, 2017), 273.

of *dissonances*" that can be heard clearly by anyone with ears attuned to the first-century context.[40] Again, the expectations with respect to phenomena of the text that might be explained as the result of such a process differ widely from those one should entertain on the basis of Wright's original subtext-hypothesis—which explains why the text I was looking at, 2 Cor 2:14, had not played any significant role in prior conversations on Paul and Empire.

In what follows, I will basically remain within the framework sketched in my earlier work and summarized in the previous paragraphs. However, I think that in light of Robinson's article I can now add sharper contours to my proposal, hopefully making it more fruitful for exegesis. I am especially thinking of a passage in which Robinson interacts with both Wright and me and in which she considers the different options that scholars face with respect to Paul and Empire:

> However, this still leaves us with one kind of speech that Heilig believes that Rome could not abide—the proclamation of a rival for imperial power. Heilig is on steadier ground when he claims that naming a competitor for Caesar's titles and lordship was far riskier than simply criticising the emperor. After all, the authors of the Gospels all seem to think that this was the crime for which Jesus was executed. However, here we fall into another trap. If Wright is correct that the "echo" of imperial propaganda is so strong that the claim "Jesus is Lord" declares that "Caesar is not," then Paul's letters already contain a bare-faced threat to Rome. Why would we need to search further for hidden criticism when Paul has already courted a death sentence and proclaimed a king besides Caesar? We are left with two options. Either Paul's coded subversion of the Roman government was so subtle that Romans would not hear it (in which case, it would be useless as a code for Roman Christians) or Paul was capable of drawing metaphorical language from the political sphere without actually attacking it. The latter solution seems likely. After all, Christian apologists of the second century regularly refer to Jesus as Lord in their texts that are meant to demonstrate what peaceable Roman subjects they are.[41]

So, basically what Robinson is saying is that we are faced with *two* options. The first is that Paul is a genius when it comes to concealing his critical message. That would explain why only Wright and a handful of his followers have been able to decode these critiques. However, this option has the downside

---

40. Heilig, *Paul's Triumph*, 273.
41. Robinson, "Hidden Transcripts?," 66.

that such an anti-imperial subtext would be communicatively ineffective. If modern experts cannot uncover the hidden message, why should mostly il-literate addressees in a Pauline church in the first century, who never had the accessible, birds-eye perspective from a wide range of sources about the Roman Empire available to modern scholars, have the necessary abilities? The only alternative that Robinson seems to recognize is that there is indeed nothing to uncover.

Interestingly, in the very same paragraph she herself hints at yet another option. Reading authors like Wright—who emphasize that the act of hiding critique is aimed at remaining under a sanctionable threshold—one cannot escape the impression that in their reading Paul is in the end quite blunt. At least *their* paraphrases of what Paul "actually" said are outright denials of important aspects of Roman ideology. There is certainly no ambiguity with respect to the alleged opinion itself. And time and again we are told how "ob-vious" the connection to Roman propaganda is.[42] Even assuming that a tiny fraction of these conclusions were justified, the question would arise: "Why would we need to search further for *hidden* criticism?" Exactly! Perhaps there is a third option after all—more *open* criticism of the Roman Empire than has been recognized so far.

At least the *Wirkungsgeschichte*, which Robinson adduces herself, seems to offer thorough support for such an idea. To be sure, if we are looking for sophisticated attempts to decode the political mysteries of Paul's letters, we will be disappointed. However, the very fact, which we have noted above (p. 23), that the conflict between emerging Christianity and the Roman Empire was "inevitable"[43] is rooted not least in the Pauline writings and their specific Christology. We will later (pp. 120–25) take a closer look at the claim that Christological titles such as κύριος were not judged to be problematic from a Roman perspective (and, vice versa, at the question of whether Christians really had no problem with the application of such terminology to the em-perors). For the moment, I want to focus on how to adequately integrate the insight that "Christian apologists of the second century" appear to be so keen on demonstrating "what peaceable Roman subjects they are."

It seems notable to me that when reference is made to later Christian au-

---

42. To give just one example, see Wright, *Paul and the Faithfulness of God*, 1291 on 1 Thess 5:3: "A wealth of evidence, including coins, points in one rather obvious direction: this was a standard boast of the Roman Empire."

43. Cf. Udo Schnelle, *Die ersten 100 Jahre des Christentums: 30–130 n. Chr.*, 3rd ed. (Göt-tingen: Vandenhoeck & Ruprecht, 2019), 444.

thors in discussions about New Testament writings in their Roman context, the works that are adduced regularly belong to the *public* transcript. If we fail to take this into account sufficiently, we will misinterpret texts that had to navigate public scrutiny by relying on works that are even meant to influence public discourse directly. To be sure, Tertullian is trying to paint the Christians as good citizens in, e.g., *Ad Scapulam*, a letter to a Roman governor, or in his *Apologeticus* (written to either Carthaginian or Roman elites). There he emphasizes what Paul in Rom 13:1–7 also already had maintained and what he might have emphasized even more in his appearances before Roman officials (cf. Acts 25:8 for a small glimpse). At the same time, in *De idololatria*, written to a Christian audience, Tertullian leaves no doubt about the incompatibility of emperor and Christ worship (15). Right before that (14), he adduces the apostle Paul and makes fun of those who might argue that his principle of trying to "please" everyone (1 Cor 10:33) might have extended to his willingness to take part in idolatry. It is treated as a *matter of course* that Paul opposed idolatry, including cultic veneration of the Roman emperors. There is no question that this was very controversial within the context of the wider society, nor is there any need to first uncover this problematic stance. To the contrary—those who might try to make Paul *less provocative* are the ones who are exercising *obscure interpretive moves*. Exactly the same logic lies behind Tertullian's discussion of the saying by Jesus on paying taxes a few sentences later (cf. Matt 22:15–22 // Mark 12:13–17 // Luke 20:20–26). He even admits that he is happy (*Bene quod apposuit...*) that the text does not just talk about obligations to the emperor but also to God and thus makes it absolutely clear what is meant. Notably, it is taken to be the *self-evident* reading (*Scilicet...*) that Jesus here marks the person as God's property in contrast to the money that belongs to the emperor.

If the general conflict at the basis of early Christian beliefs—fueled not least by Paul's writings—and basic tenets of the Roman Empire is recognized appropriately, the variegated attempts of early Christian authors, in the New Testament and beyond, to negotiate relations with their surroundings make good sense in their respective contexts. Defense of Christian loyalty toward the state and reference to past demonstrations of Roman goodwill toward the Christians have their place (as part of the public transcript or as an integral part of the hidden transcript, aiming at securing the lasting existence of the faith) just as much as harsh critique of practices that are widespread and yet unacceptable for Christians. The former cannot be adduced as argument against the latter, as Robinson wrongfully implies. Rather, the latter—the unquestioned controversial status of Christians in their Roman context—offers the necessary context for understanding the former emphases. It is only when public (Roman) and hidden (Christian) transcripts begin to merge that these realities cease to form the background of the whole discourse. If anything, in contexts of experiences of persecution the effective history of Paul's writings shows a tendency to overemphasize his arguably not-so-subtle qualifications of the scope of Roman authority (particularly in the Martyrdom of Paul).[44] To be sure, such texts probably do not reflect accurately how Paul would have framed his case in Rome, but it is important to note that they constitute an intensification of what is actually already there in the text. What is there is neither a completely new development, as one might think if one regards the Pauline epistles to be politically harmless,[45] nor a successful attempt to unlock a previously hidden subversive potential, as one might argue on the basis of the assumption that at least on the surface of Paul's letters they are (disappointingly) harmless.

Admittedly, my suggestion that the solution to the whole debate about hidden criticism in Paul's letters is ultimately that it is not well concealed at all but rather out there in the open might seem absurd, especially to those who have followed the nuanced discussions about proper sets of criteria and subtle textual allusions up to now. After all, the whole *premise* of the subtext-hypothesis is that while we would, for whatever reason, expect Paul to have said critical things about the Roman Empire, he apparently did not do so explicitly in his letters—thus, the perceived need to look elsewhere. But I maintain that we do not need to look elsewhere, just *closer*. If confirmed, this development would be not that unparalleled within Pauline studies. With respect to "implicit" narrative

44. Adduced as an argument from effective history by, e.g., Michael F. Bird, *An Anomalous Jew: Paul among Jews, Greeks, and Romans* (Grand Rapids: Eerdmans, 2016), 213–14.

45. Against, e.g., Harry W. Tajra, *The Martyrdom of St. Paul: Historical and Judicial Context, Tradition and Legends*, WUNT 2/67 (Tübingen: Mohr Siebeck, 1994), 121. The characterization by Glenn E. Snyder, *Acts of Paul: The Formation of a Pauline Corpus*, WUNT 2/352 (Tübingen: Mohr Siebeck, 2013), 64, as "an early, politically engaged form of Pauline faith and practice" is more to the point. The question is just how early that is. It is of course controversial whether the Mart. Paul actually offers us authentic (and even independent) insights into the persecution of Christians under Nero, as claimed by Willy Rordorf, "Die neronische Christenverfolgung im Spiegel der apokryphen Paulusakten," *NTS* 28 (1982): 365–74. In any case, it is hard to debate that they reflect a sentiment that would already fit very well in the time immediately after 64 CE. Cf. also Glenn E. Snyder, "History of the Martyrdom of Paul," in *The Last Years of Paul: Essays from the Tarragona Conference, June 2013*, ed. Armand Puig i Tàrrech, John M. G. Barclay, and Jörg Frey, with the assistance of Orrey McFarland, WUNT 352 (Tübingen: Mohr Siebeck, 2015), 343–73, for the case that the version in the Mart. Paul has at least as much claim to historicity as Acts and other legends (whatever that might ultimately imply).

structures in Paul's letters too, the justified attempt to save the category of 'story' for the interpretation of Paul's letters elicited the very unnecessary fundamental concession that there are basically no explicit, real, narratives in these texts.[46] (Alternatively, one could say perhaps that my suggestion proves only that I am guilty of the same unconvincing move in two different subject areas.)

I am thinking here of passages like 1 Cor 2:6, which I have adduced from the beginning as evidence for Paul being blunt on at least one occasion (see pp. 10–11, above). I would now just add that it no longer seems to be such an isolated phenomenon to me. In fact, Wright, in *Paul and the Faithfulness of God* (next to his assessment of 1 Thess 5:3 quoted above), also now adduces this verse as another "obvious" reproach of Rome (I agree!).[47] This tells me that in the end it might well be that quite a bit of what Wright has argued for as the result of some rather elaborate coding might eventually be explicable without reference to any such activity, which many find implausible.

At the same time, it is notable that, put in perspective, a passage like 1 Cor 2:6 has kept a rather low profile in the initial debates about an anti-imperial subtext in Paul.[48] How is it possible that such a clear deviation from public protocol has not featured more prominently in our conversation? Even though its existence is sometimes acknowledged, I think it is often not discussed in detail because it would not contribute very much toward arguing for *hidden* criticism. Claiming that such passages were meant to contain a *coded* message would indeed "understimat[e] potential censors' abilities to read between the lines."[49] Rather,

46. See in detail Heilig, *Paulus als Erzähler?*, chapter 2, section 4.

47. Wright, *Paul and the Faithfulness of God*, 1291. See also p. 1285.

48. It is sometimes mentioned as part of a general argument that Paul is more critical of the Roman Empire than one might think, for example, on the basis of Acts. Cf. Neil Elliott, "The Apostle Paul and Empire," in *In the Shadow of Empire: Reclaiming the Bible as a History of Faithful Resistance*, ed. Richard A. Horsley (Louisville: Westminster John Knox, 2008), 100. As far as I can see, the most attention the passage has received is in Neil Elliott, "The Anti-Imperial Message of the Cross," in *Paul and Empire: Religion and Power in Roman Imperial Society*, ed. Richard A. Horsley (Harrisburg: Trinity Press International, 1997), 172–76. Implications for the subtext-hypothesis that depend on coding as a means of avoiding persecution are not addressed, however.

49. With these words, Omerzu, "Paul," 455, specifically comments on the proposal by Standhartinger, "Greetings from Prison and Greetings from Caesar's House (Philippians 4.22): A Reconsideration of an Enigmatic Greek Expression in the Light of the Context and Setting of Philippians," *JSNT* 43 (2021), according to which Phil 4:22 is an attempt to *conceal* the identity of coprisoners. I agree with her that the explicit mention of the emperor would unnecessarily draw attention to these people that Standhartinger believes to be in great danger and that Paul is said to be protecting with his wording. Moreover, I think that her objection can be applied more generally to theses of anti-imperial subtexts. While these

1 Cor 2:6 constitutes a case of what one might, by contrast, call *casual* criticism, i.e., criticism that occurs in passing. Passages like this one do not fit the mold of elaborately concealed provocations and, thus, fly under the radar if what we are interested in is the sophisticated cover-up of anti-imperial intentions.

Thus, it is safe to say that there is undoubtedly a certain tension between what I have in mind and what Wright is suggesting. Paul can hardly be the *careful concealer* of his critical intentions and the *careless provocateur* at the same time. But between these two prototypical poles exists a broad spectrum of possible manifestations of mental interaction with Roman ideology. If Scott's concepts of hidden and public transcripts teach us anything then it is how *dynamically* these two conceptions relate to each other. We have already discussed this above pp. 37–38) in relation to 1 Cor 2:6. Paul might have avoided unnecessary risks in some places if he was sure that his audience would understand him even if he only referenced something by means of an allusion—with a more explicit discussion of the matter perhaps even having already occurred in person. In other cases, he might have felt it necessary to go out on a limb, or might simply have been moved by his emotions to do so. Or he might, rightly or not, have felt relatively safe in frankly speaking his mind in some situations (cf. Phil 4:22?), misjudging either the applicable protocol or the rules currently in place in that realm. In any case, it should be clear that arguing for how boldly provocative Paul is in some cases can hardly be an argument against a critique of Rome in general—it might just lower the background plausibility for intentionally coded criticism in specific letters.[50]

The cases of "casual" criticism or criticism "in passing" that I have in mind and to which I would encourage us to give greater attention constitute more or less deliberately granted insights in the Pauline hidden transcript. I have above (p. 32 n. 102) already cited Angela Standhartinger's point that in Philippians Paul speaks about his imprisonment only in "Andeutungen und mehrdeutige

---

claims might be correct with respect to the identification of an inherent challenge of the empire, they might be better understood as actually quite explicit, more or less intentional, outbursts of the hidden transcript on the stage of public discourse.

50. For example, Lynn H. Cohick, "Philippians and Empire: Paul's Engagement with Imperialism and the Imperial Cult," in *Jesus Is Lord, Caesar Is Not: Evaluating Empire in New Testament Studies*, ed. Scot McKnight and Joseph B. Monica (Downers Grove: IVP Academic, 2013), 175, makes a big deal of how unimpressed Paul seems to be by imperial power in his letter to the Philippians. So be it. It by no means implies that Phil 2:6–11 (cf. pp. 171–72) could not be a deeply subversive text from a Roman perspective. To the contrary, in my opinion it probably takes Paul's undaunted stance to pen such a provocative confession, possibly in Rome itself.

Aussagen."[51] Just like Wright has postulated with respect to criticism of Roman ideology, Standhartinger thinks that being more detailed in writing could potentially be dangerous for him. By contrast, I would like us to gain an even broader perspective on this phenomenon. To me, it seems like Paul is taciturn not only here; as exegetes we are frustratingly confronted with "hints and ambiguous statements" at almost every turn.

One of the main reasons why narratives in Paul's letters were overlooked for such a long time, even though they are of great importance for grasping his communicative aims, is that Paul is not a typical storyteller who narrates stories in order to inform the recipients about the occurrence of certain events in the past.[52] Rather, he regularly wants to affect the reevaluation of circumstances that are already known to his readers—or even wants to call them to action directly with the aid of stories. He can do this with incredibly succinct narratives because he can draw on implicit stories that stand behind his letters, stories that he already told explicitly in the congregations in earlier times. This shared knowledge affects a "pragmatic relief" of Paul's narration, i.e., he does not have to tell his stories the way he would tell them if he were informing the recipients of his letters of certain events for the first time (which he also does sometimes in other places).[53]

It seems plausible to me that something very similar might be going on with Paul's references to Roman ideology. It stands to reason that the topics Wright and others want to identify in Paul's letters were at least an issue that the early Christians struggled with in private (see above, pp. 39–43). It is because of the discussions that will have inevitably ensued within the Christian communities that Paul can pick up such themes in passing—simply because there is no need any more for elaborate discussions about how Christ and Caesar relate to each other. Even if new circumstances might arise (see above, p. 43, on Winter's thesis on the imperial cult in Corinth), Paul could comment on it against the backdrop of associated shared experiences.

51. Standhartinger, "Die paulinische Theologie im Spannungsfeld römisch-imperialer Machtpolitik: Eine neue Perspektive auf Paulus, kritisch geprüft anhand des Philipperbriefs," in Religion, Politik und Gewalt, ed. Friedrich Schweitzer, Veröffentlichungen der Wissenschaftlichen Gesellschaft für Theologie 29 (Gütersloh: Gütersloher Verlagshaus, 2006), 376.

52. On this issue and on everything that follows in this section see Heilig, Paulus als Erzähler?, chapter 1, section 3 and chapter 8, section 3.

53. Interestingly, the very same dynamic can be observed in the disputed letters, i.e., at least in the narrated world of these letters we are encouraged to imagine a prior shared prehistory between sender and recipients.

The more details Paul would have felt compelled to add to a potentially subversive statement, the more potentially looming sanctions might have played a role in inhibiting his first instincts when writing. It is here that Wright's thesis might still be applicable. But I also think that left to this threshold there is a zone on the spectrum of Pauline statements where "omitting" certain information (i.e., information that from *our* perspective seems to be lacking) is not even part of a conscious process but simply the result of the contextual factors that are involved in the pragmatics of Paul's letters. (And, it deserves to be repeated, such resonances do not depend on the fulfillment of either necessary condition number 1 or number 2!) For Paul to be cryptic (to us!) in relation to elements of discourses relating to the Roman Empire is not a circumstance to be explained by elaborate theories of coding—but should rather be our default expectation unless there are clear indications of situations that might have triggered a more explicit discussion.

Perhaps the biggest obstacle to enabling the discussion to continue in a constructive way is the term "criticism" itself. It is defined as 'the act of expressing disapproval and of noting the problems or faults of a person or thing: the act of criticizing someone or something.'[54] I have used it in such a wide sense myself.[55] For many, however, it will undoubtedly come with the association of confrontation: we usually express said problems in front of the affected persons. Perhaps it would be better to say that certain passages allow us to get a better idea of Paul's *unease* or *discontent* with the Roman Empire. ("Unmut" in German captures it really nicely.) We need to be careful not to make too ambitious statements about what Paul "really wants to say." In fact, in such an approach we are leaving interpretation proper (what did Paul mean?)[56] and venturing into an assessment of the Pauline letters as sources for historical reconstructions (what did Paul think?)—providing us, to be sure, with new background information that helps us address the question of how to understand Paul (that is, reconstruct the intended meaning of his texts) in many other places.

I am convinced that if we can move on from the idea that Paul somehow actively hid his Rome-critical opinions in his letters, the question of simply

---

54. *Merriam-Webster*, s.v. "criticism," accessed May 26, 2021, https://www.merriam -webster.com/dictionary/criticism.

55. Heilig, *Hidden Criticism?*, 129–38.

56. Cf. Theresa Heilig and Christoph Heilig, "Teaching Biblical Exegesis: The Distinction between Methods of Description and Interpretation," *Didaktikos* (forthcoming).

Figure 1. An "elephant tree" (marula tree, *Sclerocarya birrea*) in the shape of the actual animal (photo by Georg Grabowski)

overlooked criticism—or overlooked indications for Pauline discontent with the Roman Empire—will impose itself upon us in a powerful way. Perhaps—adapting Robinson's illustration—our focus on finding elephants hiding in trees has caused us to overlook the beautiful elephant trees (figure 1) right in front of our eyes.[57]

In the second half of this book, I will present just such a beautiful "elephant tree" to you in more detail: Paul's interaction with Roman ideology in 2 Cor 2:14.

57. The joke works better in German, where the marula tree (*Sclerocarya birrea*) is commonly called "Elefantenbaum," whereas in English "elephant tree" seems to be an alternative designation of mainly local relevance. Though the specimen in figure 1 truly resembles the large mammal, it must also be added that the name apparently is not due to the suggestive shape but to the preference elephants show for its fruits.

Finding—and Ignoring—Rome in a Pauline Passage

In this chapter, my aim is to illuminate the *contemporary Roman background* of 2 Cor 2:14—a background that is missed surprisingly often by modern readers of that letter. As I think this example demonstrates, Paul was indeed an *active observer* of his Roman context, and the fact that it does not regularly shine through in our interpretation of his letters tells much more about our lack of sensitivities than about his supposed ignorance toward the Roman Empire.

Looking at 2 Cor 2:14 in many English versions, I recognize that the Roman element that I have claimed to be there is admittedly not easily discernable. The KJV renders the Greek Τῷ δὲ θεῷ χάρις τῷ πάντοτε θριαμβεύοντι ἡμᾶς ἐν τῷ Χριστῷ as "Now thanks be unto God, which always causeth us to triumph in Christ." Most readers will understand the action implied by "to triumph" in the sense of 'to obtain victory.'[1] In American English, the verb "to triumph" can also express the celebration of a previously secured victory ('to celebrate victory or success boastfully or exultingly'). Nothing about that sounds particularly Roman either.

There is, however, a definition that is a bit more concrete, apparently specifying the kind of celebration: 'to receive the honor of a triumph.' It can be debated whether most readers have a good idea of what said "triumph" is. Usually, the noun will be understood simply as a synonym for other words like "victory"—perhaps, though certainly not necessarily, even with military overtones.[2] To be sure, it is difficult to see how the "honor" of such a victory could

---

1. *Merriam-Webster*, s.v. "triumph," accessed May 26, 2021, https://www.merriam-webster.com/dictionary/triumph.

2. *Merriam-Webster*, s.v. "triumph": 'a victory or conquest by or as if by military force'

be "received." In order to make sense of the definition for the verb, we thus need to turn again to the celebration of prior victory. Besides a more general meaning ('the joy or exultation of victory or success'), *Merriam-Webster* now lists a meaning that seems pretty specific—and Roman: 'a ceremony attending the entering of Rome by a general who had won a decisive victory over a foreign enemy.'

Whether or not this military concept is meant in English Bible versions is difficult to discern for the reader, however, because phrases like "who always leads us in triumph" (e.g., RSV) can easily be understood along the lines of the KJV (the collocation with the words in the context does not give as many indications as the verb "to receive" in the *Merriam-Webster* dictionary quoted above). Others, like the ESV, translate the Greek participial phrase as "who in Christ always leads us in triumphal procession." The military—or even Roman—dimension is still not entirely clear, since for many the language of triumphal processions has become a dead metaphor that can now be used for any kind of victory celebration that resembles a parade.[3]

The *military* connotation finds expression clearly in versions such as the NIV: "who always leads us as captives in Christ's triumphal procession." One might, however, ask whether the NIV has managed to make the specifically *Roman* dimension visible too. After all, the fact that the ritual that the *Merriam-Webster* definition has in view is often called a "*Roman* triumphal procession" is a revealing indication that speakers today feel a need to specify which of several possible "triumphal processions" is meant. The way that William J. Webb introduces his discussion of the Pauline passage in question is symptomatic: "Does the apostle have a *Roman* triumphal procession specifically in mind? Or is he drawing from the general practice of triumphal processions (common to Rome and many other cultures)?"[4]

Versions like the ESV demonstrate an interest in communicating the first of several definitions that BDAG, the standard dictionary for the New Testament,

---

and 'a notable success,' accessed May 26, 2021, https://www.merriam-webster.com/dictionary/triumph.

3. Cf., e.g., Crede H. Calhoun, "Panama Joyously Greets Lindbergh, after 4-Hour Flight from Costa Rica," *The New York Times*, January 10, 1928, https://www.nytimes.com/1928/01/10/archives/panama-joyously-greets-lindbergh-after-4hour-flight-from-costa-rica.html.

4. William J. Webb, *Returning Home: New Covenant and Second Exodus as the Context for 2 Corinthians 6.14–7.1*, JSNTSup 85 (Sheffield: Sheffield Academic Press, 1993), 78. Italics in the original.

offers for the Greek verb θριαμβεύω: 'to lead in a triumphal procession.'[5] They add the explanatory note that this meaning occurs "in imagery of the Roman military triumph" and add that when it occurs with an accusative object, this leading activity relates to captives. On the basis of a rather gracious reading, one could understand them to suggest the following definition: 'to lead someone as a captive in a Roman triumphal procession.'

However, this is not the only option that BDAG lists. The lack of clarity in the Bible versions reflects a general unease biblical scholars seem to have with respect to having Paul use imagery of the Roman military world in 2 Cor 2:14. In the only other occurrence of θριαμβεύω in the New Testament—Col 2:15— the direct object is not "us" but "them," namely the principalities and powers, which for most interpreters makes it pretty clear that Christ's victory over them is in view (see below, pp. 125–27, on this passage). But how could *Paul* be either one who has been defeated by God or, even stranger, be presented in a Roman triumphal procession?

The editors of BDAG list several definitions for transitive θριαμβεύω that are just as ambiguous as the glosses adduced above from various Bible versions, giving an idea of how uncomfortable biblical scholars are with this idea.[6] How are we, for example, supposed to understand 'to cause to triumph'? Does this mean 'to enable a Roman triumphal procession'? Probably not. Instead, it is probably to be understood as the causative variant of the option 'to triumph over,' which—by means of the preposition—seems to fall pretty clearly on the side of the spectrum of definitions that do not focus on *any* kind of parade, but rather on the prior victory itself.

Even the explanatory note "in imagery of Roman generals leading their troops in triumph" after the definition 'to lead in triumph' does not make the kind of triumph particularly clear—some exegetes apparently understand it to specify the kind of "victory" (triumph) that is in view, namely a military one (with the specifically Roman element simply being ignored in that case).[7]

Frederick W. Danker, the lead editor of the revision that BDAG constitutes,

5. BDAG, s.v. "θριαμβεύω."

6. BDAG 3604 (s.v. "θριαμβεύω").

7. The option is taken over from LSJM 50507 (s.v. "θριαμβεύω II"), where "as a general does his army" is added to 'to lead in triumph' as an alternative to "of conquered enemies." As their reference to Josephus, *B.J.* 7.123–157 and the comment that there is "no lexical support" make clear, the editors of BDAG correctly understood what the editors of LSJM had intended. However, the paraphrase they offer is ambiguous at best and probably even misleading: "thanks be to God, who always leads us as partners in triumph in Christ."

is even more confusing in his *Concise Greek-English Lexicon*, where he defines the verb in a similarly vague way as 'to lead in a triumphal procession.'[8] However, here the adjective "Roman" does not even feature at all. He adds an etymological note that glosses the noun θρίαμβος with "religious procession" (which is a terrible translation equivalent for the Roman *triumphus*, assuming that this is what is meant) and for later occurrences "festive triumph," whatever that might be. On 2 Cor 2:14, he says that "precise details cannot be determined; in any event the focus is on the assurance of triumph for the gospel." This sounds like he is trying to decode the metaphor while still using the figurative language to decipher the content side. It is basically impossible for students to determine what imagery is supposed to be in view here and whether it contains a military or even Roman component.

Other definitions that are adduced in BDAG assume a variety of semantic shifts that led to a concentration on one aspect inherent in the Roman triumphal procession, such as the status of the captives ('to expose [somebody] to shame'), the effect on the watching crowd ('to display, publicize, make known [somebody/something]')[9] and the effect the triumphator has on the captives ('to lead [somebody] around').[10] In each of these cases, the *triumphus* is no longer in view at all. In fact, they are all *demilitarized completely*. Other suggestions in the secondary literature at least keep in view the parameter of a parade, but *deny any Roman associations*: 'to lead in a Jewish merkabah procession' / 'YHWH's eschatological victory celebration' or 'to lead in a pagan epiphany procession.'[11]

Against this backdrop, it might seem strange for me to choose 2 Cor 2:14 as an illustration for overlooked Pauline unease with the Roman Empire. After all, even the question of whether the Roman military triumphal procession is in view at all (as will be discussed in this chapter)—let alone critically (as will be discussed in the next chapter)—seems to be highly debated. Plenty of semantic suggestions have been put forth that do not evoke a Roman context at all. And

---

8. Frederick W. Danker, with Kathryn Krug, *The Concise Greek-English Lexicon of the New Testament* (Chicago: University of Chicago Press, 2009), 171.

9. Rory B. Egan, "Lexical Evidence on Two Pauline Passages," *NovT* 19 (1977): 41, even considers the possibility that the semantic shift might have occurred in the other direction.

10. The editors of BDAG decided to lump the last definition together with the one before. This clearly does not make sense. In this proposal, θριαμβεύειν τινα is synonymous with παράγειν τινα. Again, no procession is in view, but this time it is the aspect of leading that is picked out as an alleged further semantic development, as an alternative to the dynamics implied behind the previous suggestions (which focus, e.g., on the effect of making somebody/something visible to the watching crowd).

11. Cf. Christoph Heilig, *Paul's Triumph: Reassessing 2 Corinthians 2:14 in Its Literary and Historical Context* (Leuven: Peeters, 2017), 105–7, for references.

this multitude of proposals certainly contributes to the impression that this might be a bad place to start if one is looking for a rather obvious critique of Roman ideology. Then again, what we are looking for is not simply examples of rather blunt critique of the Roman Empire but specifically cases in which this critique has been overlooked but is actually there. And indeed, all the proposals listed above face one big problem: A simple search of transitive θριαμβεύω in the *TLG* corpus demonstrates that in the time leading up to Paul *none* of the suggested alternative contexts is *ever* in view in *any* of the occurrences.

Some scholars recognize that it is difficult to make the Roman dimension go away and try to make the sense of Paul's metaphor less offensive by changing the role of the accusative object in the triumphal procession. Perhaps—so an influential suggestion by Breytenbach from the early 1990s—the presence in the triumphal procession is just a matter of reference, not of lexical meaning.[12] In other words, it is claimed that even though the person referred to by the accusative object in some texts is also taking part in the procession (as a captive), the verb itself does not demand such a constellation. All it is supposed to imply is a prior victory (think Damascus!) and the granting of a triumphal procession to the triumphator for that victory. In this view, the defeated person can then be either absent or walk in the procession in any role—also as a joyful participant, perhaps as an incense bearer. The problem with this proposal is that while it may fit some occurrences, it is completely impossible in other cases. There are, for example, passages where people go to great lengths in their attempt to avoid getting into a situation in which one could speak about them as the direct object of θριαμβεύω—efforts that even include suicide. While this effectively prevents them from having to march in the triumphal procession, it does not change the *celebration* of a triumphal procession at all; it is only the circumstance that one is not presented as a captive to the watching crowd in this event that is avoided.[13] Vice-versa, there are also occurrences of the transitive verb where the person behind the direct object is shown around in the procession even though their defeat was not instrumental to the victor being awarded the honor of that ritual (usually because the captive was simply too irrelevant).[14]

12. Cilliers Breytenbach, "Paul's Proclamation and God's 'Thriambos': Notes on 2 Corinthians 2:14–16b," *Neot* 24 (1990): 257–71; and Cilliers Breytenbach, "Christologie, Nachfolge/Apostolat," *BTZ* 8 (1991): 183–98.

13. See Heilig, *Paul's Triumph*, 51–101, for very clear examples. The most obvious ones are Strabo, *Geogr.* 7.1.4, 12.3.6; Plutarch, *Ant.* 84.7 (cf. on this also, not included in the *TLG* corpus, the fragment from Livy, *Ab urb. cond.* 45 in Pomponius Porphyrio, *Carm.* 1.37.30; Heilig, *Paul's Triumph*, 95) and *Aem.* 36.9 as well as *Comp. Cim. Luc.* 3.2 (with the referent being a diadem!); and Appian, *Hist. rom.* 12.77 and 12.105.

14. See Appian, *Hist. rom.* 12.105–117. Cf. Heilig, *Paul's Triumph*, 70.

While Breytenbach's analysis comes from a time when such analyses were still quite difficult to perform (he had to rely on help from the Tyndale House, Cambridge, to identify the relevant occurrences; cf. below, pp. 127–28), it is surprising to see that even with the technical possibilities we have today, variations of such attempts simply do not cease. As recently as 2015, George Guthrie, in a *New Testament Studies* article, suggested the very general meaning 'to lead someone in the triumphal procession.' This meaning would—in a vein similar to Breytenbach's suggestion—allow for participation as, for example, victorious soldiers or incense bearers.[15] There is just one thing Guthrie fails to mention: The verb is always used in connection with persons who are presented to the watching crowd as prisoners of war (and in the one case in which an object is in view, it is booty that is shown around) and *never* with respect to the parties that Guthrie adduces.[16] Moreover, it must not be forgotten that for these persons too there are extremely well-established lexical patterns (as shown by the very passages that Guthrie quotes). Thus, if Paul *would have* wanted to say anything like that, we would expect him to have chosen from among these options. In other, more technical terms, the likelihood (the explanatory potential) of this hypothesis is incredibly small and articles putting forward such suggestions can only make a convincing impression by artfully ignoring this important parameter entirely.

Even if one is willing to allow for totally unattested meanings to compete in the exegetical decision, the conclusion is inevitable. The explanatory potential of all these hypothetical meanings is extremely slim.[17] Not only is θριαμβεύω not attested with these meanings (at least in the relevant time frame), but we are always faced with well-attested alternative lexical options that would make the suggested point very clearly and which thus constitute much more expectable choices. Thus, one must conclude that the verb in 2 Cor 2:14 indeed portrays the subject of the verb—here: God—to be the triumphator in a triumphal procession and that Paul and his coworkers[18] appear as captives who are presented to the watching crowd.[19]

---

15. George H. Guthrie, "Paul's Triumphal Procession Imagery (2 Cor 2.14–16a): Neglected Points of Background," *NTS* 61 (2015): 79–91.

16. See Plutarch, *Comp. Cim. Luc.* 3.2. Cf. Heilig, *Paul's Triumph*, 66–67. Unfortunately, the new entry in the *CGL* (s.v. "θριαμβεύω") still gets it wrong.

17. Heilig, *Paul's Triumph*, 194–217.

18. See Heilig, *Paul's Triumph*, 219–23, on the plural. The idea that Paul only thinks of himself here and uses an "apostolic plural" is not supported by evidence.

19. See Heilig, *Paul's Triumph*, 247–54, for this element of being perceived by the spectators.

Evoking Rome and the Emperor

We will touch upon the question of how this image—which is indeed very strange—fits into the larger context of the Corinthian correspondence below (pp. 67–77 and 138–39). Here I want to draw attention in particular to two implications of the semantics of the verb that are of great importance for our analysis.

First, the verb implies the *city of Rome* as the context of the action. Something like a Ῥωμαϊκός θρίαμβος ("Roman triumph") does not exist in antiquity. More generally, it is very rare for the noun to be used for other victory celebrations at all. What might be its very first occurrence, Polybius, *Hist.* 1.88.6, might be an exception. But we also need to keep in mind that it might have been Polybius himself who was responsible for creating the Latinism in the first place,[20] so some flexibility at this stage should not surprise us. Later, Plutarch, *Crass.* 32, is very telling in that he describes a Parthian victory celebration that was obviously meant as a parody of the *triumphus*, including Roman heads, abusive songs, and a captive dressed in female clothing. For Plutarch it clearly is "insulting" that this "laughable procession" was referred to as a "triumph" (32.1: παρεσκευάζετο πομπήν τινα γελοίαν ὕβρει προσαγορεύων θρίαμβον).[21] To be sure, θρίαμβος is not only attested as a Latinism for *triumphus* but also as a byname of the god Dionysos and a song sung in his honor (both the Latin word and the Dionysiac usage have a common root).[22] Even though ancient authors recognized this connection, there was simply no need to *distinguish* between these two spheres by means of the adjective as we commonly do in English.[23]

Analogously, the verb is almost never used with the local specification ἐν Ῥώμη ("in Rome") because this would be pleonastic.[24] Where else would one want to celebrate the *triumphus?!* It is difficult to stress this enough because it is not easy to get rid of the more relaxed reading that is possible in English. But if there is an exception in ancient literature and the lexemes are used with reference to a victory celebration that is not staged in Rome itself, these cases are very remarkable indeed. One passage in the work of the historian Appian from Alexandria includes talk about the celebration of a triumph in New

20. See Heilig, *Paul's Triumph*, 37.
21. Cf. Heilig, *Paul's Triumph*, 264.
22. Cf. Heilig, *Paul's Triumph*, 32–37. See below, p. 93.
23. Cf. Heilig, *Paul's Triumph*, 195–201.
24. Heilig, *Paul's Triumph*, 234.

Carthage (*Hist. rom.* 6.23: . . . ἔθυε τῆς ἐπιούσης καὶ ἐθριάμβευε). This has caused historians, who are familiar with the ancient sources and who are aware of how strange this usage is, to assume that the author either simply made a mistake or intentionally wanted to offer a kind of prolepsis.[25] Plutarch, *Ant.* 50.6, is also very telling. Here, the confrontation of Antony with Artavasdes the Armenian is followed by a remarkable event: "But afterwards, when he once more invaded Armenia, and by many invitations and promises induced Artavasdes to come to him, Antony seized him, and took him in chains down to Alexandria, where he celebrated a triumph (. . . καὶ δέσμιον καταγαγὼν εἰς Ἀλεξάνδρειαν, ἐθριάμβευσεν)."[26] Historically, it is much more plausible that Antony had intended to cast himself as a Dionysos, but it certainly fit Octavian's propaganda (and Plutarch's literary intentions) to present Antony's procession as a *triumphus*. The exception thus clearly proves the rule.[27] Antony's act is so unpatriotic precisely because he does the unthinkable and stages a Roman triumphal procession outside Rome—an oxymoron!—because he is so enamored with Cleopatra.

Second, in a first-century context, the use of θριαμβεύω implies no less a person as the triumphator than the Roman emperor himself. In the secondary literature on 2 Cor 2:14, we often read about how frequent Roman triumphs were, a claim usually substantiated with reference to the number 320 known from ancient sources.[28] And Itgenshorst in her recent analysis lists almost as

25. John S. Richardson, *Appian: Wars of the Romans in Iberia; With an Introduction, Translation and Commentary* (Warminster: Aris & Phillips, 2000), 125, thinks this usage is quite confusing and comments: "If that [a Roman triumph] is what he means here, he is clearly wrong, since a triumph can only take place in Rome." Cf. Christoph Leidl, *Appians Darstellung des 2. Punischen Krieges in Spanien (Iberike c. 1–38 § 1–158a): Text und Kommentar*, Münchner Arbeiten zur Alten Geschichte 11 (Munich: Editio Maris, 1996), 213, and Heilig, *Paul's Triumph*, 68.

26. Translation from Perrin (LCL).

27. And it does not, to be sure, establish a new, "figurative" meaning 'to behave as if celebrating a triumph' as the new entry in *CGL*, s.v. "θριαμβεύω"—most certainly on the basis of this passage—assumes. First of all, adding this category at all seems very problematic as a separate lexical sense because in principle every action can of course be portrayed "as if" happening, without this implying an established metaphor whatsoever. Second, Octavian's propaganda only works of course if the sense is not weakened to expressing just an event "similar" to the *triumphus*. The point is precisely that it was *meant* to be the Roman ritual, though in the entirely wrong place.

28. Scott J. Hafemann, *Suffering and the Spirit: An Exegetical Study of 2 Cor 2:14–3:3 within the Context of the Corinthian Correspondence*, WUNT 2/19 (Tübingen: Mohr, 1986), 22. Cf. Orosius, *Hist.* 7.9.8.

many triumphal processions: 297.[29] These, however, all date from the period of 340 to 19 BCE. During the Republic there were indeed times of frequent celebrations. A total of twelve triumphs took place between 260 and 251 BCE and there were four in 71 BCE alone. Things changed dramatically, however, with the early principate. From 19 BCE onward, the triumph was a privilege reserved for the emperor and his family.[30] Thus it is safe to say that 2 Cor 2:14 is the one passage in the *corpus Paulinum* that evokes the Roman emperor most clearly in the imagination, even in comparison to the explicit mention of the household of Caesar in Phil 4:22.[31]

Claudius's Triumphal Procession from 44 CE

In fact, I want to suggest that Paul has a very specific emperor and a very specific triumphal procession in mind when he creates this metaphor. I think it is highly plausible that he uses this image because he is reminded of the triumphal procession that Claudius celebrated in 44 CE for his victory in Britannia.[32] For this military success, Claudius was granted the name "Britannicus," which he passed on to his son, known initially as Tiberius Claudius Germanicus after his birth in 41 CE.[33] Obviously, this conquest was a very important matter for the emperor. It is famously depicted in a relief from Aphrodisias that shows the personification of Britannia being defeated by Claudius (figure 2).[34]

The reason I am so specific is that when we say the triumph was limited to "the emperor" and his family in the first century, we need to be careful not to give the impression that we are dealing with a highly abstract category in the minds of the inhabitants of the Roman Empire, synthesized on the basis of a multitude of different experiences and accounts. Rather, we need to be very clear about one thing: Claudius's triumph in 44 CE is the *first* by an

29. Tanja Itgenshorst, *Katalog der Triumphe von 340 bis 19 vor Christus*, accompanying CD-ROM of *Tota illa pompa: Der Triumph in der römischen Republik*, Hypomnemata 161 (Göttingen: Vandenhoeck & Ruprecht, 2005).

30. On all this, cf. Heilig, *Paul's Triumph*, 121–22.

31. Cf. Heilig, *Paul's Triumph*, 263.

32. See the detailed account of the military operation by Jorit Wintjes, *Die Römische Armee auf dem Oceanus: Zur römischen Seekriegsgeschichte in Nordwesteuropa*, Mnemosyne Supplements: History and Archaeology of Classical Antiquity 433 (Leiden: Brill, 2019), chapter 5.

33. Initially in position to be Claudius's heir, he was later replaced by Nero—who probably had him killed as a teenager. Cf. below, pp. 74–75 n. 10.

34. See R. R. R. Smith, *The Marble Reliefs from the Julio-Claudian Sebasteion at Aphrodisias*, vol. 6 of *Aphrodisias* (Darmstadt: von Zabern, 2013), C 10.

incumbent emperor. (Octavian had celebrated his triumphs in 29 BCE, two years before being elevated to "Augustus.")

Admittedly, this might be taken as relativizing the certainty with which the metaphor would evoke "the Roman emperor," as suggested in the last section.[35] I find it more plausible, however, to take it simply as an argument for a *very specific* background. Claudius's triumph was the only potential source for contemporary knowledge about the *triumphus*. When the next triumph took place—in 71 CE—Paul was already dead. To be fair, during the earlier phase of Paul's life triumphal processions were also granted to Tiberius and Germanicus as a means of establishing them as successors, and there were several smaller victory celebrations known as "ovations."[36]

Figure 2. Claudius defeating Britannia, in a relief from the Sebasteion, south building, in Aphrodisias, Roman province of Asia (modern-day Turkey) (© 2019 The Aphrodisias Excavations Project)

And I do not think we should completely rule out these ovations as a potential source for Paul's knowledge about the Roman triumphal procession. True, the Romans usually distinguished between the two rituals rather strictly, and this is reflected in the terminology. This can be seen, for example, in Augustus's autobiography (*Res gest. divi Aug.* 4.1), where *ovationes* and *triumphi* are adduced separately. However, the comparison between the Latin and Greek versions and the obvious difficulties in the attempt to communicate what is meant demonstrate that the difference was probably not that clear in the eastern provinces of the Roman Empire.[37] Still, it seems that we should approach

35. In other words, "the emperor" was admittedly not connected in the public imagination with the triumphal procession in the same way as he had become with, for example, coinage in the early principate. On the latter, cf. Heilig, *Hidden Criticism? The Methodology and Plausibility of the Search for a Counter-Imperial Subtext in Paul* (Minneapolis: Fortress, 2017), 106.

36. See Heilig, *Paul's Triumph*, 130.

37. It is possible that Paul is familiar with this very text through the Greek version in

the triumph of Claudius in 44 CE at least with the warranted suspicion that it might constitute the historical backdrop for Paul's use of the triumph metaphor. After all, the inscription demonstrates that "*both* triumph and ovation would be alien to a provincial readership."[38] Yet, rather shockingly, Claudius's triumphal procession is not even mentioned, let alone considered in any detail, in almost all commentaries.[39] The only exception that I am aware of is J. Paul Sampley's commentary in the *New Interpreter's Bible*. He does include the following short remark: "At least some of the Corinthians, residents of an official Roman colony city and, therefore, especially attuned to Rome, would have Claudius's triumphal procession in memory."[40]

To be sure, having it "in memory" presupposes that they somehow learned about the event in the first place. "Triumphs and other forms of ceremony," so says Olivier Hekster in an article on the Roman army and propaganda, "were only visible to those who were there to witness." He concludes: "Both, therefore, were limited as forms of propaganda."[41] Claudius apparently not only called the governors back to Rome in order for them to witness his celebration but even invited exiles to see him marching in the triumphal procession (Suetonius, *Claud.* 17). Obviously, being *present* was of great importance for the ritual to have its intended effect. Thus, Paul, too, would have been dependent on eyewitnesses for him to know anything specific about this victory celebration.

Ancyra. Cf. Heilig, *Paul's Triumph*, 129.

38. Alison E. Cooley, *Res Gestae Divi Augusti: Text, Translation, and Commentary* (Cambridge: Cambridge University Press, 2009), 121. Italics added.

39. Cf. Heilig, *Paul's Triumph*, 131 and 263.

40. J. Paul Sampley, "The Second Letter to the Corinthians," in vol. 11 of *NIB*, ed. Leander E. Keck et al. (Nashville: Abingdon, 2000), 58–59. Douglas A. Campbell, *Framing Paul: An Epistolary Biography* (Grand Rapids: Eerdmans, 2014), 188, wants to date the Corinthian correspondence to the year 51 CE and for that purpose refers to the presentation of Caratacus in Rome (on which see pp. 75, 78, and 92). In a footnote he also mentions the actual triumphal procession. Even though he does not explicate this background any further, he is at least one of the few scholars who seems to be aware of the event and is open to seeing a connection: "It would be interesting if an imperial triumph occurred just prior to the middle of 51 CE, thereby explaining the allusion in 2 Cor 2:14–16. And arguably, one did. Claudius celebrated the final capture of Cara[c]tacus, the guerrilla leader of British opposition to Roman rule, who was apprehended around 51 CE. The emperor famously pardoned him. . . . However, it is important to appreciate that Claudius celebrated triumphs in relation to the conquest of Britain repeatedly. The first probably took place shortly after the campaign in 43 CE. The Arch of Claudius at Rome, voted in his honor in 43, was dedicated in 51 CE, or perhaps early in 52."

41. Olivier Hekster, "The Roman Army and Propaganda," in *A Companion to the Roman Army*, ed. Paul Erdkamp, Blackwell Companions to the Ancient World (Malden: Blackwell, 2007), 349.

And at this point we enter territory that is quite rare in historical reconstructions like these. We actually have good contemporary evidence for Paul having met potential eyewitnesses! As we learn from Acts 18, Paul meets Priscilla and Aquilla at the beginning of 50 CE—in *Corinth* of all places. Of course, we do not know for sure what they talked about while they were working as "tentmakers," but it is hard to imagine that *Claudius* did not feature in these discussions. Those conversations are part of a "very hidden" transcript (cf. above, p. 42, on different layers of hidden transcripts) and thus lost to us. But we must not forget that the couple had just left *Rome* a few months earlier due to an edict of said emperor—something Paul probably will have cared about if his initial plan had indeed been to travel from Corinth to Rome directly.[42] Speculation, to be sure—but historically very plausible speculation!

In any case, the situation is far better than it is with respect to the only other specific suggestion that I am aware of, put forward by Roger David Aus.[43] According to Aus, Paul is comparing himself to his namesake Paulus Macedonicus and his triumph—which took place two hundred years earlier, in 167 BCE![44] To suggest such a connection based on the name of the triumphator and Paul's mention of Macedonia in v. 13 but not to take seriously the event that had happened just a decade prior and to which Paul might have had access through actual eyewitnesses seems deeply problematic to me.[45]

To simply point in a general way to "the evidence from the period"[46] in order to prove a *widespread and general cultural knowledge* of "the" triumph will not suffice either, because even though these claims are frequent in the secondary literature they are *never* substantiated by actual historical evidence. They simply reflect textbook accounts of a generalized concept of "the" triumph that *we* as modern historians have come to synthesize on the basis of depictions like the ones on the triumphal arch of Titus and on the basis of accounts like the one by Josephus.[47]

42. Heilig, *Paul's Triumph*, 132.

43. Roger David Aus, *Imagery of Triumph and Rebellion in 2 Corinthians 2:14–17 and Elsewhere in the Epistle: An Example of the Combination of Greco-Roman and Judaic Traditions in the Apostle Paul*, Studies in Judaism (Lanham: University Press of America, 2005).

44. Cf. Heilig, *Paul's Triumph*, 131. I have similar reservations concerning Dodson's thesis on the significance of Marcus Atilius Regulus's death in the third century for understanding Col 2:15. See Joseph R. Dodson, "The Convict's Gibbet and the Victor's Car: The Triumphal Death of Marcus Atilius Regulus and the Background of Col 2:15," *HTR* 114 (2021).

45. Cf. Heilig, *Paul's Triumph*, 153.

46. Ben Witherington III, *Conflict and Community in Corinth: A Socio-Rhetorical Commentary on 1 and 2 Corinthians* (Grand Rapids: Eerdmans, 1995), 366.

47. Cf. Mary Beard, *The Roman Triumph* (Cambridge: Harvard University Press, 2007), 82–83, on this issue.

Unfortunately, this idea seems to have become the default option in the secondary literature—at least in the portion that does not deny the Roman reference altogether. Even though these authors are right in what they affirm (the Romanness of the metaphor), they still miss very fundamental parameters due to unrealistic assumptions about the shape of Paul's knowledge about the event. For example, Guthrie thinks the Roman triumphal procession would have been known in antiquity just like the "Super Bowl parade" (which I—living in the "far east"—had never heard of, by the way!): "Paul's metaphor would have been immediately recognized in first-century Corinth"[48]—which makes it easier for him to assume that Paul knows about the different parties marching on the side of the victorious party. Guthrie's far-reaching claim in the end is based on nothing but the widespread assumption that the triumph was simply "part of the cultural fabric of the time," and thus, as David E. Garland agrees, "was widely known."[49] In short, as Marshall claims: "The triumphal procession must have been a familiar institution to Greeks and Romans of all levels of society."[50] However, if one actually looks at the "Roman arches, reliefs, coins, statues, medallions, paintings, and cameos" that are supposed to support such strong claims but never adduced with specific references, it becomes clear that such ideas do not have any foundation in the historical evidence.[51] This, by the way, has to do in large part with the fact that the *triumphus* was a fleeting honor and triumphators usually preferred to commemorate the actual military victories behind them—as demonstrated, for example, by figure 2 above (for details see below, pp. 86–87).

Undoubtedly, the way this issue is treated in the secondary literature casts a rather critical light on the genre of biblical commentaries—a topic to which we will return later (pp. 129–34). The last commentator who genuinely—and justifiably so!—seems to have wondered how an "Anatolian" like Paul might have known both the word and the ritual was Philipp Bachmann, an entire century ago.[52] Only authors who discuss the Roman triumphal procession as

---

48. Guthrie, "Triumphal Procession," 80.

49. George H. Guthrie, *2 Corinthians*, BECNT (Grand Rapids: Baker Academic, 2015), 158; David E. Garland, *2 Corinthians*, NAC 29 (Nashville: Broadman & Holman, 1999), 143.

50. Peter Marshall, "A Metaphor of Social Shame: ΘΡΙΑΜΒΕΥΕΙΝ in 2 Cor. 2:14," *NovT* 25 (1983): 304.

51. Scott J. Hafemann, *2 Corinthians*, The NIV Application Commentary (Grand Rapids: Zondervan, 2000), 107. Statements such as Hafemann's usually are followed by a reference to other pieces of the secondary literature, which usually do not offer any primary material either. Cf. Heilig, *Paul's Triumph*, 124–29, 136–41.

52. Philipp Bachmann, *Der zweite Brief des Paulus an die Korinther*, 4th ed., Kommentar zum Neuen Testament 8 (Leipzig: Deichert, 1922), 127–28.

a potential backdrop for *other* New Testament passages sometimes point to the problem by implication, namely when they try to back up their exegetical claims by arguing for Rome as the place of composition or knowledge of the triumph of Vespasian/Titus in 71 CE.[53]

If this consensus is questioned at all, it is by authors who deny the Roman connection altogether. For example, George G. Findlay in the nineteenth century already raised the issue of how Paul could have known about the Roman triumph, pointing to the fact that he had, after all, not yet been to Rome.[54] The historical evidence for Paul having some knowledge of the alternatively suggested contexts—such as pagan Dionysius processions—is indeed far better than for the view that the Roman triumphal procession was as pervasive a phenomenon as it is claimed.[55] The prior-probability (background plausibility) of such hypotheses is thus not bad at all. Their problem—which rules them out as serious interpretive options—lies with the likelihood factor, the extremely weak explanatory potential of the hypotheses. There is no reason to assume that Paul would have used θριαμβεύω to express these concepts.[56]

This is not to say that it is impossible that Paul might also have had other sources for his knowledge of both the usage of the Greek verb θριαμβεύω and the Roman ritual. Still, the Priscilla/Aquilla connection itself should be enough for us to seriously consider the option that seems to be a pretty obvious one anyway, even without that additional piece of evidence. However, it gets even better! Claudius's British victory has left archaeological traces in Corinth. First, we can note the fact that Britannicus is mentioned with this

---

53. So far, I have not been convinced that the Roman triumphal procession is in the background of any of these passages. See Heilig, *Paul's Triumph*, 119–20. Cf. Heilig, *Paul's Triumph*, 130–31n71. On the importance of the defeat of the Jews and the subsequent triumphal procession for the consolidation of the Flavian dynasty, see Johanna Leithoff, *Macht der Vergangenheit: Zur Erringung, Verstetigung und Ausgestaltung des Principats unter Vespasian, Titus und Domitian*, Schriften zur politischen Kommunikation 19 (Göttingen: Vandenhoeck & Ruprecht, 2014), section II.2.

54. George G. Findley, "St. Paul's Use of ΘΡΙΑΜΒΕΥΩ," *Expositor* 10 (1879): 413.

55. Heilig, *Paul's Triumph*, 141–42.

56. Heilig, *Paul's Triumph*, 195–201. In my opinion, this is unfortunately still not sufficiently taken into account by Dietrich-Alex Koch, "Gottes Triumph und die Aufgabe des Apostels: Überlegungen zu 2Kor 2,14," *Sacra Scripta* 16 (2018): 7–20. Cf. also Dietrich-Alex Koch, review of *Paul's Triumph: Reassessing 2 Corinthians 2:14 in Its Literary and Historical Context*, by Christoph Heilig, *TLZ* 143 (2018): 623, who emphasizes the "literarische und vor allem ikonographisch sehr wirksame Tradition vom Triumph des Dionysos im Zusammenhang seines mythischen Zuges nach Indien."

name in at least one inscription, as is the victory itself.[57] Second, and even more impressive, we must not overlook the fact that excavators of ancient Corinth have found a series of inscriptions that talk about a certain Tiberius Claudius Dinippus.[58] In some of them he is referred to as the *sacerdos Victoriae Britannicae*.

On the basis of these inscriptions, we thus know that there was a priest of the personified goddess Victoria Britannica[59] in Corinth—and accordingly a cult centered on the very military victory that had secured Claudius his triumphal procession! Parallels to similar cults suggest that Dinippus would have made yearly sacrifices to Victoria Briannica on the anniversary of Claudius's British victory. As Standing stresses in an article from 2003: "The true focus of the cult, however, was the emperor Claudius himself, for it was his victory which was personified and venerated at Corinth. . . . The anniversary of Claudius' victory may thus have constituted an Imperial

Figure 3. Latin inscription (West no. 86), including the words SACERDOTI VICTORIAE | BRITANN (see lines 3 and 4); now in the Archaeological Museum of Ancient Corinth (https://edh.ub .uni-heidelberg.de/edh/foto/F036266, © E. Roels)

57. Kent no. 77. Probably also in Kent no. 76; West no. 11. Only an unspecified "victory" is attested in the inscription, but the spelling VICTORIAI suggests a date under Claudius.

58. See West nos. 86–90 and Kent nos. 158–64. For Pauline studies, Tiberius Claudius Dinippus is also of interest as the potential curator of the grain supply (*curator annonae*) during the food shortage around Paul's visit in 51 CE that might be reflected in 1 Cor 7:26. Cf. Barry B. Danylak, "Tiberius Claudius Dinippus and the Food Shortage in Corinth," *TynBul* 59 (2008): 231–70.

59. On the goddess Victoria with epithets referring to conquered people, see foundationally Robert O. Fink, "*Victoria Parthica* and Kindred *Victoriae*," YCS 8 (1942): 81–101.

festival funded by the wealthy Tiberius Claudius Dinippus, with religious processions and feasts for the civic community (based, in part, on the meat of the sacrificed animals)."[60]

Since Dinippus probably already began his service around 45 CE,[61] we have archaeological evidence for Claudius and his victory over Britannia being celebrated in a very public—and cultic!—way in Corinth during the exact time that Paul was active there. If this is not considered excellent historical evidence for a contemporary historical background of Paul's use of the triumph metaphor in 2 Cor 2:14, we must at least admit that according to this standard the vast majority of tradition-historical arguments would need to be rejected.

---

60. Giles Standing, "The Claudian Invasion of Britain and the Cult of *Victoria Britannica*," *Britannia* 34 (2003): 286.

61. Originally, the series of inscriptions mentioning Dinippus was dated to the second century. On the history of research, see pp. 71–74 in West.

4 | RECONSTRUCTING UNEASE

Claudius's Triumph as an Opportunity for Glory and Scorn

In the previous chapter, I tried to establish that Paul, as an active observer of his contemporary context, presupposes Claudius's triumphal procession in the imagery of 2 Cor 2:14—even though this Roman dimension does not feature as prominently in the secondary literature as it should, based on the evidence. But I used this example to demonstrate that there might be cases of "over-looked unease" concerning the Roman Empire in Paul's letter. So far, we have only addressed the issue of the figure of the emperor Claudius having been ignored in the exegesis of 2 Cor 2:14. Now we need to address the question of whether it is indeed possible to *reconstruct Paul's unease with the Roman Empire by reading 2 Cor 2:14 in the context of the public Roman transcript.*

Paul writes his letter in the autumn of 55 CE, approximately one year after Emperor Claudius's death on October 13, 54 CE—probably as the result of being poisoned by his wife Agrippina,[1] who thereby successfully installed Nero as the new emperor. This change in Rome would also have affected Corinth,

---

1. Years later, Paul spent just one day on the island of Kos, according to Acts 21:1. If he had a chance to read some of the inscriptions there, he might very well have encountered Claudius's triumph again. The Greek word θρίαμβος does not occur in inscriptions very often. But there is a notable cumulation on Kos, where it occurs in honorary inscriptions for Gaius Stertinius Xenophon, who had served as the physician of the emperor Claudius and who had received honors connected with Claudius's triumph (*IG* XII 4.2.952 and 1143; *Iscr. di Cos* EV 219; IRhodM 475; IKosPH 345). Ironically, tradition has it that before Xenophon returned to Kos as a respected citizen under Nero, he was the one who actually carried out the assassination of Claudius (Tacitus, *Ann.* 12.67). On Xenophon on Kos, cf. Kostas Buraselis, *Kos between Hellenism and Rome: Studies on the Political, Institutional and Social History of Kos from ca. the Middle Second Century B.C. until Late Antiquity*, TAPS 90 (Philadelphia: American Philosophical Society, 2000).

especially if the establishment of the imperial cult of the Achaean League, stationed in Corinth, falls into this exact period.[2] As I will seek to demonstrate in what follows, I think that Paul's metaphor in 2 Cor 2:14 picks up elements of the variegated discourses surrounding the triumph of Claudius, creating *dissonances* between the picture painted by the apostle and the public transcript of the Claudian reign.

At first sight, the idea that Paul would use the ritual of the *triumphus* to "critique" the emperor Claudius might seem implausible. After all, was not the Roman triumphal procession the most glorious event imaginable for the emperor, a unique opportunity to appear before the citizens even in the costume of Jupiter? Thus, one might argue that it would be quite counterproductive for Paul to draw attention to Claudius's big success if he really wanted to cast a shadow on him. It is indeed true that the triumph was an honor that carried a lot of weight with respect to public recognition. However, this opportunity also came with the risk of making a fool of oneself.[3] For example, a pompous celebration of victory that was not matched by an equally impressive military achievement could draw derision just as easily as a procession that was rather unspectacular with respect to the spoils and captives that were presented.

Claudius's triumph was certainly prone to being met with such scorn. After all, the emperor had left Rome for just half a year. In fact, his presence in Britannia was limited to not more than sixteen days! And this short duration was of course also noticed by contemporaries. We are in the extraordinary situation that a single manuscript from the ninth century, Latinus Vossianus Q86 (figure 4), hands down to us what may well be the only surviving song performed during a Roman triumphal procession (or in its immediate context).[4] Even this *Laus Caesaris*—a "praise" of the emperor Claudius—contains the line (fol. 95v, col. 2, l. 1) *conspectu devicta tuo, Germanice Caesar*, i.e., the mere sight of the emperor is said to have caused Britannia to strike her colors. This is, to be sure, a very diplomatic way of expressing a circumstance that could also be formulated with much more scorn! Emphasizing Claudius's *blitzkrieg* while not making it too obvious that the whole campaign was merely an

---

2. Cf. above, p. 43.

3. Cf. Mary Beard, *The Roman Triumph* (Cambridge: Harvard University Press, 2007), chapter 7, and Christoph Heilig, *Paul's Triumph: Reassessing 2 Corinthians 2:14 in Its Literary and Historical Context* (Leuven: Peeters, 2017), 264–68.

4. See Anthony A. Barrett, "The *Laus Caesaris*: Its History and Its Place in Latin Literature," *Latomus* 59 (2000): 596–606. On the debate over the historical context cf. Heilig, *Paul's Triumph*, 134–36, with references.

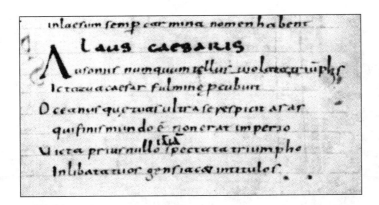

Figure 4. Beginning of the *Laus Caesaris*, a song praising Claudius after his return from Britannia (Latinus Vossianus Q86, fol. 95r; Leiden University Libraries)

attempt to secure a triumphal procession without any real investment was undoubtedly a balancing act.[5]

The Captives

If we read Paul's metaphor with an eye to the controversial nature of Claudius's triumph, we will notice a series of elements that suggest themselves as potential provocations. It begins with the fact that Paul portrays himself and his coworkers as *captives* in the procession.[6] Presenting famous and exotic rulers in Rome was an important part of staging a successful show. Apparently, Claudius's efforts in that regard were not very convincing.[7] To be sure, Claudius did not come back from his visit to Britain entirely empty-handed, as can be seen, for example, by the mention of *reges* ("chieftains") in the fragment of his triumphal arch, which is depicted in figure 5 and shown in its original place in figure 6.[8]

At the same time, it remains extremely suspicious that the capture of the

5. Cf. Heilig, *Paul's Triumph*, 265.

6. Heilig, *Paul's Triumph*, 219–23.

7. Heilig, *Paul's Triumph*, 132–36.

8. *CIL* VI 920a. The text and the complicated history of the archaeological evidence connected with the triumphal arch is discussed in a fascinating account by Anthony A. Barrett, "Claudius' British Victory Arch in Rome," *Britannia* 22 (1991): 1–19. Cf. Heilig, *Paul's Triumph*, 36. On captives see also Tacitus, *Agr.* 13.5.

Figure 5. Inscription from the Arch of Claudius, Capitoline Museums, Rome (photo by Jenni Ahonen; *CIL* VI 920a)

Figure 6. Drawing of the Arch of Claudius, by Stephen Copp (figure 5 of Anthony A. Barrett, "Claudius' British Victory Arch in Rome," *Britannia* 22 [1991]: 1–19)

British chieftain Caratacus years later caused so much enthusiasm that—in something like a remake of the actual triumph—he was presented to the Romans in a procession in 51 CE (at the end of which he was pardoned). It was as if the triumph of 44 CE had only found closure with this event.[9]

Another contemporary work that helps shed light on the perception of Claudius's military success against Britannia is the *Apocolocyntosis* by Seneca, written in the aftermath of Claudius's death. It is full of cruel scorn[10] and reflects

9. Heilig, *Paul's Triumph,* 138–39.
10. It probably had some very real, destructive consequences—facilitating an atmo-

the author's frustration with the deceased emperor who had sent him into exile for some time.[11] Here too we find a section (12.3) on Claudius's military achievements. The clearest satirical element in what is otherwise almost indistinguishable from the hyperbole that we find in official statements from Claudius's reign itself (see below, pp. 83–84) is a comment on the Brigantes, a tribe in what is today northern England. Claudius did not put their necks in Roman chains (*et caeruleos scuta Brigantas / dare Romuleis colla catenis*). Significant military advancements were not made in this area prior to the time of Vespasian. The only chains involved were those put around Caratacus, when Cartimandua, queen of the Brigantes, decided to hand him over to Rome after he had sought refuge in her area (Tacitus, *Ann.* 12.36). Not quite a heroic story of conquest!

Figure 7. Cameo showing Augustus as Alexander-Zeus (Kunsthistorisches Museum, Vienna; Antikensammlung, IXa 54; © KHM-Museumsverband)

It is fitting that one cameo (figure 7) that was previously believed to depict a British captive from Claudius's campaign is now by and large viewed (on the basis of the hairstyle) as actually portraying Augustus (with the captive either being a Dalmatian or simply an unspecified barbarian)—so that we have even less tangible evidence of Claudius's success.[12]

---

sphere that led to the murder of Britannicus. Gerhard Binder, *Apokolokyntosis*, Sammlung Tusculum (Düsseldorf: Artemis & Winkler, 1999), 92, emphasizes that the work is not simply an attempt to exact revenge on Claudius by literary means but also a political pamphlet meant to influence the new ruler according to Seneca's own ideas, probably published very soon after Claudius's death. He adds: "Wenn dies richtig ist, wird man Seneca nicht davon freisprechen können, am Entstehen eines Klimas am Kaiserhof mitgewirkt zu haben, dem schon im Februar des Jahres 55 der 14jährige Britannicus zum Opfer fiel."

11. See Christoph Heilig, *Hidden Criticism? The Methodology and Plausibility of the Search for a Counter-Imperial Subtext in Paul* (Minneapolis: Fortress, 2017), 82–84, for more details.

12. Erika Zwierlein-Diehl, ed. *Magie der Steine: Die antiken Prunkkameen im Kunsthistorischen Museum* (Vienna: Brandstätter, 2008), 80–83.

Figure 8. The Great/Hague Cameo, showing an emperor with his
family on the triumphal chariot (National Museum of Antiquities
in Leiden, GS-11096)

This leaves us—if I have not missed anything—only with the controversial
Great/Hague Cameo that many believe dates from the time of Constantine (it
is also referred to as the *Gemma Constantiniana*), but that in fact might portray
Claudius's triumph (figure 8). Here too (cf. above, p. 87) we see the intrusion
of the motif of victory (the barbarians being trampled down) into a depiction
of the later triumphal procession (with the imperatorial family in the chariot).
(On the mythical elements, see below, pp. 95–96.)[13]

Paul places a lot of rhetorical weight on the role of the captives. The most
plausible reason for why he bursts into thanksgiving in 2 Cor 2:14 is the fact
that he mentions giving up a promising evangelistic opportunity in v. 13 in
order to find Titus. Here Paul anticipates the accusation of fickleness (ἐλαφρία)

13. Another relief from Aphrodisias shows an emperor, who in the past has been identified with Claudius, with a female captive. However, this identification is no longer maintained. See C 18 in R. R. R. Smith, *The Marble Reliefs from the Julio-Claudian Sebasteion
at Aphrodisias*, vol. 6 of *Aphrodisias* (Darmstadt: von Zabern, 2013), 156–58. For a recent
interpretation of the Great/Hague Cameo in the framework of the time of Constantine,
see Ruurd B. Halbertsma, "*Nulli tam laeti triumphi*: Constantine's Victory on a Reworked
Cameo in Leiden," *BABESCH* 90 (2015): 221–35. For the proposal that it dates to the time of
Claudius, see the recent work by R. R. R. Smith, "*Maiestas Serena*: Roman Court Cameos
and Early Imperial Poetry and Panegyric," *JRS* 111 (2021): 18–21.

that was already leveled against him earlier in light of his constant changes of travel plans (1:17).[14] Portraying his team as captives in a Roman triumphal procession offers him a powerful opportunity to take up the perception of his mission by the Corinthians and at the same time challenge it.[15] The no doubt shameful aspect of being presented to the watching crowd as prisoners of war reflects the way that the Corinthians look down on the missionary movements of Paul and his coworkers. At the same time, the metaphor also emphasizes the role of the triumphator, who is the one who is ultimately in charge—and, thus, to be blamed if the Corinthians have a problem with how Paul and his supporters act.

This is also how the triumph imagery is employed by Ovid in *Am.* 1.2.[16] There, the poet portrays himself as subject to the triumphator, Cupid, who has brought him under his control—forcing him to write about his romantic misery instead of more appropriate, more patriotic, subjects (cf. *Am.* 1.1). Paul's metaphor also stresses the side-effect of "being made known," which is developed in further detail through the imagery of scent in the rest of the verse and in 2:15 (a notion to which some, illegitimately, have reduced the semantics of θριαμβεύω itself).[17]

Finally, there is also an inherent challenge to the association of shame itself. We have already mentioned how noble captives reflected well on the triumphator—which is why one would not want to have a ragged, miserable-looking person in one's procession but might even take care for the captives to be

---

14. Heilig, *Paul's Triumph*, 156–61.

15. For more details, see Heilig, *Paul's Triumph*, 254–59.

16. Beard, *Roman Triumph*, 113, says that "this clever allegorizing, this manipulation of the conventions of the ceremony to explore the idea of erotic capture, must count as the closest we get to a surviving first-person account from a triumphal victim." Second Corinthians 2:14 demonstrates that the basic idea is not that unique (cf. Heilig, *Paul's Triumph*, 271). In fact, if we also take into account merely *potential* presence in the triumph, we can see that the scenario is entertained several more times. Seneca has a desperate man say in *Ben.* 2.11.1 that in a triumphal procession he would have been presented only once (*Semel in triumpho ductus essem!*)—whereas his benefactor in real life cannot stop parading him around as the recipient of his goodwill. And in *Vit. beat.* 25.4 he creates a—quite anachronistic—speech for Socrates in which the great philosopher emphasizes that as someone celebrating a triumph (connected here too, see below, pp. 93–94, with the one by Liber/Bacchus), he would be just as humble as he would be in the contrary case of being a captive in another victor's triumphal procession (*in alienum imponar fericulum exornaturus victoris superbi ac feri pompam; non humilior sub alieno curru agar quam in meo steteram*).

17. See Heilig, *Paul's Triumph*, 255–56. On the scent imagery, see in detail Heilig, *Paul's Triumph*, chapter 4, section 3.

put into impressive clothing. The goal of the triumphator is to impress the watching crowd, not cause them to feel pity. That is exactly the impression Caratacus had made in this strange procession just a few years earlier, when "not a downcast look nor a word requested pity" (Tacitus, *Ann.* 12.36: *at non Caratacus aut vultu demisso aut verbis misericordiam requirens*).

As we can see, Paul's rhetorical strategy is clearly directed *toward the Corinthians.* He is criticizing them—and not Claudius for the bad show he put on. At the same time, remarks in that regard by eyewitnesses might indeed explain why Paul comes up with this metaphor in the first place. Plus, talk about captives in the triumphal procession might have reminded people about this being a rather sensitive topic with respect to the recent triumph by Claudius. We are presented here with an admittedly small and cloudy window into the Pauline hidden transcript, but it nevertheless gives us a fascinating tentative insight into discussions surrounding contemporary political mega-events.

Space and Time

A second aspect of Paul's metaphorical language that we need to address is the role of *Christ.* The triumphator's action is said to take place "in Christ."[18] First, we have to note that the use of θριαμβεύω with the preposition ἐν is extremely rare.[19] One interpretation that merits some attention locates the sphere of "Christ" *within* the triumph, analogous to formulations like "among the captives," and so on.[20] This would allow for a substitutionary reading with the Christians being represented by the crucified Christ.[21] And there is in fact a parallel in the ancient sources. In Plutarch, *Ant.* 84.7, Cleopatra does not want the already deceased Antony to be presented by Octavian "in her." In the end, the attractiveness of this interpretation depends a lot on broader theological presuppositions.[22]

Another option that merits more scrutiny would be that "in Christ" refers to the *context* of the leading activity—either as an alternative to the ritual of

---

18. I.e., an attributive reading, connecting the prepositional phrase with the pronoun, is not plausible. See Heilig, *Paul's Triumph*, 227–31.

19. Though it is not true that it occurs only in Paul, as Andreas Hock wrongly claims in "Christ Is the Parade: A Comparative Study of the Triumphal Procession in 2 Cor 2,14 and Col 2,15," *Bib* 88 (2007): 111.

20. See Heilig, *Paul's Triumph*, 235.

21. Heilig, *Paul's Triumph*, 236.

22. Heilig, *Paul's Triumph*, 236–37.

the triumph itself ("not in a triumphal procession, but in Christ") or as an alternative to the location where it normally took place ("not in Rome, but in Christ").[23] Both of these options are certainly very appealing from the perspective of arguing for a direct confrontation with the Roman Empire. Since they come with the largest communicative contribution, however, it runs into the problem that we would expect a more specific spatial adjunct (such as "in Christ's procession").[24]

In the end, I think it is most plausible that the locative specification is influenced by the content side of the metaphor, strengthening the idea of divine agency behind Paul's mission.[25] This is supported well by how the image of the triumph is already dropped even within v. 14 and makes room for the more general imagery of scent that then ends in v. 16 with a discussion of the reality that stood behind the previous figurative language (see below, pp. 80–83, for more details on why I think this is the case).[26]

By contrast, if one is willing to read ἐν Χριστῷ *instrumentally*,[27] this would allow for yet another interpretation with a lot of provocative potential. Perhaps Christ is imagined as a victorious soldier who co-triumphs with God and is directly responsible for the movement of the captives?[28] A beautiful *aureus* struck in 71 CE in Lyon immediately comes to mind in that regard (*RIC* II.1² 1127; figure 9). On its reverse, the coin shows the triumphator in the quadriga. In the eighteenth century, Johann Baptist Otte, in his work on Josephus in relation to the New Testament, already adduces this coin in his discussion of Col 2:15.[29] Otte's numismatic source[30] speaks of two captives (i.e., Simon and John), but, as Otte correctly remarks, the second person from the right seems to be a soldier (Otte: *lictor*), who leads the captive. Again, the attractiveness of this reading from the perspective of an anti-imperial approach to Paul is obvious. I remain unconvinced, however, mainly on the grounds that I cannot thus far see evidence that would suggest that this accompa-

---

23. Heilig, *Paul's Triumph*, 234–35.

24. See Heilig, *Paul's Triumph*, 236.

25. Heilig, *Paul's Triumph*, 237.

26. See Heilig, *Paul's Triumph*, 185–90.

27. Something I am reluctant to do. See Heilig, *Paul's Triumph*, 231–32.

28. Cf. Heilig, *Paul's Triumph*, 232–33.

29. Johann Baptist Otte, *Spicilegium, sive, Excerpta ex Flavio Josepho ad Novi Testamenti* (Leiden: Hasebroek, 1741), 417.

30. Jean Foy-Vaillant, *De Aureis et Argenteis*, 3rd ed., vol. 2 of *Numismata imperatorum Romanorum* (Paris: Jombert, 1694), 94.

Figure 9. A Roman *aureus*; the reverse depicts Vespasian on the triumphal chariot and a captive being led by a soldier before him (Lyon, 71 CE; *RIC* II.1² 1127; photo by Ira and Larry Goldberg Auctioneers / Lyle Engleson)

nying role of soldiers would have been an element particularly prominent to either Paul or the Corinthians. Further, why did Paul not use the less ambiguous preposition διά?

Next, we need to discuss the temporal adjunct πάντοτε in v. 14a and the spatial adjunct ἐν παντὶ τόπῳ in v. 14b, the latter of which is connected not to θριαμβεύω but to the verb φανερόω, which is coordinated with the former. Here, we are moving from possible resonances with discourses surrounding Claudius's triumphal procession into the realm of highly plausible conceptual overlaps—and clashes.

First, we will take a closer look at the subversive potential of the prepositional phrase from v. 14b. To many, talk about "revealing the scent of the knowledge of him through us everywhere" (cf. καὶ τὴν ὀσμὴν τῆς γνώσεως αὐτοῦ φανεροῦντι δι᾽ ἡμῶν ἐν παντὶ τόπῳ) is a clear reference to the incense that is burnt in the Roman triumph, adding an olfactory dimension to the visual spectacle. If that were indeed the case, this spatial emphasis would undoubtedly constitute a very controversial remark from a Roman standpoint—for the very same reasons that "in Christ" as a sphere of the procession that would replace the common route in Rome would be very provocative. We have already seen how Octavian used Antony's procession in Alexandria to paint him as being un-Roman (see above, p. 62). Having the victory celebration occur in *all* places would have been an immense downgrading of the city of Rome.[31] (If we

---

31. Cf. Christian Strecker, "Taktiken der Aneignung: Politische Implikationen der paulinischen Botschaft im Kontext der römischen imperialen Wirklichkeit," in *Das Neue Testament und politische Theorie: Interdisziplinäre Beiträge zur Zukunft des Politischen*, ed. Eckart

are still within the image of the triumph, we most certainly are not encouraged to think about the scent reaching everywhere from this single location.) One might even consider whether the prepositional phrase could perhaps further encourage this confrontation by conceptualizing the spatial dimension not monolithically—"everywhere"—but in a way that points to an encompassing sum of all the *individual* places that would receive that honor.[32]

In the end, what makes me cautious with respect to these resonances is that it is by no means clear that the metaphor of the Roman triumph runs through the whole of 2 Cor 2:14. My doubts are based in particular on how the olfactory language develops in 2:15–16. First, 2:14b is grounded in v. 15 in the statement that "we are Christ's fragrance to God among those who are being saved and those who are perishing" (ὅτι Χριστοῦ εὐωδία ἐσμὲν τῷ θεῷ ἐν τοῖς σῳζομένοις καὶ ἐν τοῖς ἀπολλυμένοις). Verse 16a continues this bifurcation with "to the ones a smell from death to death, to the others a smell from life to life" (οἷς μὲν ὀσμὴ ἐκ θανάτου εἰς θάνατον, οἷς δὲ ὀσμὴ ἐκ ζωῆς εἰς ζωήν). The whole passage beginning with 2:14 is then concluded in v. 16b with the question "And who is sufficient for these things?" (καὶ πρὸς ταῦτα τίς ἱκανός;). If we approach the whole issue beginning from the end, it seems pretty clear that everything runs toward this question—which focuses on Paul's apostolic mission, i.e., on the content side of the figurative language. The same quite obviously is also already true for the preceding statements on the different effects of scents. To be sure, εἰς θάνατον might be understood as a reference to the eventual execution of some captives, and "it takes little interpretative reflection to draw the parallels between the liberated of the *pompa triumphali* and 'those being saved,'"[33] i.e., οἱ σῳζόμενοι, who are εἰς ζωήν. The problem is that it would take a bit more "interpretative reflection" to also confirm what is otherwise mere speculation. What would ἐκ ζωῆς even refer to in this interpretation? To the life in captivity? So far, no interpretation of vv. 15–16 has been proposed that even begins to successfully integrate all the elements into the metaphor of the Roman triumph.[34]

On top of that, we also run into the problem that these proposals regularly presuppose untenable meanings of θριαμβεύω. The only proposal that keeps Paul in the role of a prisoner of war and still allows for the scent imagery to

---

Reinmuth, ReligionsKulturen 9 (Stuttgart: Kohlhammer, 2011), 160, on the importance of the *location* of Rome for Roman religion.

32. See LN 83.8 on πανταχῇ, πανταχοῦ, πάντοθεν, and πάντῃ.

33. George H. Guthrie, "Paul's Triumphal Procession Imagery (2 Cor 2.14–16a): Neglected Points of Background," *NTS* 61 (2015): 90.

34. See Heilig, *Paul's Triumph*, 185–90.

be understood entirely within the framework of the triumph is the suggestion by Witherington that it "may just refer to the smell of the captive himself."[35] Fortunately, this overly creative suggestion for integrating the scent imagery into the triumph imagery does not seem to have gained acceptance in the literature. To be sure, *if* the verb merely expressed a leading activity of someone in *any* role in the triumphal procession, there would be no obstacle for Paul presenting himself as an incense bearer throughout 2:14. But as we have seen, this is not really an option (see above, pp. 59–60).

Moreover, the assumption that Paul is somehow *spreading* the scent through his involvement in the triumphal procession does not fit well with Paul *identifying* himself and his coworkers with the fragrance in 2:15.[36] He can hardly be the incense carrier and the incense itself at the same time.[37] Hafemann has put forward an interpretation that is more successful in integrating this particular aspect: Paul identifies himself (Hafemann thinks we are dealing with an "apostolic plural" here, i.e., coworkers are not involved) with the "sacrificial aroma of the crucified Christ."[38] The connection with the Roman triumph is only an indirect one. Just like captives of war were regularly executed at the end of the procession (so Hafemann), Paul depicts himself here as being sacrificed (see Phil 2:17 and 2 Tim 4:6 for very explicit references to being poured out as a drink offering). However, in this interpretation too, a lot is based on questionable assumptions concerning θριαμβεύω, namely that it implies leading a captive *to death*. Even though this sometimes happened to captives—though by no means as frequently as Hafemann supposes (and as we have seen, Caratacus in 51 CE was pardoned too)—such an end is clearly not part of the semantics of the verb itself.[39] Even if it were, however, the *sacrificial* overtones would not fit the character of these executions as *punishment* well.[40] Lastly, Hafemann's interpretation faces the problem that his supporting argument that the use of

---

35. Ben Witherington III, *Conflict and Community in Corinth: A Socio-Rhetorical Commentary on 1 and 2 Corinthians* (Grand Rapids: Eerdmans, 1995), 366.

36. Heilig, *Paul's Triumph*, 175.

37. One would have to postulate a shift to metonymy (*AGG* 205).

38. Scott J. Hafemann, *Suffering and the Spirit: An Exegetical Study of 2 Cor 2:14–3:3 within the Context of the Corinthian Correspondence*, WUNT 2/19 (Tübingen: Mohr Siebeck, 1986), 52.

39. Cf. Heilig, *Paul's Triumph*, 136–41, 74–101.

40. Heilig, *Paul's Triumph*, 171.

ὀσμή and εὐωδία here serves to remind readers of the phrase ὀσμὴ εὐωδίας cannot be maintained.[41]

All this leads us to the conclusion that the scent imagery that Paul uses in 2:14b–16a is pretty much unrelated to the Roman triumph and, in a more general way, simply makes use of different qualities attributed to scent in antiquity.[42] In our analysis of what Paul implies with respect to the Roman triumph, we thus need to be careful not to read too much into Paul's assertion that through his and his coworkers' activity the gospel is made known "in every place." It seems unlikely that Paul is explicitly contrasting Claudius's triumph in Rome with a series of triumphs or an unceasing triumph (see below, pp. 88–93, on πάντοτε) taking place in *all* the cities of the Roman Empire.

Still, I remain convinced that the locations associated with the triumphs of the two triumphators cannot be meticulously kept apart from each other. The spatial dimension of the Roman triumph is just too important to this ritual—and to the specific event in 44 CE—for there not to be any dissonances audible to the Corinthians.

First, we can note that Claudius himself, in a speech before the Senate from 48 CE, which has survived as a bronze inscription (figure 10), does not fail to mention "the glory of having advanced the Empire beyond the Ocean."[43] The "re-invention" of Britain as untouched soil "beyond the Ocean" that was first subdued by Claudius is a central element of Claudian propaganda, which

41. On apparent "parallels" adduced in support see Heilig, *Paul's Triumph*, 247–54. Note that Hafemann argues that ὀσμὴ εὐωδίας—the typical rendering in the LXX for the Hebrew ניחח ריח, the "pleasing aroma" of sacrifices—is "broken up" in 2 Cor 2:14. But see Heilig, *Paul's Triumph*, 164–71. See also Heilig, *Paul's Triumph*, 182–84, on how these two terms regularly appear in the same contexts in ancient literature without functioning in such a way.

42. Heilig, *Paul's Triumph*, 175–91.

43. To be sure, the official goal is *not* to be accused of boasting (*et quaesisse iactationem gloriae pro| lati imperi ultra Oceanum*; CIL XIII 1668, col. 1, ll. 39–40). What Claudius actually does is portray himself as surpassing even his most famous predecessors. See Heinz Jakobsmeier, *Die Gallier-Rede des Claudius aus dem Jahr 48 n. Chr.: Historisch-philologische Untersuchungen und Kommentar zur* tabula Claudiana *aus Lyon*, Quellen und Forschungen zur Antiken Welt 63 (Munich: Utzverlag, 2019), 106. Cf. also S. J. V. Malloch, *The* Tabula Lugdunensis: *A Critical Edition with Translation and Commentary* (Cambridge: Cambridge University Press, 2020), 131–33. The above translation is from David C. Braund, *Augustus to Nero: A Source Book on Roman History 31 BC–AD 68* (London: Croom Helm, 1986), 200. For the inscription, see also no. 369 in E. Mary Smallwood, *Documents Illustrating the Principate of Gaius, Claudius, and Nero* (Cambridge: Cambridge University Press, 1967). The speech is recorded quite differently by Tacitus, *Ann.* 12.23–24.

Figure 10. The Claudian table, which preserves a speech of Claudius before the Roman senate; *Oceanus* is mentioned in l. 40 of the first column (*CIL* XIII 1668; Lugdunum Museum, Lyon)

aims at rooting the dynasty in an impressive military achievement—an obvious attempt to demarcate Claudius from Julius Caesar and Caligula, whose campaigns (55/54 BCE and 40 CE) are ignored.[44] This attitude might very well be reflected on Claudius's triumphal arch too, in the possible mention of the deed of integrating the "barbarians across the ocean" into the empire.[45] But there are other pieces of evidence too. According to Suetonius, *Claud.* 17.3, the triumphator even "set a naval crown on the gable of the Palace beside the civic crown, as a sign that he had crossed and, as it were, subdued the Ocean." And the *Laus Caesaris* (cf. above, pp. 72–73) also continuously emphasizes

44. Suetonius, *Cal.* 46, records the famous anecdote that Caligula ordered his soldiers to collect "seashells" into their clothes (*repente ut conchas legerent galeasque et sinus replerent imperavit*). David Woods, "Caligula's Seashells," *GR* 47 (2000): 80–87, argues that this actually refers to boats, more plausible candidates for serious *spolia Oceani*. On the demarcation, see P. B. C. Stewart, "Inventing Britain: The Roman Creation and Adaptation of an Image," *Britannia* 26 (1995): 4–10.

45. On the reconstruction of *CIL* VI 920a, l. 8, see Barrett, "Victory Arch," 10–13.

this theme. The personified Oceanus is no longer the border of the Roman Empire but rather has become part of it (v. 12); yes, he now even constitutes its center (v. 10: *Oceanus medium venit in imperium*). As the very last line, v. 42, emphatically summarizes: There are no longer two globes, but now they have been united.[46]

Such rhetoric would have fallen on fruitful soil in the East of the empire, where Claudius was called the "manifest savior god," divine benefactor of the whole world, in the 40s of the first century.[47] And there is even a relief from the south

Figure 11. Claudius with figures representing land and sea in a relief from the Sebasteion, south building, in Aphrodisias, Roman province of Asia (modern-day Turkey) (© 2019 The Aphrodisias Excavations Project)

stoa of Aphrodisias (figure 11) that impressively "reflects a Greek perception of the emperor as a benefactor-saviour god," ruling over the whole cosmos.[48]

Here, we see Claudius (the depiction of the emperor had originally been identified with Augustus) in his imperial rule over both earth and sea. The composition "shows the emperor as a divine superman, ruler of the cosmos and guarantor of prosperity and fortune on land and on sea."[49]

With such an emphasis on the global dimension of the military campaign that had secured Claudius's triumph and with the Corinthians being recipients of this propaganda through a cult with the function of highlighting this specific aspect, it seems hard to imagine that the Corinthians would not have recognized the parallel to another kind of "good news" of victory that was also being spread[50] in all the cities of the Roman Empire—and beyond. (The

46. On this, see Heilig, *Paul's Triumph*, 270.

47. From Arneae in Lycia, *TAM* II 760, col. 3, ll. 1–3 (Smallwood, *Documents*, no. 136): Τιβέριον Κλαύδιον Καίσαρα| Σεβαστὸν Γερμανικόν, θε| ὸν ἐπιφανῆ, σωτῆρα.

48. See Smith, *Marble Reliefs*, 173 on C 29.

49. Smith, *Marble Reliefs*, 171.

50. Cf. Philostratus, *Vit. soph.* 2.508, on conveying "the good news of the victory" with extraordinary speed: χρησάμενος ἀμηχάνῳ τάχει περὶ τὰ εὐαγγέλια τῆς νίκης.

kingdom of Nabataea—Gal 1:17—came under direct Roman rule under Trajan only in 106 CE.)[51]

We are now in the position to discuss the temporal adjunct that modifies θριαμβεύω itself. If there was a lot of booty to display, a triumphal procession

51. On Paul's stay in Arabia, see, with much unrivaled detail, Martin Hengel and Anna Maria Schwermer, *Paulus zwischen Damaskus und Antiochien: Die unbekannten Jahre des Apostels*, with a contribution by Ernst Axel Knauf, WUNT 108 (Tübingen: Mohr Siebeck, 1998), chapter 4, and Martin Hengel, *Paulus und Jakobus: Kleine Schriften III*, WUNT 141 (Tübingen: Mohr Siebeck, 2002), chapter 3. On Paul's intention in mentioning Arabia, see Christoph Heilig, *Paulus als Erzähler? Eine narratologische Perspektive auf die Paulusbriefe* (Berlin: de Gruyter, 2020), section 5.1.2. On the kingdom of Nabataea: The idea—going back in particular to Mommsen—that the establishment of the *provincial Arabia* under Trajan in 106 CE was merely a bureaucratic act after decades of gradual assimilation and that Paul, hence, never really left "Roman" territory seems no longer tenable. Cf. Peter Funke, "Rom und das Nabatäerreich bis zur Aufrichtung der Provinz Arabia," in *Migratio et Commutatio: Studien zur Alten Geschichte und deren Nachleben, Festschrift Th. Pekáry*, ed. Hans-Jochaim Drexhage and Julia Sünskes (St. Katharinen: Scripta Mercaturae, 1989), 1–18. On the annexation, see Fahad Mutlaq Al-Otaibi, *From Nabataea to Roman Arabia: Acquisition or Conquest?*, BARIS 2212 (Oxford: Archaeopress, 2011). Paul's mission is usually understood within the framework of his movements *within* the Roman Empire (for a recent overview, see Volker Rabens, "Paul's Mission Strategy in the Urban Landscape of the First-Century Roman Empire," in *The Urban World and the First Christians*, ed. Steve Walton, Paul Trebilco, and David Gill [Grand Rapids: Eerdmans, 2017], 99–122).

To me, the fact that Paul spent most of his life in the fuzzy zone of what we might call today the "eastern border" of the Roman Empire has not yet been considered sufficiently. Besides his visit to Arabia and potential earlier journeys that we do not know anything about, he would have been in contact with the "outside" world through merchants and Jewish pilgrims from territories not ruled (directly or indirectly) by Rome. It is sometimes argued that Rom 15:23 seems to imply that in Paul's view he had evangelized the East of the Roman Empire and, thus, had to move west, i.e., that he here displays an entirely imperial perspective on the world. However, he only says that there is no longer room "in this area" for him (νυνὶ δὲ μηκέτι τόπον ἔχων ἐν τοῖς κλίμασι τούτοις). It is valid to raise the question, why he did not—again—turn eastward, but Rom 15:19 demonstrates that his geographical perspective is not oriented totally to Roman categories (Ἱερουσαλὴμ καὶ κύκλῳ includes Arabia). Comparing Paul's destinations with respect to their political and cultural alliances to Rome—which might overlap only partially—would seem to be a very interesting research project. From my perspective, Paul's encounters with the "outside" world might very well have strengthened his perspective of the Roman Empire *as* empire, i.e., with this experience offering him a negative foil to possibly unify his perception of the many places he visited within its borders, thus countering the observation by Udo Schnelle, *Einleitung in das Neue Testament*, 8th ed. (Göttingen: Vandenhoeck & Ruprecht, 2013), 190, that Paul "bewegt sich . . . mit seiner Mission nicht in 'dem' Imperium Romanum, sondern immer in Sub-Kulturen (Judentum, hellenistische Städte, Provinzen, Landschaften)." On this, see also my earlier comments in Heilig, *Hidden Criticism?*, 99.

could be spread over several days (see Plutarch, *Pomp.* 45.1). Regardless of how much was available for the show, all these efforts could not hide the fact that the triumph was a rather ephemeral honor—and for good reason. At least during the Roman Republic, the triumphator in this ritual was granted an extraordinary exaltation—shining through in his famous likeness to Jupiter, for example—that had precisely the function of *normalizing* his status and reintroducing him into society as a peer among the other senators. This also explains why monuments and coins so often do not depict the triumphal procession but commemorate the military victory itself (see above, figure 2), as if the victorious generals had been trying to reverse the exchange of social capital effected by the Senate's decision to grant a triumphal procession.[52] To be sure, during the principate attempts to make "the temporary glory of the triumphal procession . . . into a permanent mark of status and prestige"[53] had developed further, with the wearing of the triumphal dress beyond the triumphal procession demonstrating that "one-man rule could be expressed as a more or less permanent triumphal status."[54] Wearing the triumphal dress only during *parts* of official events—as it is reported for Claudius—thus could draw praise from conservatives.[55] Obviously, the temporal dimension of the triumphal procession remained a very contested field. Claudius too tried to emphasize the glory of his military victory that had been the *basis* for his triumph. Suetonius (*Claud.* 21.6) relates, for example, that Claudius had a sea battle reenacted on a lake in 52 CE, including a silver mechanical Triton—and the embarrassment that the combatants apparently refused to fight after an unsuccessful joke by the emperor.[56]

Some scholars in the past have mistakenly concluded that since the triumphal procession was a rather brief event, θριαμβεύω must mean something else in 2 Cor 2:14, where the event in question seems to be portrayed specifically as being *permanent*.[57] This correctly recognizes the tension created by Paul's metaphor but draws the wrong conclusion. Paul is very obviously playing with this temporal aspect. In an earlier publication, I had thus concluded that

---

52. See Tanja Itgenshorst, *Tota illa pompa: Der Triumph in der römischen Republik*, Hypomnemata 161 (Göttingen: Vandenhoeck & Ruprecht, 2005), 198. Cf. Heilig, *Paul's Triumph*, 124–26, on Roman coinage and triumphal arches.

53. Beard, *Roman Triumph*, 30.

54. Beard, *Roman Triumph*, 277.

55. See Beard, *Roman Triumph*, 277.

56. On this fascinating Triton, see Alan Dorin and Eva Anagnostou-Laoutides, "The Silver Triton: Suetonius *Claud.* 21.6.13–6," *Nuncius* 33 (2018): 1–24.

57. Cf., with references, Heilig, *Paul's Triumph*, 223–24.

"imperatorial anxieties concerning the ephemerality of triumphal honour are
. . . subverted by the permanency of God's triumphal celebration."[58]

It was not until I worked on Col 2:15—the only other passage in the New
Testament that contains the verb θριαμβεύω, this time in the perfective aspect
(aorist)—that I revisited this conclusion.[59] The definition of the verb that I had
proposed was 'to cause [somebody] or [something] to move (before oneself) in
a triumphal procession in order to display [somebody] or [something] to the
watching crowd.'[60] The situation that is expressed by the verb is marked by a
causative act by the triumphator that primarily focuses on having the captives
move along the route of the procession. It also seems to contain, however, the
semantic element of the result of that act, namely "the display of the object to
those watching the procession."[61] With respect to its lexical aspect (*Aktionsart*), θριαμβεύω thus displays telicity and can be classified, more specifically,
as an "active accomplishment."[62] In other words, the verb expresses a situation
that contains an inherent endpoint, which is reached when the crowd has had
the opportunity to watch the captives that are on display.

In the *imperfective* (grammatical) aspect—which is used by Paul in 2 Cor
2:14—such (lexically implied) endpoints are excluded. Accordingly, these telic
verbs usually receive a "linear" reinterpretation as activities, that is, durative
events with no inherent endpoint.[63] This way an "unbounded" situation emerges,
as it is required by this aspect, which excludes endpoints from its focus. Of the
six times the transitive verb appears in the imperfective aspect in the time frame
that I have analyzed, three times such a linear re-interpretation seems plausible
(Plutarch, *Cor.* 35.6, *Ant.* 84.7, and Acts Paul 9.22).[64] In these cases, we seem to
get an internal perspective of the procession. (We can note in passing that now
the crowd too is conceptualized differently. In the perfective aspect, the end point
is reached when the *whole crowd* has witnessed the event. In the imperfective
aspect, it is the sight by *individuals* that now constitutes the repeated event.)

There is yet another option, however, that I had not considered earlier.
Especially verbs with a particularly short duration are reinterpreted *iteratively*,

58. Heilig, *Paul's Triumph*, 271.

59. Christoph Heilig, "Caesar and Paul in the Roman Triumphal Procession: Reading
Col 2:15 in Light of 2 Cor 2:14," as part of the program unit *Bible and Empire*, at the International SBL meeting in Berlin, August 9, 2017.

60. Heilig, *Paul's Triumph*, 101.

61. Heilig, *Paul's Triumph*, 101.

62. See Heilig, *Paulus als Erzähler?*, chapter 6, section 1, and 272–73.

63. See *Paulus als Erzähler?*, 280–81.

64. Heilig, *Paul's Triumph*, 64, 65–66, 72–73.

as a series of events, in the imperfective aspect. This is the case because here the so-called reference time or topic time defined by the imperfective aspect cannot fit within the situation time as stipulated by the event in question.[65] For example, we must probably imagine Jesus in Mark 14:34 throwing himself on the ground repeatedly (ἔπιπτεν ἐπὶ τῆς γῆς) for prayer, because the imperfective aspect would usually not focus on the intermediate stages of such an instantaneous event.

Admittedly, leading someone in the triumph is certainly not instantaneous. We are not, in more technical terminology, dealing with the situation type (Aktionsart) "achievement" but "accomplishment."[66] However, discrepancies between the "typical duration" of a situation on the one hand and specifications of the reference time in the context—for example, by means of adverbials[67]—on the other hand can also force an iterative reinterpretation, even in the case of (more or less) durative situations.[68] In other words, if it is clear from the context that the time that is in view is too long in order for the typically much shorter situation time to encompass this reference time, even noninstantaneous situations will be understood as a series of events.[69] If, for

65. See Heilig, Paul's Triumph, 282–83, 330.

66. See Heilig, Paul's Triumph, 271, and Heilig, Paulus als Erzähler?, chapter 6, section 1.4.

67. These temporal indications can have different forms. Cf., for example, the imperfective participles ἄγοντες in Acts 21:16 (cf. 5:27 for the perfective aspect) and ἀπαγόμενοι in 1 Cor 12:2, both having to do with the concept of 'leading,' just like θριαμβεύοντι in 2 Cor 2:14. In the first passage, the main clause specifies that what is in view is the journey from Caesarea to Jerusalem (συνῆλθον δὲ καὶ τῶν μαθητῶν ἀπὸ Καισαρείας σὺν ἡμῖν). Here, it is a single leading activity to Mnason's house that can easily be understood as having the same temporal reference (ἄγοντες παρ᾽ ᾧ ξενισθῶμεν Μνάσωνί τινι Κυπρίῳ, ἀρχαίῳ μαθητῇ). Note that the actual arrival is not yet communicated (unlike in v. 8, which similarly recounts the arrival at another house, the one of Philippus in Caesarea: . . . καὶ εἰσελθόντες εἰς τὸν οἶκον Φιλίππου τοῦ εὐαγγελιστοῦ). We stay on the road, so to speak. It is only in v. 17 that the arrival at the destination in Jerusalem is then presupposed. Cf. on such "elliptical" narration Heilig, Paulus als Erzähler?, chapter 8, section 3. By contrast, in 1 Cor 12:2, the situation of being "led" is certainly to be understood iteratively. Here, the time frame is much longer, specified by the temporal clause "when you were pagans" (ὅτε ἔθνη ἦτε) and the imperfect of ἄγω is explicitly marked by ἄν as a replacement structure for the iterative optative known from classical Greek (see AGG 198c). On the two different possibilities of resolving the syntax, see Heilig, Paulus als Erzähler?, 416.

68. What takes just a "moment" or more is not a matter of clear definitions. The distinction rests on established conceptualizations from everyday usage (cf. Heilig, Paulus als Erzähler?, 278).

69. See Heilig, Paulus als Erzähler?, 343–44. Against Buist M. Fanning, Verbal Aspect in New Testament Greek, Oxford Theology and Religion Monographs (Oxford: Oxford University Press, 1990), 152. See, for example, Herodotus, Hist. 1.65.1: "For when Leon and

example, someone said that in the year 71 BCE, the Romans were "constantly" θριαμβεύειν captives, we would immediately understand this to express an "interruptative" situation,[70] construed on the basis of four separate triumphal processions with enough time in between, during which people were not standing in the streets. It is of course not *really* the case in Roman times that "one triumph meets the other" (Plutarch, *Mor.* 323F).

I see this dynamic of an iterative reinterpretation for example in Tatian, *Or. Graec.* 26.1. While others have suggested a semantic shift for θριαμβεύω, to me there seems to be merely a figurative usage of the verb in its usual meaning.[71] Tatian wants a certain *habitual behavior* to stop, namely the behavior of "presenting utterances by others in a triumphal procession" (Παύσασθε λόγους ἀλλοτρίους θριαμβεύοντες), just like the jackdaw behaves when it adorns itself with feathers from other birds (καὶ ὥσπερ ὁ κολοιὸς οὐκ ἰδίοις ἐπικοσμούμενοι πτεροῖς). Similar interpretations seem to be suggested by the context in other passages too. Plutarch, *Aem.* 36.9 looks forward to a specific triumphal procession but embeds it into a discourse on how Fortune *generally* treats "the triumphator" and the one who is being led in triumph (οὐκ ἀφανέστερον ἔχουσα παράδειγμα τῆς ἀνθρωπίνης ἀσθενείας τοῦ θριαμβευομένου τὸν θριαμβεύοντα).[72] Appian, *Hist. rom.* 12.77 probably also expresses a rule of *generally* not leading a Roman citizen in the procession (οὐ γὰρ ἐδόκει Ῥωμαῖον ἄνδρα βουλευτὴν θριαμβεύειν).[73]

Against this backdrop, it might be appropriate to reconsider the typical interpretation of 2 Cor 2:14 as painting the picture of a single, permanent triumphal procession.[74] In fact, one might raise the question of whether πάν-

---

Hegesicles were kings of Sparta, the Lacedaemonians, while successful in all their other wars, *suffered defeats* (προσέπταιον) only against the Tegeans." The translation is taken from Corien Bary and Markus Egg, "Variety in Ancient Greek Aspect Interpretation," *Linguistics and Philosophy* 35 (2012): 126, who comment on this passage as follows: "The bounded predicate [πρὸς Τεγεήτας μούνους προσέπταιον] 'to suffer a defeat (literally, to bump into) only against the Tegeans' could not receive a progressive [i.e., linear] reinterpretation, since the topic time (the reign of Leon and Hegesicles over Sparta) could not fit into the runtime of an eventuality characterised by the progressive of this predicate. In contrast, an iteration of losing against the Tegeans can have a runtime that is long enough to comprise the time of the reign of Leon and Hegesicles" (p. 131).

70. See Heilig, *Paulus als Erzähler?*, 344.
71. See Heilig, *Paul's Triumph*, 74.
72. Heilig, *Paul's Triumph*, 62.
73. Heilig, *Paul's Triumph*, 69.
74. This assumption seems hardly ever questioned. See, however, the following modern Greek translation of 2 Cor 2:14, which speaks of a plurality of "triumphal processions"

τοτε perhaps even necessitates such an iterative interpretation? If the usage of θριαμβεύω were not metaphorical, it seems this would indeed be the case. The "typical duration" of a normal triumph cannot be stretched to last "forever," i.e., to make room for the reference time defined by πάντοτε. However, we have to keep in mind that in 2 Cor 2:14 we are dealing with metaphorical usage.[75] Paul might indeed want us to imagine all the chaotic movements of 2:12–13 to be part of an unceasing triumphal procession of God, based perhaps on the singular victory achieved by Jesus.

However, one could counter this reference to the metaphorical nature of the triumph in 2 Cor 2:14 by pointing out that the specific journeys of 2:12–13 are in turn only part of a larger problem the Corinthians have with Paul and that has already surfaced in 1:17.[76] In other words, Paul might just as well think of a variety of different events in the real world that he wants to recast in new light by means of the metaphor. It thus seems also plausible to me that Paul would portray the many voyages of him and his team to different places as a *series* of triumphal processions—taking place not only in Rome, not even only in one additional city as it was the case with Antony, but in every city that they visited.

Again, the conceptualization of "everywhere" as the sum of many individual places through the phrase ἐν παντὶ τόπῳ in v. 14b might add further plausibility to such an understanding. The fact that Paul and his coworkers move to many different locations and in so doing are "always" part of God's triumph(s), automatically reinforces the potential spatial provocation that we have already identified with respect to v. 14b and the Roman understanding of the *triumphi*. In this iterative/interruptative understanding, that challenge might be even stronger, because the different places Paul and his coworkers visit would now be individually recipients of the greatest and most Roman honor the city of Rome had to offer.

Having an indefinite series of triumphs to celebrate would also challenge the spatial dimension of Rome in another way. Rather than being based on a single military victory, such a series of triumphs would imply God's nonstop successes—presumably in many different campaigns, subduing a wide variety of areas. Here it is particularly evocative to see what Plutarch, *Pomp.* 45.4 has

---

(TGV; italics added): Ας είναι δοξασμένος ο Θεός, που μας οδηγεί *πάντοτε σε θριάμβους* με τη δύναμη του Χριστού.

75. For details, see Heilig, *Paul's Triumph*, 233–35 and 247–48, with reference to Ernst Leisi, *Der Wortinhalt: Seine Struktur im Deutschen und Englischen*, 4th ed. (Heidelberg: Quelle & Meyer, 1971).

76. Discussed in detail in Heilig, *Paul's Triumph*, 156–61.

to say about Pompey (Perrin): "But that which most enhanced his glory and had never been the lot of any Roman before, was that he celebrated his third triumph over the third continent. For others before him had celebrated three triumphs; but he celebrated his first over Libya, his second over Europe, and this his last over Asia, so that he seemed in a way to have included the whole world in his three triumphs."

The *number* of triumphs and ovations—and, thus, underlying military successes—is also emphasized already by Augustus (*Res gest. divi Aug.* 4.1: Δὶς πεζ[ὸν ἐθριάμβευσα καὶ] τρὶς [ἐ]φ᾽ ἅρματος).[77] If we read the participle θριαμβεύοντι in 2 Cor 2:14 iteratively, as saying that Paul and his coworkers are part of "all of God's triumphs," the contrast with contemporary emphases by Roman triumphators would be glaring indeed. Especially since Claudius had celebrated only a single triumph—despite Seneca (*Polyb.* 16.2) wishing him a multitude of triumphal processions (*Hic Germaniam pacet, Britanniam aperiat, et patrios triumphos ducat et novos;* "May he bring peace to Germany, open up Britain, and celebrate again both his father's triumphs and new ones!"). In fact, the ostentatious show he put on with the display of Caratacus in 51 CE could easily be understood as a faint attempt to celebrate something like a second triumphal procession.[78] The triumphator God in Paul's metaphor does not need such shabby tricks.

A note of caution is necessary here too. In 2 Cor 2:14, the verb θριαμβεύω is not used intransitively. The metaphor is not primarily about God's triumph(s). Rather, the celebration of the triumph(s) is only the context for the action that is focused on, the presentation of captives. From their perspective, the only good thing about the triumphal procession was that you would only have to bear the shame *once* (that is the clear point of another figurative usage of triumph imagery that is often adduced in discussions of 2 Cor 2:14 and sometimes grotesquely misunderstood).[79] While it makes sense for Paul, the former enemy of God, to march joyfully in the triumphator's procession after

77. Cf. Heilig, *Paul's Triumph*, 53 and 129.

78. Douglas A. Campbell, *Framing Paul: An Epistolary Biography* (Grand Rapids: Eerdmans, 2014), 188, thus might have good reasons for emphasizing this event as a backdrop to 2 Cor 2:14 (see above, p. 65 n. 40). However, for this assumed reference we lose the documentation of potential eyewitnesses.

79. Seneca, *Ben.* 2.11.1. See Heilig, *Paul's Triumph*, 224, on *semel*. On this often-misused passage, see generally Heilig, *Paul's Triumph*, 113–14. See also above, p. 77 n. 16. Cf., by contrast, Pliny the Elder, *Nat.* 7.43.135: *bis in triumpho ductum,* and Plutarch, *Comp. Cim. Luc.* 3.2 for a diadem that "has already been presented" in the triumph before.

his defeat at Damascus,[80] it is unclear why he would be presented in this role in a series of processions, celebrating victories in battles that he was not involved with, at least not on the hostile side.[81]

But perhaps this already stretches the metaphor too far. In my view, the iterative reading remains possible—and, in light of the many potential resonances that force themselves on the reader, when he or she takes into account the public discourse on Roman triumphs, even likely. Although we are not dealing with intransitive θριαμβεύω, i.e., with a focus on simply executing the triumphal procession, the triumphator is indeed put into the spotlight. After all, the participle construction explicates the one toward the thanksgiving is directed. And, as we will now discuss, it is this role that in light of public Roman discourse would be most shocking and draw most attention.

The Triumphator

The fact that in Paul's metaphor God takes the role of the triumphator is absolutely remarkable. In all the occurrences of the verb from the second century BCE to the third century CE, even references to *other humans* who are not Roman generals are extremely rare and mostly occur in much later fragments of earlier works with very questionable textual status.[82] The verb is never used for the activity of a god. To be sure, there is a strong conceptual and lexical link with one god in particular, Dionysos/Bacchus/Liber. According to one etymological theory, the acclamation θρίαμβε, meant to summon the god Dionysos (who thus later received the byname θρίαμβος), has a common pre-Greek basis—mediated by the Etruscans—with the exclamation *triumpe*, which could be heard in the Roman triumphal procession.[83] Latin *triumphus* and *triumphare* then entered—and in the first case, re-entered—Greek as θρίαμβος and

---

80. Cf., e.g., Heilig, *Paul's Triumph*, 227–28.

81. Note that the semantics of the verb do allow, however (and against Breytenbach; see above, p. 59), for a rather loose connection between the one who is presented and the prior victory. I.e., the defeat of the presented person does not have to be instrumental in being granted a triumph. See Heilig, *Paul's Triumph*, 97–99.

82. Heilig, *Paul's Triumph*, 51–74; and cf. the critique in Christoph Heilig, "Biblical Words and Their Meaning: An Introduction to Lexical Semantics in the *NIDNTTE*," *Reviews of Biblical and Early Christian Studies*, June 15, 2015, https://rbecs.org/2015/06/17/nidntte/ of Moisés Silva, "θριαμβεύω," *NIDNTTE* 2:467–68.

83. See Heilig, *Paul's Triumph*, 33.

Figure 12. The triumph of Bacchus with echoes of the Roman ritual, from a sarcophagus at the Villa Medici, Rome

θριαμβεύω.[84] Earlier ideas about the god as a conqueror were then intensified in analogy to the conquests of Alexander the Great in India—with the latter then being portrayed more and more as Dionysos (and probably not the other way around). It is on the basis of the lexical link and the strong military profile that some then came to see Dionysos, in retrospect, as the "inventor" of the Roman triumphal procession.[85] This led to the now famous motif of the "Triumph of Bacchus," depicting the god's return from India—with, switching the direction of influence once again, sometimes very clear visual resemblance to the current Roman procession (see figure 12).[86]

This does *not* mean, however, that the semantics of θριαμβεύω somehow changed to now incorporate divine processions. In the very rare cases of gods being portrayed as celebrating a *triumphus*, the other parameters beyond the triumphator remain decidedly within the boundaries of what one would expect of the Roman triumphal procession. This is very clear in the most striking example, Ovid, *Am.* 1.2, where the poet presents himself as part of the procession of the god Cupid (cf. below, p. 96).[87] Therefore, one must conclude that attempts to soften the Roman overtones of 2 Cor 2:14 by postulating a more general lexical meaning for the verb on the basis of such texts

84. Heilig, *Paul's Triumph*, 35.

85. See Heilig, *Paul's Triumph*, 33.

86. Beard, *Roman Triumph*, 317, shows a picture of apparently the same sarcophagus, but the reference given in Beard appears to be incorrect. It should be D-DAI-ROM-63.1238. However, the condition of the scene in that picture is much worse. Figure 12 seems to show a different sarcophagus with the same motif but in much better condition. Both are obviously spolia but integrated in different ways in the surrounding wall. Apparently the object shown in figure 12 is also part of the garden façade of the Villa Medici in Rome, just like the object shown in D-DAI-ROM-63.1238.

87. See Heilig, *Paul's Triumph*, 201.

Figure 13. Cameo showing Augustus in a chariot drawn by Tritons
(Kunsthistorisches Museum, Vienna, Antikensammlung, IXa 56;
© KHM-Museumsverband)

has no basis in the sources.[88] When the vocabulary that is associated with
the Roman triumphal procession is used in such a way, we are dealing with
metaphors that explicitly *draw on the military realm.*

Still, researchers are right to point out this connection between the military
and divine realm. For the influence also worked the other way around, allow-
ing Roman triumphators to draw on mythical elements. This line of reasoning
can already build on what might be remnants of an Etruscan prototype of the
triumphus, the portrayal of the triumphator as Jupiter.[89] The cameo in figure 13,
which shows Augustus in the likeness of Neptune in a triumphal chariot drawn
by Tritons, gives an insight into the ancient creativity in combining politics
with mythological elements.[90]

88. Heilig, *Paul's Triumph,* 195–201.

89. See Heilig, *Paul's Triumph,* 264–65. Cf. Beard, *Roman Triumph,* 233–38.

90. Correctly noted by Dietrich-Alex Koch, "Gottes Triumph und die Aufgabe des Apostels: Überlegungen zu 2Kor 2,14," *Sacra Scripta* 16 (2018): 15–16, whose interpretation of
2 Cor 2:14 I find implausible, however. See generally on the visual interplay between Roman
and bacchic "triumphal" procession John Boardmann, *The Triumph of Dionysos: Convivial
Processions, From Antiquity to the Present Day* (Oxford: Archaeopress, 2014), 19–27.

The Hague Cameo (see figure 8, p. 76 above)—which might even depict *Claudius's* triumphal procession!—also incorporates such mythical elements: "Both the krater and the centaurs transpose military victory into a Dionysian cavalcade."[91] To be sure, one needs to be very careful with evidence like this because such cameos probably mostly served as status symbols. Whether such mythological speculations had much effect outside of the hidden transcript of the elites remains doubtful.[92]

Still, I am willing to grant that, perhaps, Paul was *inspired* by this merging of divine and human elements in the Roman triumphal procession. Ideas about YHWH as celebrating an eschatological victory similarly might have helped him make the connection.[93] Even if all that were the case, however, it would not make his metaphorical replacement of the emperor with the Jewish god YHWH any less provocative. In Ovid's portrayal of Cupid as triumphator (*Am.* 1.2),[94] the military realm is not merely a source for the figurative language—rather, it is at the same time also challenged by the divine sphere, to which this language is applied. The picture that emerges is "dazzlingly subversive," not the least by "pok[ing] fun at the militaristic ethos of the ceremony."[95] Moreover, linking Cupid with his "cousin" Augustus may only appear to be a compliment at first sight. A closer examination suggests that it actually trivializes the mercy of the princeps and perhaps even comments "on the growing restriction of this honorific procession to members of the imperial family."[96]

To be sure, Paul's metaphor is all the more "dazzlingly subversive," for he

91. Smith, "*Maiestas Serena*," 45.

92. Koch, "Gottes Triumph," 16, quotes Patrick Schollmeyer, "Kleopatras Preziosen: Das hellenistische Schatzerbe der römischen Kaiser," *Antike Welt* 5 (2017): 12, but seems to miss the relevance of his concluding remark: "Mit dieser spezifischen Form politischer Bildpropaganda [as in the case of the Tazza Fanese], die in ihrer Komplexität wohl nur gebildeten Hofkreisen voll verständlich gewesen ist, und auch nur dort in entsprechenden Zeremonien sinnvoll eingesetzt werden konnte, haben die Ptolemäer schließlich den Grund für die in gleicher Weise anspruchsvolle Kameenkunst der römischen Kaiser bereitet. Auch diese nutzten die kostbaren Steine zum metaphorischallegorischen Herrscherlob, bestimmt für die Eliten des Kaiserhofs, weshalb die Kameen in ihrer Bildsprache wohl um so vieles verschlüsselter sind als die einfachen und noch dazu beschrifteten Münzdarstellungen der Massenpropaganda."

93. Heilig, *Paul's Triumph*, 204.

94. Cf. Heilig, *Paul's Triumph*, 271–72.

95. Beard, *Roman Triumph*, 52.

96. John F. Miller, "Reading Cupid's Triumph," *CJ* 90 (1995): 294. By contrast, according to William Turpin, *Ovid "Amores": Book 1*, Dickinson College Commentaries (Cambridge: Open Book, 2016), 33, the mention of Augustus is to be read as a counterbalance to having made fun of the Roman triumph throughout the poem, thus having further cast doubt on his patriotism after having first given up the plan of writing patriotic poetry due to Cupid's influence (cf. *Am.* 1.1).

Figure 14. Arch of Titus, Rome

chooses to replace the emperor with a deity that had always been suspect to the Romans—and whose cultic instruments would be presented in another triumphal procession (figure 14) just a few years later.

Paul's appropriation of the triumph will also have been viewed as being incredibly problematic from a Roman perspective due to yet another factor, the issue of reference. In Ovid's case, the image functions basically to underscore the poet's submission to Cupid, who in the previous poem (*Am.* 1.1) was introduced as the one who was trying to keep the poet from writing patriotic poetry. Having been shot with Cupid's arrow, the poet is now crazy in love and forced to write elegy, totally under the control of the god of love, just like a prisoner of war. The triumph imagery thus merely explains what the poet is presently doing, indulging in his pain of love. In Paul's case, however, the metaphor stands for his and his coworkers' concrete activities throughout the Roman world—which would have been suspicious enough already for Roman observers (see above, chapter 1). It cannot get much more controversial than portraying these actions as part of a military victory procession by the Jewish God, not only mimicking the Roman *triumphus* but also surpassing it in several ways and, in so doing, simply pushing the emperor out of his *quadriga.*[97]

97. Against Thomas Schmeller, review of *Paul's Triumph: Reassessing 2 Corinthians 2:14*

Robinson's claim that when "Paul draws vocabulary from political metaphors, the evidence just does not exist that this is Paul at his most subtly subversive" is clearly incorrect, at least with respect to 2 Cor 2:14.[98]

Transcripts

Therefore, I conclude that, if analyzed carefully within its historical context, 2 Cor 2:14 does indeed give us valuable insights into the contemporary discourse concerning Claudius's triumphal procession. Are there also more general conclusions that we can draw with respect to Paul's interaction with his Roman environment? As I have emphasized above (pp. 77–78), Paul's rhetorical strategy is clearly aimed at the Corinthian Christians, and it is certainly not his primary aim to "attack Caesar." This, however, does not change the fact that 2 Cor 2:14 seems to be the one passage in Paul's letters where the emperor (and even, more specifically, Emperor Claudius) is most vividly evoked in the imagination of the reader—only to be immediately replaced again by God. We are now in a position to flesh out in more detail what shape the critical potential of this passage takes. In what follows, I will adduce a number of conclusions that I believe we can draw from the previous exegetical discussion.

First, we can note (conclusion number 1) that, with respect to the pragmatics of the passages, there seems to be at least a secondary function relating to the imperial context of the recipients: the metaphor offers the Corinthians some comfort and guidance with respect to their new alienated status within their society. The way monuments and rituals would have contributed to making them feel their status as outsiders in their city is difficult to appreciate for Christians today in western societies. Paul helps them to cope with the overwhelming impact of the many aspects of their pagan environment by integrating the recipients of his letters into a surpassing framework.[99] Paul's metaphor

---

in Its Literary and Historical Context, by Christoph Heilig, BZ 63 (2019): 341: "Von einer Kritik am Imperium Romanum und seinen politisch-religiosen Ausdrucksformen kann ich hier nichts entdecken."

98. Laura Robinson, "Hidden Transcripts? The Supposedly Self-Censoring Paul and Rome as Surveillance State in Modern Pauline Scholarship," NTS 67 (2021): 72.

99. Heilig, Paul's Triumph, 277. Tom Holland, Dominion: How the Christian Revolution Remade the World (New York: Basic Books, 2019), 92, integrates this passage in a remarkably similar way. He focuses on Paul himself (and misinterprets v. 14b in my opinion; see above, pp. 80–83) but rightly—and eloquently—captures the hermeneutical significance. He writes: "Even Corinth itself, seen through Paul's eyes, appeared transfigured. Its theatres and stadia served as monuments, not to the honouring of the city's ancient festivals, but to the radical novelty of his message. To preach the gospel of Christ was to stand like an actor before the gaze of an entire people; it was to train for the great games staged on the Isthmus, as a

does not constitute "criticism" in a confrontational sense—as if it were directed to Claudius himself—nor does it call the Corinthians to take up their arms in a revolution. It does, however, seem to challenge basic assumptions of Roman ideology and can thus be classified as at least potentially "subversive."[100]

We may now return once again to the issue of Scott's "hidden transcripts," put into focus so decisively by Robinson. As I have argued above (pp. 44–54), I think the concept of the "hidden transcript" as something to be reconstructed from a wide variety of fragmentary expressions in Paul's letters seems to be more promising than the idea of actively "hidden criticism," which needs to be decoded. And I do think that 2 Cor 2:14 is an excellent example in that regard. The concept of the hidden transcript allows us (conclusion number 2) to reconstruct a *critical attitude* toward the Roman Empire—or at least a specific event in recent Roman history. The passage reflects a sense of unease in relation to Roman demonstrations of military power. Or, to put it more carefully, the fact that Paul embraces the possibility of creating rather stark dissonances with respect to Roman expectations concerning the discourse on *triumphi* can be taken as an indication of such unease. Just like the refusal of a Roman general to celebrate a triumphal procession can be understood as a reflection of his worldview,[101] the dissonances created by Paul's metaphor within the broader discourse of his time are indicative of his rejection of at least the cultically elevated expression of Roman military conquest.[102]

So, whose hidden transcript are we getting a glimpse of in 2 Cor 2:14? We need to be careful not to answer this question too quickly. It would be easy to just speak of the "Pauline" hidden transcript, the private opinion circulating in his churches. However, the very fact that we are offered this window into an otherwise largely invisible sphere in a document subject to the rules of public

---

runner, as a boxer. Once, back in the darkest year of the city's history, it had been a Roman general who led the Corinthians in long lines as the mark of his triumph; but now it was God. There was no shame in joining such a procession. Just the opposite. To walk incense-perfumed in the divine train was not to be a captive, but truly to be free."

100. "Subversion" is defined as 'a systematic attempt to overthrow or undermine a government or political system by persons working from within' (*Merriam-Webster*, s.v. "subversion," accessed May 27, 2021, https://www.merriam-webster.com/dictionary/subversion). Paul's metaphor cannot be taken as a direct attempt toward these ends. However, he clearly "subverts" standard Roman assumptions (*Merriam-Webster*, s.v. "subvert," accessed May 27, 2021, https://www.merriam-webster.com/dictionary/subvert: 'to pervert or corrupt by an undermining of morals, allegiance, or faith'). As we have just discussed, Paul's metaphor contributes toward helping the Corinthians realize their allegiance in the case of conflict.

101. Cf. Cicero, *Pis*. Cf. Heilig, *Paul's Triumph*, 262–63.

102. Heilig, *Paul's Triumph*, 262.

discourse[103] calls for an explanation. Is Paul casting prudence to the wind? Is he forgetting, for a moment at least,[104] that he might put his congregation in danger by being too blunt in his letter? Or is he simply making an error of judgment with respect to the boundaries between hidden and public transcript, in regard to what is allowed and what might be sanctioned?

There might be yet another option: What if Paul is very aware of the conditions of his writing but is interested in testing—and perhaps carefully stretching—the boundaries of the public transcript? After all, we must not forget the fact that Seneca's *Apocolocyntosis* can be attributed with high certainty to Seneca because of the circumstance that it probably never circulated anonymously. Thus the most plausible assumption is that it was written for and received with enthusiasm among the elites at Nero's palace. No one will have found the biting scorn for his predecessor more humorous than the new emperor himself. The early principate was a tumultuous time and there will have been many "dislocations" in the public transcript, making its precise boundaries an issue of constant debate and renegotiation—with the suppressed taking every opportunity to fill the space that became available. In fact, "testing the limits" seems to be yet another explicit emphasis in the original work of James C. Scott that has played a rather minor role in the application to New Testament texts so far.[105] It might very well be the case that we get some insight into a Pauline hidden transcript from Claudian times simply because it was now more acceptable in the public transcript. In any case, especially when compared with works like the *Apocolocyntosis* and the *Laus Caesaris*, it becomes clear that Paul not only (conclusion number 3) attentively observes his Roman environment, but also (conclusion number 4) proactively engages in a broader societal discourse, with (conclusion number 5) hidden transcript and public transcript being in a very dynamic relationship.[106] Even just integrating this realization—that Paul demonstrates interest in contemporary political events and takes a position that can be related to other statements

---

103. See above, pp. 8–9. For details cf. Heilig, *Hidden Criticism?*, chapter 2.

104. The question of how Paul dictated his letters and to what extent first drafts would have been subject to revision is of vital importance but so far rarely addressed in Pauline studies. Cf. Heilig, *Paulus als Erzähler?*, chapter 4, section 1 and conclusion, section 12. There are some textual phenomena that might suggest a rather unfiltered attestation of Paul's spoken words. Cf. the entries in the index on "Pseudepigraphie, Sekretärshypothese" (Heilig, *Paulus als Erzähler?*, 1093).

105. James C. Scott, *Domination and the Arts of Resistance: Hidden Transcripts* (New Haven: Yale University Press, 1990), 192–97.

106. Heilig, *Paul's Triumph*, 275–77.

from public figures of his time—into our background knowledge should go a long way in increasing the background plausibility of critical engagement with Roman ideology when approaching other passages.[107] This is particularly the case if we have previously fed Bayes's theorem with Barclay's assumption that Paul *deliberately ignores* the Roman Empire![108]

Finally, we need to emphasize (conclusion number 6) what might have become obvious by now: that the critical subtext I have identified behind 2 Cor 2:14 was not in any meaningful way *"hidden."* To the contrary, if viewed through a historically informed lens it actually seems quite obvious. It is clearer than many other exegetical conclusions concerning the semantics and pragmatics of biblical texts that are not adduced as the result of obscure detective work aimed at "decoding" a secret message. At the same time, there can be no doubt that the dimension of a critical interaction with "Rome"—or rather, with a specific event of contemporary politics that is indicative of larger ideological structures—has been almost completely *overlooked* in the past.[109] As we have seen (see above, p. 65), Claudius is not even mentioned in most commentaries on this passage. And even N. T. Wright, arguably the most important figure in the debate that sparked this whole conversation (see above, chapter 1), does not recognize that the metaphor has a Roman dimension at all, speaking only of "a king, a general, or some other great leader" returning after military victory to his respective city.[110] To be sure, decoding ancient enigmas would be more heroic than identifying blind spots in current scholarship. But if the clear political implications of 2 Cor 2:14 can be missed so easily, even in a context where "Paul and Empire" is a hotly debated issue, this is a clear indication that we need to stop looking for the elephants hiding in trees and start appreciating their beautiful botanical counterparts.

107. Heilig, *Paul's Triumph*, 276. Cf. Heilig, *Paulus als Erzähler?*, chapter 16, section 4.1 for another example of how more debatable passages can be gradually substantiated.

108. The central thesis of John M. G. Barclay, "Why the Roman Empire Was Insignificant to Paul," in *Pauline Churches and Diaspora Jews*, ed. John M. G. Barclay, WUNT 275 (Tübingen: Mohr Siebeck, 2011).

109. See Heilig, *Paul's Triumph*, 263.

110. N. T. Wright, 2 *Corinthians*, Paul for Everyone (London: SPCK, 2003), 24. Of course, the passage is sometimes adduced, but usually only in passing. See references in Heilig, *Paul's Triumph*, 263. See also Neil Elliott, "The Apostle Paul and Empire," in *In the Shadow of Empire: Reclaiming the Bible as a History of Faithful Resistance*, ed. Richard A. Horsley (Louisville: Westminster John Knox, 2008), 100, who at least makes the more specific statement that Paul "parodies the ceremonial of Roman triumphs."

5 | Sharpening Our Exegetical Senses

Exegetical Blind Spots

In closing, I want to provide an outlook on how we might proceed from here. In particular, it seems important to me to take a moment to reflect on the potential reasons that might have made large parts of scholarship on 2 Cor 2:14 blind for an aspect of background information that clearly has a lot of potential.[1] My guiding question in these concluding remarks is: *What has caused our blindness and how can we sharpen our senses so that we do not miss important aspects of the text?* My comments are not meant to be exhaustive. Nor do I claim that they are of equal value (nor that the respective detail of my treatment corresponds to their significance). They mostly reflect a growing self-awareness of my own limitations and blind spots and are meant to stimulate a debate about what is actually needed to create the preconditions for a fruitful discussion about Paul's unease with the Roman Empire. In any case, I am very confident that if taken into account they will provide a powerful challenge to the idea that in Paul's letters we almost never find "external reference to Roman society."[2]

---

1. See Christoph Heilig, *Paulus als Erzähler? Eine narratologische Perspektive auf die Paulusbriefe*, BZNW 237 (Berlin: de Gruyter, 2020), chapter 1, section 2, on the heuristic significance of such analyses.

2. Michael Flexsenhar III, "Paul the Trojan Horse: The Legacy of Triumph in Philippians," *JSNT* 43 (2021): 439, thinks there might only be three occasions (Rom 16:23; Phil 1:13; 4:22). Perhaps the statement is less reductionistic and, thus, more plausible if we replace "society" with "administration." But it seems important to me to distinguish, on an even more fundamental level, between the (a) *narrative distance/the degree of "vividness"* of Paul's narration—which might be low at points—and (b) the *degree of specificity of the mental proto-narratives created by his audience*—which might be high at the same time, because they would have been able to understand the concrete reference of statements that might seem rather general to us. For examples (including one from Greco-Roman society, 1 Cor 7:32), see Heilig, *Paulus als Erzähler?*, 770–74.

Misled Focus on "Code"

I find Robinson's critique (see above, chapters 1 and 2) to be ultimately un-convincing. She seems to be beating a dead horse—and yet at the same time missing it with her stick. (And, to make things more complicated, in the end the object of her discipline even turns out to still have some life left in it.) Still, it is difficult to blame her for not interacting in a more fruitful way with proponents of the anti-imperial subtext-hypothesis. In the end, her failed cri-tique is only a symptom of the continued emphasis on fear-induced hidden criticism. To be sure, it will be hard to drop the notion of "coded" attacks on the Roman Empire. It is, to some extent, what makes the work of exegetes—the decoding—exciting. During the time of my dissertation, when I was asked about my then-current project (narratological and text-linguistic analyses of Paul's letters) by nonacademics, I quickly pivoted to this other research focus of mine, which could be communicated with reference to Dan Brown and a conspiratorially raised eyebrow or a lowered voice. (I was once even selected by my university to talk about this topic with Prince Andrew, who seemed surprised that the apostle Paul might have something to say about the issue of imperialism.) And many of us have come to treasure the modern analogies that we have assembled and which might sometimes give us a much-needed and refreshing break from the dust of antiquity. There is much to lose—and what might be gained seems to be rather difficult to reach. Still, I hope that my analysis of 2 Cor 2:14 has demonstrated the potential of aiming at less spectac-ular but still very enlightening overlooked criticism of or unease toward the Roman Empire. In the end, it is only a shift of emphasis that I am proposing; there might still be room for more spectacular theories.

Lack of Postcolonial Sensitivities and Romans 13:1–7

It will serve us well in this endeavor to take into account the insights from *post-colonial hermeneutics*. Robinson is very critical of how Horsley can ignore, in her opinion, the specifics of the Roman public protocol by simply locating Paul "in an underclass that has existed from eternity past and has always needed to mask its discontent."[3] I do not agree with this disparaging assessment. To be sure, postcolonial interpretation presupposes its own interpretation theory with a distinct conception of meaning, a meaning that arises in a specific con-temporary context. Thus, it fundamentally differs from the search for authorial

---

3. Laura Robinson, "Hidden Transcripts? The Supposedly Self-Censoring Paul and Rome as Surveillance State in Modern Pauline Scholarship," *NTS* 67 (2021): 59.

intent in historical-critical scholarship,[4] and hence it is not possible to evaluate postcolonial readings with reference to their "anachronistic" elements—nor is it legitimate to deny the validity of historical meanings with reference to specific needs in other contexts.[5] While Robinson seems to correctly recognize this distinction,[6] I think she overlooks the potential benefits that historical-critical scholars can reap from interacting with postcolonial scholarship—namely, by using it as a means for sensitizing us to typical dynamics experienced by subordinate groups. For whenever we draw conclusions concerning the communicative intentions of historical figures, we do so against the backdrop of our life horizons, including—but not limited to—our educational biographies. Due to the confinements of our individual experiences, we do well to take into account insights from people for whom oppression is part of daily life. For there can be no doubt that in some sense they share a range of experience with Paul that most of us who are privileged enough to pursue these research questions are relatively or totally unfamiliar with. To be sure, we—scholars focused on the historical circumstances—still need to avoid being anachronistic when switching between the contexts.[7] But the danger of missing important dimensions of the text because we are blind to—or only acknowledge theoretically—basic conditions of Paul's letter-writing is just as real (and often very apparent to us when looking at the scholarship of *previous* generations).

One area where this lack of sensitivity still shows itself pretty clearly is, in my opinion, the exegetical discussion of Rom 13:1–7. Frequently, the notion of an anti-imperial subtext in Paul is rejected with reference to this passage alone. Kim, for example, stresses—generalizing to an astonishing degree—that it "is the Achilles' heel for *all* anti-imperial readings of Paul."[8] Similarly, he later claims that his discussion of Wright's and Elliott's treatment of the passage shows "that *any* anti-imperial reading of Romans or Paul's gospel is bound to stumble at Rom 13:1–7, exposing only its self-contradiction."[9] Can Rom 13:1–7 really bear that argumentative weight?

---

4. The designation "historical-critical method" is very problematic in that the framework rather constitutes an interpretation *theory* and thus does not come automatically with a fixed methodology.

5. See on the whole issue Heilig, *Paulus als Erzähler?*, chapter 3, section 6, and Theresa Heilig and Christoph Heilig, "Teaching Biblical Exegesis: The Distinction between Methods of Description and Interpretation," *Didaktikos* (forthcoming).

6. Robinson, "Hidden Transcripts?," 57n5.

7. Here the criticism by Robinson, "Hidden Transcripts?," 61, is spot-on.

8. Seyoon Kim, *Christ and Caesar: The Gospel and the Roman Empire in the Writings of Paul and Luke* (Grand Rapids: Eerdmans, 2008), 36. Italics added.

9. Kim, *Christ and Caesar*, 42. Italics added.

First of all, we need to note that it is of course very appropriate to begin explorations into Paul's views on the Roman Empire with the *clearest* statements we find in his letters in order to shed light on the more difficult ones. This principle is already deeply imbedded into Protestant views on the *claritas scripturae* and can be maintained definitively within a Bayesian framework.[10] In making exegetical judgements we approach passages with our background knowledge and the further we are able to draw conclusions on specific parts of a text—or other, related texts—the more our background knowledge grows, with which we can then tackle more difficult formulations (hopefully avoiding circularity in so doing).[11]

However, we must be careful not to confuse the "clearest" passages with those that deal merely in the most "explicit" way with a certain topic. In discussions about the Roman Empire and Paul it is often presupposed[12]—also by

10. See Christoph Heilig, *Paul's Triumph: Reassessing 2 Corinthians 2:14 in Its Literary and Historical Context* (Leuven: Peeters, 2017), 5–6.

11. It would be an example of (a) *circular reasoning* to say that passages like 1 Cor 2:6 or 2 Cor 2:14 should not be understood as creating dissonances with respect to Roman ideology because we know from Rom 13:1–7 that Paul is uncritical of the Roman Empire—while at the same time maintaining this interpretation of Rom 13:1–7 with reference to the lack of anti-imperial passages in Paul. What must by no means be confused with circular reasoning is (b) a *hermeneutical spiral*, which in the end is unavoidable because our arguments never start from scratch. It is, thus, entirely acceptable to begin explorations on the topic of Paul and Empire with the assumption of a low background plausibility for anti-imperial resonances in passages like 1 Cor 2:6 or 2 Cor 2:14 on the basis of a traditional understanding of Rom 13:1–7. It would then, however, be important to be aware of the fact that this interpretation of Rom 13:1–7 is itself only an *initial* conclusion. If we are then confronted with a series of passages for which the explanatory potential of an empire-critical subtext is just so good that it trumps the initial skepticism based on the initial interpretation of Rom 13:1–7, this will gradually change the contours of our background knowledge—to an extent that in the end it might become necessary to see whether the outcome of the inference to the most probable interpretation of Rom 13:1–7 might be affected by that shift. On circular reasoning, see Christoph Heilig, *Hidden Criticism? The Methodology and Plausibility of the Search for a Counter-Imperial Subtext in Paul* (Minneapolis: Fortress, 2017), 32–33, and Christoph Heilig, "The New Perspective (on Paul) on Peter: How the Philosophy of Historiography Can Help in Understanding Earliest Christianity," in *Christian Origins and the Establishment of the Early Jesus Movement*, Christian Origins and Greco-Roman Culture 4, ed. Stanley E. Porter and Andrew W. Pitts (Leiden: Brill, 2018), 468. On the correct process for the updating of probabilities, see Heilig, *Paulus als Erzähler?*, chapter 16, section 4.1. On a case of incorrect updating by Joel R. White, "Anti-Imperial Subtexts in Paul: An Attempt at Building a Firmer Foundation," *Bib* 90 (2009), see Heilig, *Hidden Criticism?*, 29–30.

12. Interestingly, Stefan Krauter, *Studien zu Röm 13,1–7: Paulus und der politische Diskurs der neronischen Zeit*, WUNT 243 (Tübingen: Mohr Siebeck, 2009), 253, who is very critical of anti-imperial readings of Rom 13:1–7, recognizes this principle very clearly: "Das ist freilich

Robinson, it seems[13]—that Rom 13:1-7 is Paul's only explicit comment on the subject and that it, hence, needs to serve as the point of departure for evaluating other claims about implicit statements about Rome's status. This would be a legitimate procedure if the meaning of Rom 13:1-7 were indeed as clear as it is often presupposed. Admittedly, to some extent those of us who are interested in the *subtext* of Paul's letters have at times contributed to this image of Rom 13:1-7 by referring to it as a contrast foil for what we were interested in with phrases like "surface of the text."[14] This masks the fact that the meaning of Rom 13:1-7 too is not a matter of course but also needs to be established by means of inference, against the backdrop of some kind of background knowledge. In analyzing texts there is no "obvious" meaning from which to proceed; all that there is are some cases where we as modern readers do not need to make recourse to debated reconstructions as part of the background knowledge.

Now, I would argue emphatically that Rom 13:1-7 is *not* such a case. To be sure, there can be no question that the reference to ἐξουσία right in v. 1 raises the question of how the Roman Empire and emperor(s) fit in here. The same could be said, to be sure, with respect to passages like 1 Cor 2:6 and 2 Cor 2:14. The difference is that in Romans this statement is followed by a quite lengthy discussion—with the natural assumption being that we might learn more details here about Paul's ideas about Rome than in any other single passage. However, just as explicitness does not necessarily translate into clarity, the same can be said with respect to detail. There is some value to the idea that redundancy and variation with respect to expressing the same thought help to eliminate misunderstandings, and this can be seen indeed in vv. 3-4.[15] But all in all, Rom 13:1-7 must count as a very difficult passage to interpret.

If we look at one end of the spectrum of interpretations, we find a postu-

ein problematisches Vorgehen. Weniger darum, weil hier eine für sich genommen sehr klare Aussage mit Hilfe von umstrittenen und teilweise etwas unklaren Texten ausgelegt wird. Denn zwar scheint das umgekehrte Vorgehen logischer, aber es wäre ja durchaus möglich, dass Paulus sich bei der expliziten Behandlung eines Themas eher bedeckt hielte, während er sich in beiläufigen Anmerkungen zum selben Thema offener äußerte." Cf. also Heilig, *Paulus als Erzähler?*, 76-77.

13. Robinson, "Hidden Transcripts?," 72: "Ultimately, this is the final shortcoming of the hunt for hidden criticism in Paul's letters. The question that this scholarship asks is, 'If circumstances had been different for Paul as a man in the first century, what different things might Paul have said?' The only clues, though, are what Paul did say about the Empire, and outside Romans 13, it wasn't much."

14. Cf., e.g., Heilig, *Hidden Criticism?*, 19, 22, and 112.

15. See Heilig, *Paulus als Erzähler?*, 826-27, against Ulrich Wilckens, *Röm 12-16*, vol. 3 of *Der Brief an die Römer*, 3 vols., EKKNT 6.3 (Zurich: Benziger, 1982), 33.

lated meaning that—if true—would indeed undermine every attempt to find fundamental criticism of the Roman Empire in other parts of Paul's letters. It would also have to cause us to understand 2 Cor 2:14 in an entirely positive way, probably as an affirmation of Roman imperial aspirations, and to find alternative explanations for passages like 1 Cor 2:6, such as claiming that it is only demons who are in view there. I am not criticizing such consecutive exegetical decisions as they are the natural consequence of the background plausibilities as fixed by such an extreme interpretation of Rom 13:1–7. Rather, the problem lies with the exegesis that provides the starting point itself. In order to maintain it, we first have to presuppose a distinct shape for our background knowledge before we begin the endeavor, with which we approach Rom 13:1–7 in the first place. And I do not think this is a very reasonable construct. Consequently, the *background plausibility* of such interpretations of Rom 13:1–7 (and, again, we are talking about a meaning that would rule out all dissonances with Roman ideology elsewhere in Paul's letters) seems extremely questionable to me too.

Is Paul really (a) demanding complete submission to governing authorities and (b) encouraging the Roman Christians to seek out recognition within society, grounding all this in (c) divine legitimation of state authority, including brutal force? In order to come to such an extreme conclusion, one must ignore or classify as more ambiguous than seems reasonable to me other information that is available to us. Even just looking at Acts, a book probably not interested in highlighting the illegal actions of its main proponents, one recognizes that Paul and his colleagues do not emerge precisely as the kind of model citizens that would seem to correspond to the standard of (a). Right in the beginning, in Acts 5:29, the apostles emphasize that obedience to human beings is relativized by obedience to God. A little later, in 9:23–24, Paul does not simply stay in Damascus to be lynched but rather flees (just like Peter in 12:6–19, who escapes from prison—something Paul might actually also have considered).[16] Thanks to 2 Cor 11:32–33 we know that Paul's spectacular flight

---

16. As far as I can see, the argument by Mark J. Keown, "Did Paul Plan to Escape from Prison? (Philippians 1:19–26)," *Journal for the Study of Paul and His Letters* 5 (2015): 89–108, that the combination of looming death and certainty of vindication in Philippians is best explained by the expectation of a negative verdict but a safe escape plan has not yet been countered effectively. Keown structures his argument in a way that perfectly lends itself as a test case for a Bayesian analysis. Even if his conclusion might not be justified in the end, the way he presents the evidence is certainly highly effective. I remember very well listening to the original paper at the International SBL meeting in Vienna in 2014 with a full room of Pauline scholars reacting to the presentation with both skeptical looks and astonishing

was diametrically opposed to an official's intention. Now, in this—and many other instances that one might adduce[17]—one can indeed raise the question of which actual local or imperial laws were broken. But that is beside the point. After all, is it not supposed to be exactly the point of Rom 13:1–2 that there is *no* government authority that would act without God's consent and that *everything but complete submission* is an act of rebellion against his will?

Analogously, addressing (b), the idea that in Rom 13:3 ἔπαινος stands for noncultic honors like honorary inscriptions[18] also seems to stand at odds with much of what Paul seems to say rather "obviously" elsewhere. Keeping a low profile and not giving fellow citizens too much reason to complain and potentially destroy the congregation (cf., e.g., 1 Thess 4:11)? Sure. But even aiming at blameless moral conduct and thus "shining light" into society presupposes the utter darkness it constitutes (Phil 2:15). Are we really supposed to believe that Paul was under the impression that it was realistic for his followers to gain such worldly recognitions (a world that, mind you, he says in 1 Cor 5:10 they would have to leave if they wanted to completely refrain from immorality)? Of course, Paul wants the members of his congregations to keep peace with

---

silence. Cf. Mart. Paul 4.3 for an ancient witness to the idea that Paul might escape with the help of converts in the prison. The Paul of this work rejects this suggestion, emphasizing that he is not a "runaway" (δρηπέτης).

17. Cf. above, p. 11 n. 24, on Acts 17. If it does not document punishment but "just" a bail, it would still imply that Paul fled official procedure. Cf. Cédric Brélaz, "The Provincial Contexts of Paul's Imprisonments: Law Enforcement and Criminal Procedure in the Roman East," *JSNT* 43 (2021): 490: "The believers in Thessalonica were aware of the legally binding nature of the forthcoming procedure and of the risks faced by the apostle in the event of an arrest, and for that reason helped Paul and Silas escape secretly from the city at night. . . .The first time he could have been charged before a court and risked formal detention under the law, the apostle evaded judgment." For this very reason I remain doubtful that we can detect an elaborate strategy of exonerating Paul as a law-abiding citizen in Acts (as suggested by Brélaz, "Provincial Contexts," 498–503)—deviating explicitly from the historical reality, which is of interest for our purposes and would, if the thesis were right, have to be judged even *more* subversive than the picture that we can get from Acts.

18. Cf. Michael Wolter, *Röm 9–16*, vol. 2 of *Der Brief an die Römer*, 2 vols, EKKNT 6.2 (Göttingen: Vandenhoeck & Ruprecht, 2019), 315: "In V. 3d steht 'Lob' (ἔπαινος) summarisch für die unterschiedlichen Formen der Anerkennung, mit denen Bürger, die sich um das Gemeinwohl verdient gemacht haben, ausgezeichnet werden konnten (Ehreninschriften, Geldzuwendungen, Beförderungen). Für welche, bleibt offen." Recht ähnlich bereits Wilckens, *Röm 12–16*, 34: "Paulus scheint die römische 'laudatio' im Blick zu haben, d. h. die Sitte der römischen Provinzverwaltung, Wohlverhalten durch offizielle Belobigung in Gestalt von Kaiserbriefen zu honorieren und es so auch weiterhin zu provozieren."

the wider community, but he is also fully aware that this is only partially within their power (cf. Rom 12:18).

Paul is often accused of being naïve in Rom 13:1–7. To me it seems that the assumptions required to allow for an interpretation that in turn would allow for such a judgment are even more naïve. They betray a lack of understanding for the manifold forms of oppression that Paul and his congregations would have endured on a daily basis. The idea that (c) Paul in v. 4 would say that Rome is "not carrying the sword in vain" in order to not only point to the obvious fact

Figure 15. Alexamenos graffito, Rome, ca. 200 CE

that Roman officials could command executions but also to emphasize that they would do so in accordance with God's will truly seems mindboggling to me. Are we really to believe that Paul "simply, indeed naively, expresses a positive or optimistic view that they—again, most immediately the Roman rulers—'are not a terror to good conduct, but [only] to bad'"?[19] If Paul really did say *that*, we would have to call him not only naïve but incredibly ignorant of what was happening around him all the time. In fact, we would even have to conclude that he was outright stupid, incapable of even the basics of communication. After all, the more than just obvious counterquestion would be: "So, Paul, I guess Rome is also not carrying 'the cross' in vain?" Jesus, it seems, can only blame himself for having experienced the "justice" of Rome. Paul shows such an excellent sense for the objections his statements would provoke among his readers in 2 Cor 2:14.[20] Even in Romans itself Paul is constantly emerged in simulating complicated dialogues with his readership.[21] The idea that he would not know that the followers of a crucified Messiah

---

19. Kim, *Christ and Caesar*, 38.
20. See above, p. 77.
21. See, for example, Heilig, *Paulus als Erzähler?*, 490, on Rom 9:19 and 11:19.

in Rome—where a little later a Christian would be mocked for praying to a donkey on a cross (figure 15)[22]—would come up with such an objection in a heartbeat, is absurd.

It is sometimes remarked that in comparison to Romans, 1 Peter is "a good deal more reserved, even implicitly critical" with respect to Roman imperial rule.[23] And it is admittedly true that in 1 Pet 2:13–17 God's involvement seems to be expressed much more cautiously, and the possibility of governmental failure seems to be considered more openly (v. 15; cf. 4:14–16). Some alleged differences, however, seem to be identified by circular reasoning. For example, both Πᾶσα ψυχὴ ἐξουσίαις ὑπερεχούσαις ὑποτασσέσθω in Rom 13:1 and Ὑποτάγητε πάσῃ ἀνθρωπίνῃ κτίσει in 1 Pet 2:13 have been interpreted as relativizations of imperatorial claims to divinity. In order to accept this interpretation in the second case but to reject it in the first place (as many do), one needs to assign significantly differing background plausibilities to both versions of this hypothesis because the wording is so similar. This is only possible if the attitude toward Roman rule that is assumed for the authors is assumed to diverge, mostly on the alleged ground that Paul writes before the "criminalization" of Christianity and thus lacks an awareness of the (still future) problem. This later date for 1 Peter is then, in a circular move, sometimes grounded in the fact that this letter relativizes the emperor's status but Romans does not do so.[24] The more fundamental problem I see, however, is that any comparative statement in the end remains very problematic because it depends on the assumption that both authors are speaking about basically the *same issue*. But can we actually assume that Paul wants to make a general statement about the "king" (1 Pet 2:13) and his "governors" (1 Pet 2:14)? That he basically speaks about the same subject, just less critically—perhaps because he lacks the foresight to recognize how the Roman politics toward Christians would change under the promising new emperor, Nero, in 64 CE? This view has the problem (see above, pp. 17–27) that the whole idea of an alleged development of "criminalization" of Christianity after Paul's death, which is presupposed as the backdrop of 1 Peter, is itself an ahistorical construct. In other words, our "excuse" for Paul's failure to mention the possibility of injustice by Roman officials would be limited to the possible circumstance

---

22. See Heikki Solin and Marja Itkonen, *Paedagogium*, vol. 1 of *Graffiti del Palatino* (Helsinki: Institutum Romanum Finlandise, 1966), 209–12, no. 246.

23. David G. Horrell, *Becoming Christian: Essays on 1 Peter and the Making of Christian Identity*, LNTS 394 (London: Bloomsbury, 2013), 187.

24. Cf. Heilig, *Hidden Criticism?*, 32–33. On circular reasoning see also above, pp. 22–23 n. 65 and p. 105 n. 11.

(a very forthcoming admission on behalf of the argument I critique here) that, at the time of the composition of Romans, Christians in the East had largely remained lucky in the face of the capriciousness of Roman governors. However, the fundamental danger behind a purely hypothetical[25] increase of sanctions at the time of 1 Peter would already have existed in the 50s too. (And, again, in the 30s, as Christians of all people should know.) I would thus argue that the comparison between Romans and 1 Peter in combination with the realization of the *shared* lived realities actually points toward the opposite direction. *If* Paul were commenting on the same thing as 1 Peter, we would expect him to display just the same nuance. Thus, the comparison raises the background plausibilities of hypotheses that either assume that Paul is displaying the same awareness or that argue, alternatively, that he is talking about a sufficiently distinct matter—two options that we will look at in what follows.

It needs to be kept in mind that all these considerations so far show merely what is problematic about the aspect of the background plausibility. The *explanatory potential* of such an interpretative hypothesis is also far from convincing. For example, we would certainly not expect Paul to refer in such a strange manner to "superior authorities" and command "every soul" to practice submission toward those respectively above them (Rom 13:1: Πᾶσα ψυχὴ ἐξουσίαις ὑπερεχούσαις ὑποτασσέσθω) if he simply wanted to make clear that the emperor had to be obeyed in all cases. Nor would we expect the sudden reference to people collecting taxes in v. 6 (is he referring to the rulers, ἄρχοντες, of v. 3 or introducing a new group acting on their behalf?) or so much confusion about taxes and revenues (cf. φόρος in v. 6 and 7 and τέλος in v. 7) and lack of clarity with respect to "honor" and "fear" (cf. φόβος and τιμή in v. 7) as things being owed to a party or several different parties.

Against this backdrop, it seems only logical that other scholars would in an act of abduction[26] come up with an alternative suggestion that marks the

25. I.e., unless one dates it to the time of Trajan, something Horrell, *Becoming Christian*, explicitly does not want to do. His emphasis on the same danger existing earlier is entirely correct. He too, however, presupposes a shift in policy (although not in codified form) as the issue that created the risk of the Christians in the first place. By contrast, the problem probably never was policy but politics, the political practice of Roman governors when faced with potential unrest.

26. See Theresa Heilig and Christoph Heilig, "Historical Methodology," in *God and the Faithfulness of Paul: A Critical Examination of the Pauline Theology of N. T. Wright*, ed. Christoph Heilig, J. Thomas Hewitt, and Michael F. Bird, WUNT 2/413 (Tübingen: Mohr Siebeck, 2016; Minneapolis: Fortress, 2017).

other end of the spectrum, claiming that the whole passage is ironical.[27] Some
have argued in response that the text simply lacks clear signals of irony that one
would expect in comparison with ironic praise in contemporary texts.[28] This,
however, is an argument that needs to be treated very carefully. See, for example,
how Seneca describes Claudius's campaign in Britannia (*Apocol.* 11.12–17):

> Swiftly the striped barbarians fled:
> With one little wound he shot them dead.
> And the Britons beyond the sea-shores which one sees,
> Blue-shielded Brigantians too, all these
> He chained by the neck as the Roman's slaves.
> He spake, and the Ocean with trembling waves
> Accepted the axe of the Roman law.

This is undoubtedly meant to be a satirical exaggeration,[29] but with the
exception of the reference to the Brigantians (see above, p. 75), the text actually
remains squarely within the public transcript as attested by other sources (see
above, pp. 72 and 84–85, on the *Laus Caesaris*, which displays an incredibly
similar tone). Assuming the same referents for the "authorities" as in the just
rejected interpretation, it seems valid to suggest that Rom 13:1–7 might be an
ironic exaggeration, considering how redundantly Paul seems to emphasize
subordination and cast it in divine light. Poe's law (which refers to the fact
that with extreme views it is often very difficult to distinguish between serious
statements and parody) not only applies in the times of the internet but also in
antiquity. Moreover, besides this little boost, which the *explanatory potential*
of the irony-hypothesis receives from this comparison with Seneca's satirical
work, one might point to the excellent *background plausibility* one might construe for such a communicative content on the basis of other passages such as
1 Cor 2:6. And indeed I think that the message that people like Carter assign
to Rom 13:1–7 is indeed something Paul very well *could have* said (see above,
pp. 40–42).

In the end, though, I remain doubtful with respect to whether these ideas
are in fact conveyed in Rom 13:1–7. The ultimate problem I have with this

27. E.g., T. L. Carter, "The Irony of Romans 13," *NovT* 46 (2004): 209–28.

28. Cf., e.g., Krauter, *Studien zu Rom 13,1–7*, 72–81.

29. Cf. Gerhard Binder, *Apokolokyntosis*, Sammlung Tusculum (Düsseldorf: Artemis &
Winkler, 1999), 161–62.

solution is twofold, and it affects exclusively the explanatory potential. First, at least in the *literary* context there are no indications that Paul is switching to irony here. The passage from Seneca's pamphlet against the deceased emperor Claudius is situated very differently. If Paul really wanted to communicate said ironic message in this passage, one would expect him to somehow make that clear in the introduction. Second, Rom 13:1–7 on the content level not only consists of a series of propositions but also contains a pragmatic dimension.[30] It is one thing to parody claims. Understanding that they are ironic, Paul's readers would have had no problem decoding the author's real opinions. But what would follow for the apostle's instructions? Would they still be encouraged to submit to orders by the authorities—even though it would only be due to pure pragmatism, knowing, and perhaps being comforted by that knowledge, that their authority was without any real basis? Or would they not rather conclude that since the justification of said authority is laughable there would also be no reason to follow these instructions? If Paul did not want to create chaos with an ironic passage, we would expect him to be less confusing in that regard.[31]

Thus, in the end we will probably have to come to the conclusion that the interpretative hypothesis that displays the best combination of *both* background plausibility and explanatory potential will lie somewhere in between these two extremes. On the one hand, such an interpretation will not deny that Paul indeed saw concern to encourage going along with certain specific demands by Roman officials—probably connected with the φόροι in v. 6. At the same time, it will acknowledge that these specific circumstances will have prompted an exhortation by Paul that was tailored *so specifically* to the concrete situation in terms of function[32] that the natural objections he would have

30. On this fundamental distinction see Heilig, *Paulus als Erzähler?*, chapter 4, section 5.

31. Admittedly, the relationship between mood (imperatives) and communicative function (illocutionary act) is only an indirect one. Cf. Heilig, *Paulus als Erzähler?*, 162–63 and chapter 8, section 4. Oda Wischmeyer, "Staat und Christen nach Römer 13,1–7: Ein neuer hermeneutischer Zugang," in *Kirche und Volk Gottes: Festschrift für Jürgen Roloff zum 70. Geburtstag*, ed. Martin Karrer, Wolfgang Kraus, and Otto Merk (Neukirchen-Vluyn: Neukirchener, 2000), 161, is getting at this when she says that Rom 13:17 "ist trotz der Imperative lehrhaft—diskursiv—beschreibend." I think that the last characterization—description—is yet another parameter for the classification of texts (Heilig, *Paulus als Erzähler?*, chapter 1, section 3) but Wischmeyer is right to differentiate between the grammatical mood and the communicative intention: "Damit werden die Hörer in einen fiktiven Dialog gezogen, dessen Ziel das *Verständnis* ihrer Lebenswelt ist" (italics in the original). So perhaps my counterargument against an ironical reading here still needs more nuance.

32. One possibility that could be developed along the lines of the distinction between

faced for much more fundamental statements[33] would not have crossed either his or his readers' minds—even given the theological reasons he adduces, most certainly in good faith.

I am reminded once again (cf. above, pp. 2–3) of the riots in Washington, DC, on January 6, 2021. Even persons who strongly believe that Christian ethics encourages opposition to immoral political power might have spoken about the events in a way that, if taken out of context, might sound like a mere denunciation of "resistance" in general. To give just one example that might illuminate this consideration, I would like to point to the way late-night host Stephen Colbert, known for his Catholic faith, has commented on Rom 13 in his show. In 2018, Jeff Sessions—then attorney general under President Trump—referenced Paul's "clear and wise" command "to obey the laws of the government because God has ordained them for the purpose of order" with regard to the treatment of migrants seeking asylum at the US border.[34] Colbert made fun of that reductionistic reading, pointing in particular to the command to "love your neighbor" just a few verses later, in Rom 13:10.[35] When Pauline Beuer, a Pennsylvania pizzeria owner who was among those who stormed the capitol, appeared in court and argued that as an ambassador

---

grammatical form, strategy of text production, and text function (cf. previous footnote) is that while Paul does not want to *inform* his readers about circumstances (as Wischmeyer's formulation might suggest) he is indeed not mainly interested in motivating them to action but rather wants them to *reevaluate* behavior with a very concrete referent. That might have been controversial in Rome, specifically with respect to the *motivation* behind it. In that regard, v. 5 with its emphasis on following the demands of officials as a free choice of conscience seems to be a crucial aspect. I am grateful to Annina Völlmy for pointing this out to me. Such a reading would be very reminiscent of 2 Cor 9:7!

33. As Wischmeyer, "Staat," 159, emphasizes, what Paul actually demands ("describes"; cf. p. 113 n. 31, above) is *trivial*: "Die Textinterpretation hat deutlich gemacht, daß Paulus kein positives inhaltliches Interesse am römischen Staat und seinem Rechts- und Finanzwesen hat. Seine Aufforderung, Zölle und Steuern zu bezahlen und keine Selbstjustiz zu üben, ist geradezu trivial. Ebenso ist die Aufforderung, sich den Behörden unterzuordnen, trivial. Welcher Bürger einer Stadt, welchen Rechts auch immer, oder gar welcher Inhaber des römischen Bürgerrechtes, der Christ war, hätte sich zu der Zeit anders verhalten?" I am not entirely sure whether she gets the contours of the real-life situation that Paul references right but I agree that the factor of the background plausibility indeed strongly suggests a matter of course.

34. See Lincoln Mullen, "The Fight to Define Romans 13," *The Atlantic*, June 15, 2018, https://www.theatlantic.com/ideas/archive/2018/06/romans-13/562916/.

35. Stephen Colbert, "Jeff Sessions Cites the Bible in Separating Children from Parents," *The Late Show with Stephen Colbert*, June 15, 2018, https://www.youtube.com/watch?v=j4KaLkYxMZ8, beginning at 2:47.

of Christ she was immune to laws, the judge reportedly responded to Beuer's throwing Bible verses at her by quoting Rom 13:1: "Let every person be subject to the governing authorities"—a reaction that was quite obviously celebrated by Colbert as a gotcha moment in this particular case.[36] At least for Colbert's usual audience, these references to Rom 13, which on their surface differ quite dramatically, probably were quite coherent. Most of them certainly would not see a problem with referring to a biblical text in order to argue for some kind of law and order when the issue at stake was such an obvious threat to national security while mocking such an insistence when it implied a rather brutal treatment of immigrant children. There is still room for debate about whether it is not risky to make such unqualified statements about the rule of law when one is more reluctant to put legal standards first in other situations. Analogously, one might want to raise the question, as Gerd Theißen, for example, does, whether Paul's advice is perhaps "one-sided" and whether the inevitable reduction of complexity inherent in Paul's perspective goes too far.[37] There are no easy answers to this, because we always, necessarily, simplify in communication and do not address all theoretically possible implications; the issue that is at stake is thus one of gradation. In any case, an interpretation that

36. See Kelly Weill, "Pizzeria Owner Mounts Truly Bizarre Defense for Jan. 6 Riots," *Daily Beast,* July 11, 2021 (updated on July 12, 2021), https://www.thedailybeast.com/pizzeria -owner-pauline-bauer-mounts-truly-bizarre-defense-for-jan-6-riots; Matt Naham, "Pizzeria Owner Charged for Jan. 6 Insists She Is 'Not a Person,' Gets into Bible Quoting Exchange with Trump-Appointed Judge before Being Brought Back to Jail," *Law and Crime,* September 24, 2021, https://lawandcrime.com/u-s-capitol-breach/pizzeria-owner-charged-for-jan -6-insists-she-is-not-a-person-gets-into-bible-quoting-exchange-with-trump-appointed -judge-before-being-ordered-back-to-jail/; Stephen Colbert, "Drinking More? Having Less Sex? Throwing Tantrums in Public? Blame the Pandemic!," *The Late Show with Stephen Colbert,* October 2, 2021, https://www.youtube.com/watch?v=kjA2xu7idMc, beginning at 6:44.

37. Gerd Theißen, "Respekt vor der Verfassung: Gegenlektüre eines staatstragenden Textes (Röm 13,1–7)," in *Erlösungsbilder: Predigten und Meditationen von Gerd Theißen* (Gütersloh: Kaiser, 2002), 129–33, constitutes the interesting exercise of imagining Luke debating this text with the apostle Paul shortly before his execution in Rome. While I do not think that the situation of Christians in the East would have been much less precarious before 64 CE (see above, pp. 17–27) and while I, thus, do not think that the mass murder would either have disillusioned Paul nor have required a reevaluation of "the empire" on his side, it is very stimulating to read Paul saying things like "Ich hätte eindeutiger schreiben sollen: . . ." (p. 131). It is certainly a plausible reaction if we imagine him being confronted with the effective history of his text. And what an event like the persecution from 64 CE might have accomplished is making him aware of the possibilities of misunderstanding when cataclysmic events like this one replace much more specific considerations associated with the realm evoked by certain vocabulary.

follows the basic shape that I have sketched will not force us to commit to a series of subsequent interpretations of a multitude of passages that would in each
case require us to go with hypotheses that have incredibly small explanatory
potential. It will not force us to eliminate everything that would contradict the
simplistic picture of Paul that would be needed to plausibly have him praising
Nero here in Rom 13:1–7.

In the end, I remain skeptical about whether we will ever reach a much
more specific conclusion than this, given that the specific historical circumstances shining through in v. 6 seem to remain rather elusive to us. But what
we can say by way of approximation suffices in order not to be forced to adopt
an understanding of the passage that would undermine "*any* anti-imperial
reading of Romans or Paul's gospel" (see above, p. 104). And—coming back
to where we started this excursus on Rom 13—*learning from the sensitivities
postcolonial interpreters of the passage display* can help us to guard against
anachronistic assumptions concerning the background plausibility of such
extreme interpretations. To be sure, nowadays the passage is less often adduced
uncritically to bolster the authority of the elites without qualifications than in
previous times. Even scholars like Kim acknowledge that Paul does not offer
an abstract discussion of political ethics here and that in other places, like
1 Cor 2:6, he can be critical about Roman officials.[38] But the only way they
can admit this constellation is by accepting that Paul naively forgot about an
absolutely fundamental parameter of *his* lived reality, whose significance as
such can only be overlooked if we reason from *our* own comfortable position
as scholars of biblical texts who by and large do not experience anything even
remotely comparable to the oppressive forces active in Paul's world.[39]

---

38. See Kim, *Christ and Caesar*, 38: "As he is advising Roman Christians with their
specific situation in view, Paul applies this general principle to their situation rather than
giving a well-rounded instruction on the nature of political authority or the relationship
between the church and the state. So here he does not entertain our usual question: What
if rulers fail to be faithful to divine commission, become despotic, and commit injustice?
Nor does Paul reflect the critical view of the rulers of this world that he expresses elsewhere
(1 Cor 2:6–8; 6:1; 15:24–25; 1 Thess 2:18; etc.) and the unjust treatment that he himself has
received from some of them (1 Cor 4:9–13; 2 Cor 1:8–10; 6:5; 11:23, 25a; 1 Thess 2:2, 18; etc.),
not to mention Pilate's trial and execution of Jesus." Admittedly, Wischmeyer, "Staat," 149–55,
still finds quite a few astonishingly uncritical assessments of this passage from the 1980s
and 1990s. And even today sometimes one still encounters, at least outside of scholarly
discourses, rather uncritical use of the passage to bolster claims about state power. Cf.
above, p. 114, on Jeff Sessions.

39. This call for taking seriously postcolonial sensitivities of course also applies to the
construal of the background plausibility itself. For example, the view by Molthagen (see

Methodology and Cognitive Linguistics

A constantly missed, crucial dimension of the text can be taken as an indication that there is something wrong with the exegetical method in general. Therefore, I think it is safe to argue that yet another reason why the crucial aspects of the Roman background of Paul's metaphor in 2 Cor 2:14 were overlooked for such a long time lies in the fact that a lot of research carried out in New Testament studies is still rooted in outdated methodology. For a start, the way we teach exegesis is very problematic. This varies with respect to the various institutions, but these approaches all come with their own problems.[40]

For example, in the German-speaking context, exegesis of the New Testament and the Old Testament is taught in two seminars ("Proseminare") that aim to teach a variety of different methodological approaches. The seminars culminate in a detailed exegetical paper by the students in which they have to apply these skills to a specific biblical passage. The problem is that what is taught in these modules reflects the discontinuous growth of the "historical-critical method" over centuries and, thus, often combines methods that are not even compatible in principle with respect to their theoretical bases. For example, because different conceptions of meaning are presupposed, they require different sets of methods in interpretation. Moreover, most often the distinction between descriptive and interpretative operations on the text is lacking altogether—with students remaining confused when it comes to how exactly they are supposed to combine all these approaches. This results in, among other things, the unfortunate situation that "Traditionsgeschichte" (tradition history) is not integrated well into the process of interpretation. Rather, it is often practiced as a kind of supplementary task, detached from the actual determination of the meaning of the text. Alternatively, it is viewed as a method of interpretation in itself, which regularly results in the most absurd interpretations of all. Frequently the assessment of the background plausibility ("Could Paul have known about X?") is treated like an evaluation of the overall plausibility of the hypothesis ("Is it probable that Paul meant X in passage Z?"), while totally ignoring explanatory potentials ("Would Paul have used formulation Z to express X?").

In the English-speaking world, by contrast, there is not usually such a focus

---

above, pp. 22–23 n. 65 and 24 n. 71) of governors as law-abiding officials who would not have killed Christians without official legislation—an idea that is widespread in biblical scholarship too—is itself rooted in a lack of appreciation of the dirty dynamics in imperial rule.

40. See Heilig and Heilig, "Teaching Biblical Exegesis."

on methodology on its own. Exegesis is taught mostly as a form of advanced Koine. This leads to rather simplistic assumptions about what "meaning" can be and how it is to be determined—namely as a rather mechanistic deduction based on "grammar." The lack of theoretical reflection can be seen in, among other things, irritation about how other people can maintain certain interpretations, which are—as it seems clear on the basis of a standard Greek lexicon—"anachronistic."[41] That there might be alternative theories of interpretation and that these might identify entirely different *kinds* of meaning is often not even considered. To be sure, in some English-speaking contexts, the awareness of this issue is raised, in particular because exegesis is taught as part of hermeneutics classes and/or because contemporary issues, such as race, play an important role in the curriculum. This does have some promise. The remaining dangers are, however, that students are never introduced to a detailed and coherent set of methods within one particular framework but rather learn superficially about a variety of approaches (which, in an inversion of the German problem, might not even be exclusive but might constitute different steps toward the same goal).

What is clearly lacking is a comprehensive theoretical account of the kind of meaning that is actually pursued within the historical-critical framework and a methodological guide for students toward this goal. I have sketched elsewhere how "text grammar" could serve as one fundamental building block for such a methodology (and plan to write on this in more detail in an English textbook).[42] I am convinced of its usefulness because it allows us to analyze the propositional structure of texts and thus provides a very basic grid for interpretations. What is still lacking from a more elaborate account is a systematic integration of contextual factors—i.e., of both reference and pragmatics.[43] Because

41. For example, the interpretations of biblical texts from Jordan B. Peterson, which follow a conception of meaning that is deeply influenced by C. G. Jung, are often criticized by biblical scholars for the wrong reasons. It is possible to come to different conclusions within the framework of the same methodology. It is equally legitimate to critique the appropriateness of Peterson's methodology under the presupposition of the same psychological conception of meaning. It is likewise possible, on a hermeneutical level, to disagree on whether the choice of this conception of meaning is justified with respect to these texts at all. What is not feasible, however, is to blame interpretations that are explicitly interested in "anthropological constants" for being "anachronistic"—something that is a problem only if an intentionalist conception of meaning is presupposed. See Tilmann Köppe and Tom Kindt, *Erzähltheorie: Eine Einführung*, Reclams Universal-Bibliothek 17683 (Stuttgart: Reclam, 2014), 125.

42. Heilig, *Paulus als Erzähler?*, chapter 3, section 6. For the methodology itself, see chapter 4.

43. See the admission on a certain imbalance in von Siebenthal's text grammar (*AGG*

we are not offering students a systematic approach toward identifying authorial intentions behind biblical texts and showing them how in so doing they need to take into account the realities of the world involved in the communication process, as well as the intended and actual effects on the recipients, it is not very surprising that dimensions of the text that were of utmost importance in its original context are, likewise systematically, overlooked. Such aspects—which naturally include the parameter of contemporary politics—can come into view only if by chance one of the rather small spotlights of the different approaches currently practiced falls on them. The situation identified with respect to the secondary literature on 2 Cor 2:14 is, thus, in the end, not even that surprising but rather symptomatic of the condition of the field.

One specific aspect that awaits to be integrated into a methodology of interpretation within a historical-critical framework and that has to do with the context of utterance is cognitive linguistics. I want to briefly discuss here how it would shed light on the issue of lexical semantics and how that, in turn, could help with the apparent blindness for signs of Pauline unease with respect to the Roman Empire.[44]

Up until the 1960s the discussion of the meaning of words used by New Testament authors is often marked by several problematic tendencies that James Barr in his famous *The Semantics of Biblical Language* explicated.[45] From a semiotic perspective, "meaning" needs to be understood as part of a triangular relationship. The symbol, the Greek word in question, stands for a concrete thing in the real world. But it does so only in a mediated way, namely by symbolizing or expressing a concept, a mental category, which is in turn represented by the symbol. It is the concept that refers to the actual referent, which in turn is reflected in the concept. Barr criticized Kittel's *TWNT/TDNT* for confusing words and concepts. While the title claims that the work is a "*Wörter*buch," the authors constantly discuss concepts that are usually much more complex than the lexical meaning of the words in question. Barr thus spends a lot of energy on demonstrating how the German word "Begriff" muddies these waters.[46] In order to come up with these far-reaching concepts by means of discussing words, the authors confuse yet another relationship of the semiotic triangle:

297–54), which is mainly based on SSA, in Heilig, *Paulus als Erzähler?*, 201 and 260; see also chapter 8, which focuses on pragmatic issues.

44. For the following, see Christoph Heilig, "Lexical Semantics and Lexicography," *Zürich New Testament Blog*, March 26, 2020, https://www.uzh.ch/blog/theologie-nt/2020/03/26/lexical-semantics-and-lexicography/.

45. James Barr, *The Semantics of Biblical Language* (Oxford: Oxford University Press, 1961).

46. For more details, see Heilig, *Paulus als Erzähler?*, chapter 3, section 2.1.

they focus on referents and confuse them with words and their meanings. For example, the way the love of a specific entity is manifested—e.g., what is said about ἡ ἀγάπη τοῦ θεοῦ in a variety of contexts—was read into every occurrence of the word ἀγάπη (the well-known "illegitimate totality transfer"), even though many of these features had nothing to do with the lexical meaning. In a further step, this enriched account of the "meaning" of ἀγάπη was then presented as an exhaustive account of the concept of 'love.'

In the English-speaking world, this critique has been understood rather well. In German-speaking publications, however, it is still common to find mistakes like these, often rendering the whole work useless at worst and very tedious to decode at best. Robinson's article, to be sure, does not suffer from such failures. It is instructive to see how she embeds her discussion of the subversive potential of the Greek word κύριος:

> Either Paul's coded subversion of the Roman government was so subtle that Romans would not hear it (in which case, it would be useless as a code for Roman Christians) or Paul was capable of drawing metaphorical language from the political sphere without actually attacking it. The latter solution seems likely. After all, Christian apologists of the second century regularly refer to Jesus as Lord in their texts that are meant to demonstrate what peaceable Roman subjects they are. The invocation of the term κύριος alone was clearly not enough to make a Roman think he was reading *The Anarchist's Cookbook*. Even in our own day, Calvinist Christians are quite capable of discussing the doctrine of election without hearing a quiet critique of how Americans choose a president. The concepts are distinct. Either the proclamation of Jesus as Lord was not an actionable offence against the state, or it was and Paul is being as explicit as he wants.[47]

Robinson here distinguishes well between lexical and conceptual levels and thus puts a stop to an unjustified illegitimate totality transfer. Just because κύριος might in some contexts be used with an exclusively political meaning or have such associative meanings in these cases, this does not imply that in all occurrences early Christian authors use it in such a way. So far, so good.

There is, however, also a problem with the whole tradition following Barr, namely that it mostly overlooks the rootedness of his critique in structuralism. Thanks to Barr, the recognition that definitions are much better than glosses when it comes to the meaning of Greek words has become a commonplace

---

47. Robinson, "Hidden Transcripts?," 66.

(in English-speaking scholarship at least).[48] Rightly so. A Greek word never "means" a German or English word. It expresses a concept that might overlap in part or totally with the concept of a word in another language. It is, for example, certainly far better to offer the kind of definition I suggested for θριαμβεύω than just to adduce the glosses "lead in triumph" or "im Triumph einherführen" (see above, pp. 56–58).

However, thanks to the structuralism inherent in, e.g., Louw-Nida,[49] many of us have assumed that these definitions *are* meanings. And this can be very misleading too. For meanings are, after all, mental concepts (i.e., they exist conceptually in the mind), not strings of words. Definitions are only the tip of the iceberg, an attempt to express in more words what a word means. They themselves remain, however, lexical representations of this meaning. To apply this insight to 2 Cor 2:14, Paul did not have my definition of θριαμβεύω in his head—not even if we translated that definition into Greek. I have myself touched upon this only in outlines in the past because I too am very much part of this structuralist tradition. There were aspects that had always made me a bit uncomfortable. For example, I decided to put the location of the captive in the procession—before or behind the triumphator—in brackets in my definition because the actual practice varied so much.[50] And at various points I noted that the specific version of this meaning (or, as I would have said, of this definition) might be dependent on the particular shape of Paul's individual experience. I considered the possibility that "Paul did know θριαμβεύειν from the context of the Roman triumphal procession but that, at the same time, his implicit definition left room for it to be enriched by elements from Dionysiac cults due to the lexical link θρίαμβος." As I explained: "After all, the definition we established is built on a specific set of lexical data and we cannot simply assume that the one that was accessible to Paul had the same shape. Maybe, the narrations of the triumphal procession he heard allowed for a definition that was not tied as closely to the Roman institution itself, with the result that Paul thought its collocability . . . was broader than it actually was for other writers of his time."[51] In other words, while we employ the usage of a word

---

48. See John A. Lee, *A History of New Testament Lexicography*, Studies in Biblical Greek 8 (New York: Peter Lang, 2003).

49. They still have this effect mostly implicitly through L&N but also through their introduction to lexical semantics, Eugene A. Nida and Johannes P. Louw, *Lexical Semantics of the Greek New Testament: A Supplement to the Greek-English Lexicon of the New Testament Based on Semantic Domains*, SBLRBS 25 (Atlanta: Scholars Press, 1992).

50. Heilig, *Paul's Triumph*, 101.

51. Heilig, *Paul's Triumph*, 197.

in relation to other words in order to come up with a definition, what we are trying to get at in so doing is actually something that, as a mental category, remains categorically different—and that is very much rooted in our experience of the real world. It is rooted, in other words, in context, in *referents*. Hence, the conceptual level does not float around in lofty heights above the level of expressions but is deeply and inevitably rooted in our embodied experience of the world. And this is exactly where structuralism fails.[52]

This recognition should also have consequences for lexicography. In the end, we are again in the position to admit that the description of the meaning of a word most appropriately would occur in the form of something that would actually be quite close to an encyclopedia entry—and, thus, exactly the kind of "concept dictionary" that Barr held at arm's length from what lexicons were supposed to be! To be sure, it cannot be the goal to just collect all available information on the ritual of the *triumphus* and then to assume that the entirety is evoked in every use of the verb θριαμβεύω.[53] But we must reckon with the possibility that, depending on individual experiences, ideas about what might be involved in "θριαμβεύω someone" might have differed. (Though it is unlikely that core elements were different because in communication—if there was sufficient communication on the subject—moments of confusion would have been resolved quickly.)

A standard example for illustrating the consequences of a cognitive-linguistic approach to lexical semantics is the word "mother."[54] Its meaning entails a variety of semantic/cognitive domains: the genetic domain, the birth domain, the nurturance domain, the genealogical domain, the martial domain.

52. Michael G. Aubrey, "Linguistic Issues in Biblical Greek," in *Linguistic and Biblical Exegesis*, ed. Douglas Mangum and Josh Westbury, Lexham Methods Series 2 (Bellingham: Lexham Press, 2017), 179: "If the failure of theological dictionaries was the assumption that words and concepts are identical, then the failure of the structuralist semantics that dominated the field when James Barr wrote his critique was the assumption that words and concepts are dramatically different. If words mean anything at all, there must be a substantive relationship between them and the concepts (both associative and denotative) they evoke mentally."

53. See Heilig, *Paul's Triumph*, 102 and 128, on Roger David Aus, *Imagery of Triumph and Rebellion in 2 Corinthians 2:14–17 and Elsewhere in the Epistle: An Example of the Combination of Greco-Roman and Judaic Traditions in the Apostle Paul*, Studies in Judaism (Lanham: University Press of America, 2005).

54. This example is originally from Lakoff with differing terminology. For a helpful adaptation for biblical studies see Jeremy Thompson and Wendy Widder, "Major Approaches to Linguistics," in *Linguistic and Biblical Exegesis*, ed. Douglas Mangum and Josh Westbury, Lexham Methods Series 2 (Bellingham: Lexham Press, 2017), 131.

Together these domains make up the "mother frame." Depending on the context in which the word "mother" is used, all or only a part of these domains are activated. For example, not every person who is addressed by an English speaker as "mother" is also his or her birth mother. It is even possible for there to be disagreement on the relevant domains in a particular situation and, thus, on who is a "real" mother.[55] And it is entirely possible that two very different sets of domains are, implicitly, defended by the same person, depending on the situation. Note that this does not mean that the different domains are entirely independent of each other. The mother who is a female who gives birth to a child and the mother who is a female who nurtures and raises a child are *not* simply "distinct concepts." On the contrary, they are linked by our experience, which extracts prototypes and integrates exceptions. The fact that we can use the word "mother" in such a dynamic way reflects the way we categorize our perceptions of the world.

We would gain a lot if we thought along these lines about terms like κύριος. By this I do not mean that the use of definitions and a sensitivity to the need to avoid conflating words with meanings and larger concepts is obsolete. On the contrary, I think that, unless we actually have the appropriate linguistic training, we are well-advised to remain within the more conservative realm of our structuralist insights.[56] However, it would be good if in so doing we remained aware of the fact that the icebergs we are modeling in our definitions might be connected underwater. Note how Burk dismisses parallels as perhaps merely due to the fact "that Paul and the imperial cult were drawing from the common stock of Koine Greek, the *lingua franca* of the eastern part of the Roman Empire."[57] This is a strange way of introducing "language" as a kind of potentially neutral point of reference as an alternative to "significant" parallels.

What we rather ought to do is think about terms like κύριος as being connected with a range of cognitive domains and assess whether similar sets of domains of this frame might be activated in Paul's letters and in Roman discourse. Joel White follows Burk in emphasizing what one might call the

---

55. An impressive example is the failed dialogue between interviewer Jo Coburn and guest Jordan B. Peterson on the BBC show *Daily Politics* (May 17, 2018; https://www.bbc.co.uk/programmes/bob3kq88; a clip of the portion referred to here can be seen here: https://www.youtube.com/watch?v=MLnIkBQpo6s) that begins with her question: "Do you think a transwoman is a real woman?"

56. For some suggestions, see Heilig, "Lexical Semantics."

57. Denny Burk, "Is Paul's Gospel Counterimperial? Evaluating the Prospects of the 'Fresh Perspective' for Evangelical Theology," *JETS* 51 (2008): 317.

"religious domain" of κύριος.[58] Such an argument is of no avail against the anti-imperial approach, however,[59] if it cannot be demonstrated simultaneously that when used with respect to the emperor it is the "social domain" that is activated in isolation—as the tiresome reference to English "Lord" or German "Herr" often made in such discussions implies.[60] This is of course precisely the point that Tertullian (*Apol.* 34.1) makes when he says that he is willing to call the emperor *dominus*. This is not because, as Robinson's portrayal might suggest, he does not see the potential problem there. Rather, Tertullian explicitly makes clear that if he uses this word for the emperor, he does so in the "ordinary" sense and will not be forced to use it in the sense of God. (*Dicam plane imperatorem dominum, sed more communi, sed quando non cogor, ut dominum dei vice dicam. Ceterum liber sum illi.*) In other words, Tertullian specifies explicitly that he would exclude the religious domain— with the very fact that he addresses this so explicitly demonstrating, to be sure, how close at hand the evocation of this domain would have been![61]

Accordingly, when Polycarp is asked (Mart. Pol. 8.2) what would be so bad about simply saying Κύριος καῖσαρ (8.2), he does not simply respond: "You are right; these are distinct concepts after all." Rather, he is fully aware that

---

58. White, "Anti-Imperial Subtexts," 308–11.

59. Cf. my earlier critique in Heilig, *Hidden Criticism?*, 143–55.

60. To adduce just one example, see how J. Albert Harrill, *Paul the Apostle: His Life and Legacy in Their Roman Context* (Cambridge: Cambridge University Press, 2012), 88, makes the connection to modern English usage: "'Lord' was an epithet common of all deities in the ancient Mediterranean world, not unique to Roman emperor worship. It characterized, for example, the god of healing ('Lord and Savior Asclepius'), the Egyptian goddess Isis ('Lord and Queen Isis'), the supreme father Zeus, and even the youthful Apollo. Moreover, in Rome's fundamentally hierarchical society, *kurios* had regular use in the daily speech of slaves to masters, commoners to aristocrats, soldiers to commanders—as illustrated even in the New Testament (Luke 7:6-8); virtually all ancient people spoke this way to their social betters. Analogous are the traditional British address of a nobleman as *lord* and the aristocratic connotations of *Señor* in formal Spanish. Paul calling his Messiah Jesus 'Lord' does not prove anything about an anti-imperial stance to Rome, because the term specified not the emperor alone but was a commonplace epithet of respect for both noble society and deities." Harrill rightly notices the "linguistic flexibility of the term" but does not seem to be correct when it comes to the dynamics of how in actual communication different domains are activated. Simply pointing to usage for "social betters" is not convincing.

61. Interestingly, the example of Augustus, who did not want to be called *dominus* (cf. Suetonius, *Aug.* 53) "because" it is a name of God, might point to a very similar phenomenon, as Glover in his note of the LCL translation indicates: "The word *dominus* was associated with the ownership of slaves and with political tyranny" (T. R. Glover and Geral H. Rendall, trans., *Tertullian—Minucius Felix*, LCL 250 [Cambridge: Harvard University Press, 1931], 159).

in this context domains would be activated that would clash with claims of exclusivity of Jesus's lordship—as emphasized forcefully by Paul in 1 Cor 8:6, where there can be no doubt about the activated domains (see v. 5).[62] Even Barclay admits that here we have a clear antithesis, which allows for the safe conclusion of Paul's sensitivity regarding this title: "Given this evidence it is no surprise that Paul does not refer to political authorities as κύριοι."[63] He might, of course, have done so in other contexts where he could be sure that no domains reserved for Jesus would be implied—just like Tertullian by no means gives a cart blanche to call the emperor *dominus* without qualification.

Robinson's reference to κύριος as an example of apparently harmless parallels between Paul's letters and imperial ideology thus seems to prove precisely the opposite—if only we take into account how the "distinct" concepts are actually connected through lived experiences and how easily dimensions could be evoked that would result in a clash between the two spheres. More generally, we can note that there seems to be a lot of promise for our endeavor in thinking about the meaning of Greek words as frames consisting of different domains.

In closing, I want to adduce yet another example and sketch some reasons why I think there is at least enough evidence for an initial suspicion that, due to syntagmatic relations, domains might have been activated for the first readers that would have resulted in a conceptual clash with the public Roman transcript that they were familiar with. Colossians 2:15 is the only other verse in the New Testament in which the verb θριαμβεύω is used.[64] Here too it occurs transitively, this time with "principalities and powers"—so the translation of

62. See already Heilig, *Hidden Criticism?*, 144. As I see it, inscriptions from the southern Levant might indeed demonstrate a more localized "royal" domain at the basis of early Christian usage, as D. Clint Burnett, *Studying the New Testament through Inscriptions: An Introduction* (Peabody: Hendrickson, 2020), chapter 2, has recently argued. It seems plausible to me, however, that this usage would have been viewed as being embedded in a larger domain of political rule and that this would have become increasingly activated as a whole as κύριος was getting used more often for Roman emperors—a shift that was beginning to take place as Paul was writing his letters. In fact, it seems to me that 1 Cor 8:5, with its explicit acknowledgment of the wide set of claims associated with this title, might be taken itself as evidence for a growing awareness in that regard.

63. John M. G. Barclay, "Why the Roman Empire Was Insignificant to Paul," in *Pauline Churches and Diaspora Jews*, ed. John M. G. Barclay, WUNT 275 (Tübingen: Mohr Siebeck, 2011), 377.

64. I developed this argument in more detail in Heilig, "Caesar and Paul in the Roman Triumphal Procession: Reading Col 2:15 in Light of 2 Cor 2:14," as part of the program unit "Bible and Empire," at the International SBL meeting in Berlin, August 9, 2017.

τὰς ἀρχὰς καὶ τὰς ἐξουσίας in the KJV—as the direct object. The question of referents is very difficult here. Even if these were "political terms" they could be used metaphorically for demonic powers. Often in the secondary literature it is this political dimension itself that is denied at the outset with reference to the allegedly "spiritual" meaning of these terms.[65] However, I am wondering (and it is really just a question at this point) whether this might not be missing important contextual factors that for the recipients of the letter would have contributed toward *evoking the political domains* inherent in the frames corresponding to these words.

First, we have to reiterate that the governing verb θριαμβεύω most certainly does not communicate, as the majority of commentators still seems to think, the idea of 'victory' but actually speaks about an explicitly Roman victory procession.[66] This seems to raise the probability of an activation of the political domain significantly. Note, for example, how reminiscent the construction in Col 2:15 is of the formulation in Plutarch, *Comp. Thes. Rom.* 4.4: βασιλεῖς ἐθριάμβευσε καὶ ἡγεμόνας.

Second, it needs to be noted that in other contemporary texts even ἀρχή and ἐξουσία themselves occur with a dominant political domain in connection with θριαμβεύω and θρίαμβος. Admittedly, they are never used as direct objects of the verb, but note how the ἀρχή of Sulla is mocked in songs during his triumph over Mithridates in Appian—with the term there certainly having the political meaning of 'government' (*Bell. civ.* 1.11.101).[67] Similarly, ἐξουσία is used with a clear evocation of the political domain in direct connection with triumph imagery in a second-century letter. In the *Epistula ecclesiarum apud Lugdunum et Viennam* (as recorded by Eusebius, *Hist. eccl.* 5.1.29), we find an interesting intransitive usage with διά and Christ as the subject of the verb. It

---

65. Martin Dibelius, *An die Kolosser, Epheser, an Philemon*, 2nd ed., HNT 12 (Tübingen: Mohr Siebeck, 1927), 24, even makes the connection to 1 Cor 2:6, interpreting *both* exclusively on a *spiritual* level, however: "Indem Gott den Christus zur Herrlichkeit erhöhte . . . , hat er die Geister, die ihn unwissend gekreuzigt hatten . . . , bloßgestellt."

66. Which, by the way, allows for a re-evaluation of the whole issue concerning the relationship between destruction and reconciliation of the "powers" in Colossians. After all, note that what also does not seem to be in view here is an emphasis on execution. Cf., on the whole issue, John M. G. Barclay, *Colossians and Philemon*, New Testament Guides (Sheffield: Sheffield Academic Press, 1997), 82–88.

67. Similarly, Plutarch, *Cam.* 7.1, where πολιτικὴ ἀρχή and θριαμβεύω occur in a contrastive way. See also another use in Appian, *Hist. rom.* 8.9: A triumphal procession offers a safe context—everybody has the right to say what he wants (ἀφελὴς γὰρ ὁ θρίαμβος καὶ ἐν ἐξουσίᾳ λέγειν, ὅ τι θέλοιεν). Cf. also Strabo, *Geogr.* 12.5.2, where there is talk of Lucullus giving up his authority to Pompey in order to celebrate his triumph.

is δι' αὐτῆς [τῆς ψυχῆς ἐν αὐτῷ] that Christ could "triumph"—"through" the soul of the martyr.[68] The very next sentence describes how he was escorted to the judgment seat—by the "magistrates of the city" (παραπεμπόντων αὐτὸν τῶν πολιτικῶν ἐξουσιῶν).

Digital Humanities

For relatively young scholars like myself, it is sometimes difficult to imagine just how different research practices were just one or two generations ago. When I was first working on 2 Cor 2:14, it was only toward the end of my project that I learned about a PhD thesis from 1976 that had addressed the question of the meaning of θριαμβεύω in admirable detail.[69] In many respects, David M. Park's analysis, which has been almost entirely ignored in the secondary literature, anticipated later results several decades in advance.[70] The author told me about the difficulties he had had with respect to learning more about the papyrus *BGU* IV 1061, in which the verb ἐκθριαμβίζω occurs, and which is sometimes adduced as an argument for a semantic shift of θριαμβεύω toward a more general meaning of 'making known.'[71] While today accessing the transcription and photographs of good quality is a matter of only a few seconds, he had to wait for more than one month in order to hear back from the director of the Egyptian Museum of Berlin in East Germany.

Even Breytenbach, in writing his 1990 article, was still dependent on "the cordial help of Tyndale House at Cambridge" in order to perform "a search regarding the use of the Greek lexeme θριαμβεύειν in the *corpus hellenisticum*."[72] As Peter Head told me, back then it took around forty-five minutes to run a simple search on the whole corpus, and you usually had to run the search many times with different configurations to get the results you wanted.[73] Since you could not simply search for a whole lemma, you had to first figure out all

68. On the passage cf. Heilig, *Paul's Triumph*, 72.
69. David M. Park, "Interpretative Value of the Metaphorical Constructions in 2 Corinthians" (PhD diss., Southwestern Baptist Theological Seminary, 1976). Some of the research relevant for our question was later published in David M. Park, "The Value of Biblical Metaphors (II Cor. 2:14–17)," *Metaphor and Religion: Theolinguistics 2*, ed. Jean-Pierre van Noppen, Study Series of the Vrije Universiteit Brussel: New Series 12 (Brussels: Vrije Universiteit Brussel, 1983), 253–68.
70. Cf. Heilig, *Paul's Triumph*, 28.
71. See my discussion in *Paul's Triumph*, 108–12.
72. Cilliers Breytenbach, "Paul's Proclamation and God's 'Thriambos': Notes on 2 Corinthians 2:14–16b," *Neot* 24 (1990): 260.
73. Personal communication, May 17, 2021.

the letter strings that might be relevant.[74] In his inaugural address, published one year later, Breytenbach explicitly frames this research as an example of the fundamental question of how to "understand Paul." He attempts to illustrate on its basis a generally applicable framework for how to investigate lexical-semantic questions concerning formulations in the New Testament. Reading about the efforts that have gone into reconstructing the historical context of 2 Cor 2:14 by means of time-consuming analyses of literary and archaeological backgrounds serves as a helpful reminder, especially in light of the fact that above I criticized Breytenbach's results, of how much more effort it took back then—only three decades ago—to *evaluate* such a list of search results. This realization tempers my criticism of Breytenbach's results earlier in this volume (p. 59). Online resources come to our aid almost always when the physical library reaches its limits. Even without good linguistic competencies, it is possible today to quickly compare a variety of translations of an ancient text. It must be remembered that it was not until 2001 that the *TLG* corpus became available online and not until 2003 that efforts of lemmatization even began—with the beta version of the search engine for lemmas becoming available only in 2006![75]

So much information about historical backgrounds is now available at the tips of our fingers, with literature, coinage, papyri, inscriptions, reliefs, and so much more being searchable online. In my opinion, these advancements of the "digital humanities" contain great promise for enabling us to identify many cases of previously overlooked Pauline unease with respect to the Roman Empire. Michael P. Theophilos's recent work on how to bring together numismatics and lexical semantics—and in doing so to keep an eye on the Roman context—might serve as an example[76] of how such a broadened horizon might help us gain a much clearer picture of the ancient discourses that stand in the background of the New Testament passages that we are analyzing.[77] For example, Barclay's dismissal of the critical potential of the title "king of kings" in 1 Tim 6:15 (ὁ βασιλεὺς τῶν βασιλευόντων)[78] seems difficult to maintain against the backdrop of the numismatic evidence for βασιλεὺς βασιλέων—

---

74. This might be the reason (rather than the scope of the *TLG* corpus at that time) for why the analysis of Breytenbach, "Paul's Proclamation," does not discuss several crucial passages. Cf. Heilig, *Paul's Triumph*, 62, 63, and 66.

75. TLG, *The History of the TLG*®, stephanus.tlg.uci.edu/history.php.

76. See also, in the area of epigraphy, D. Clint Burnett, *Studying the New Testament*.

77. Michael P. Theophilos, *Numismatics and Greek Lexicography* (London: T&T Clark, 2019).

78. Barclay, "Roman Empire," 378. See my response in Heilig, *Hidden Criticism?*, 151–54.

even though such analyses might at the same time nuance the way that we refer to Rome as a relevant entity behind the text.[79]

Commentaries

To be sure, this multitude of resources and tools does not automatically generate new insights. First of all, the resources are so manifold that it is difficult even to be aware of all the existing possibilities, let alone being trained to use them adequately, especially since most of this is learned autodidactically in the course of doctoral research. Moreover, even the competence to execute these operations does not necessarily translate into new insights if the new skills are not paired with equally necessary advances with respect to knowledge. And here we might even have to attest the reverse dynamic, such as a loss of familiarity with the Greek language and texts due to software that makes answering questions that arise during studies and research apparently easier, even without prior understanding.

However, even where proper education is not the problem, electronic tools can lure researchers into a false sense of security. For example, I have demonstrated elsewhere how Moisés Silva failed to improve the state of research on θριαμβεύω in the entry of his *NIDNTTE*[80] compared to earlier editions, even though he did indeed perform a search in the online *TLG* corpus.[81] The same

---

79. Theophilos, *Numismatics*, 193–215, thinks that there is a clear challenge to Rome in Rev 7:14 and 19:16 (where the form is βασιλεὺς βασιλέων)—not directly by claiming a title of the Roman emperor but because the title is known extensively from coins of Parthian rulers, feared *enemies* of the Romans. It seems to me that this might indeed be an additional layer to the provocation. Still, there also seems to be a more direct challenge involved. If there is a king of kings, of any kind, that limits the emperor's power in an unacceptable way. Theophilos, *Numismatics*, 210, writes: "The Roman emperor was not styled or titled as 'king' or its superlative variations. The Romans, at least for the last six centuries BCE, had been defined by their anti-regal stance after the overthrow of King Tarquinius Superbus by Junius Brutus and the founding of the Roman republic in 509 BCE." However, this seems to go too quickly over the evidence for the perception of Roman emperors in the East. Cf. Heilig, *Hidden Criticism?*, 153–54n52. I do not understand why Theophilos adduces John 19:15 alongside Matt 14:9 when arguing that "regents in the provinces were sparingly permitted the title 'king' but this was not typical." In the former passage, it is clearly the Roman emperor himself who is proclaimed as the only king that the crowd accepts (οὐκ ἔχομεν βασιλέα εἰ μὴ Καίσαρα).

80. Moisés Silva, "θριαμβεύω," *NIDTTE* 2:467–68.

81. Christoph Heilig, "Biblical Words and Their Meaning: An Introduction to Lexical Semantics in the *NIDNTTE*." *Reviews of Biblical and Early Christian Studies*, June 15, 2015, https://rbecs.org/2015/06/17/nidntte/.

could be said for the new *Cambridge Greek Lexicon*.[82] If this can happen to remarkably well-qualified scholars who undoubtedly know a lot about the semantics of Greek words, there is a high risk that advancements in employed technologies might not correlate as well with new insights as one might hope.

And indeed, to give just one further example, while Roman imperial and provincial coinage is now readily available on the internet,[83] biblical scholars more often than one might hope do not use these tools properly—for simple reasons such as apparently not being aware of the fact that imperial gold, silver, and bronze coinage had vastly differing circulations in the eastern part of the empire (with local bronze coinage remaining in usage the longest before being replaced by Roman coinage).[84] Being able to search for material that in former times would have been available only in physical archives, access to which usually would have been connected with some kind of prior training, might now result in the use of evidence that is, for example, simply not even relevant for the geographical area under discussion.

The format of the biblical commentary in my view both holds promise for introducing some order amidst the chaos created by the overabundance of opportunities and is, at the same time, to be blamed in large part for the current stagnation in exegetical questions. That the genre of the biblical commentary has been in a deep crisis for a long time is obvious. Multiple cases of plagiarism in the last couple of years demonstrate how little original research goes into most commentaries and to what extent the demands of the genre force researchers to mainly restate what others have said before them. The problem here is not only that outdated research is perpetuated. Sometimes, it is even the case that the least outdated research is not even on the commentator's radar. For example, Moisés Silva in his analysis of θριαμβεύω simply missed Breytenbach's analysis (though it was discussed in the German revision of the dictionary).[85] Commentators relying on the *NIDNTTE* will therefore likely do the same. And this is not to mention a monograph by M. Margareta Gruber from 1998,[86] which had already identified crucial problems with Breytenbach's

82. See above, pp. 60 n. 16 and 62 n. 27.

83. For Roman imperial coinage, see http://numismatics.org/ocre/. For Roman provincial coinage, see https://rpc.ashmus.ox.ac.uk/.

84. See Andrew Burnett, *Coinage in the Roman World* (London: Spink, 1987), 33–65; cf. *RIC* and *RPC*.

85. Hans-Georg Link and Roland Gebauer, "θριαμβεύω," *TBLNT²* 1106–7.

86. M. Margareta Gruber, *Herrlichkeit in Schwachheit: Eine Auslegung des Apologie des Zweiten Korintherbriefs 2 Kor 2,14–6,13*, FB 89 (Würzburg: Echter, 1998).

argument—without the vast majority of commentators taking notice. Gruber's work was published in the series Forschung zur Bibel, which—although not the most famous German monograph series—contains some very important works and even has an abbreviation in *The SBL Handbook of Style*. It can thus hardly count as an obscure German source. The fact that her important contribution was missed by extension implies that research presented in the various other European series will have an even smaller chance of getting noticed. I am reminded of Oscar Cullmann, who in 1957 could not restrain his frustration about the establishment of yet another—a *third!*—journal for New Testament research (*Novum Testamentum*): "Haben die Mitarbeiter wohl daran gedacht, was sie ihren Kollegen damit zumuten, daß diese nun regelmäßig drei Fachzeitschriften lesen und vielleicht sogar abonnieren sollten?"[87] The complaint seems laughable from today's perspective with an insurmountable mass of publications now in view.

The idea that commentators actually expand our knowledge about biblical texts is, with very few exceptions, just wrong. Moreover, even the modest goal of merely reproducing the status quo is often not reached successfully. As part of my research on 2 Cor 2:14, I went through approximately twenty commentaries from both the eighteenth and the nineteenth centuries, specifically focusing on how "background material" was used for the exegesis. It is fascinating to see that ever since Georg David Kypke in 1755, the actual evidence that is adduced from interpreters who favor a "triumphant" interpretation of the metaphor is *decreasing.*[88] These days, interpreters claim that they are adducing "neglected points of background" even though they are unaware of Kypke and the actual, though highly debatable, evidence that one might adduce for such an interpretation, while not offering anything new themselves.[89]

The history of research on 2 Cor 2:14 is not only a textbook example of "exegetical amnesia,"[90] it also demonstrates painfully that the growing access to primary sources is not at all satisfactorily correlated with original incorporations of this data into interpretations of the biblical texts. The little progress

---

87. Oscar Cullmann, "Ist eine dritte neutestamentliche Zeitschrift notwendig?," *TLZ* 82 (1957): 76. On the relationship to the second journal, *New Testament Studies*, see Lukas Bormann and Hannah Kreß, "Free from German 'Schulmeinungen' and Other One-Sidedness: Die Entstehungsgeschichte der *New Testament Studies* (1936–1954)," *NTS* 66 (2020): 21–50.

88. See Georg David Kypke, *Acta, Apostolorvm, Epistolas et Apocalypsin*, vol. 2 of *Observationes sacrae in Novi Foederis libros ex ax avctoribvs potissimvm Graecis et antiqvitatibvs* (Wrocław: Korn, 1755), 243. Cf. Heilig, *Paul's Triumph*, 57–58, 63, and 105.

89. See Helig, *Paul's Triumph*, 105.

90. Cf. Dale C. Allison Jr., "Exegetical Amnesia in James," *ETL* 86 (2000): 162–66.

that had been made at times was quickly forgotten again, and fundamental questions—such as the potential role of Claudius's triumphal procession only a few years earlier—were not raised for a long time, perhaps because such issues surface only when there is sufficient time to take a deep breath and let the primary evidence take its full effect. Even if I have missed some laudable exceptions—as is very probable, given how late I became aware of the work of David M. Park—and there are other commentators besides J. Paul Sampley (see above, p. 65) who emphasize the relevance of the figure of Claudius, this would only—luckily—serve to confirm my point. Obviously, something is very wrong with our way of doing research when, in the course of such a long time that I have spent with this passage, I may still have missed bits of literature that worked out crucial aspects of background information.

A decade ago, Stanley E. Porter offered an illuminating analysis of the "linguistic competence" of commentaries on Romans, assessing them against the backdrop of his ideas about the respective contemporary linguistic state of research. While one might quibble[91] with some of the employed standards, Porter's overall conclusion[92] is very convincing indeed. Porter thinks that the aspiration of commenting on all dimensions of the text is no longer an appropriate standard for current commentary writing. Both the sheer mass of secondary literature and the broad spectrum of skills that would be necessary to give such an overall assessment overwhelm commentary writers—with the result that to a large extent "commentaries have become less commentaries on the Greek text, or even on the text in translation, and more commentaries on previous commentators—as these commentaries provide the major source of information for current commentators." Porter's own solution consists in a re-evaluation of the genre of commentaries itself:

> I believe that it is time to reassess what it is to write a commentary, and to adjust our sights to something much more manageable and attainable— commentaries that specialize in particular elements of the text, or that reflect particular viewpoints, and that can make a valid attempt to cover the most important secondary literature and actively respond to it in the commentary itself, all the while keeping the text as the center of focus. In

---

91. Cf. Heilig, *Paulus als Erzähler?*, 1014.

92. Stanley E. Porter, "The Linguistic Competence of New Testament Commentaries," in *On the Writing of New Testament Commentaries: Festschrift for Grant R. Osborne on the Occasion of His 70th Birthday*, ed. Stanley E. Porter and Eckhard J. Schnabel, TENTS 8 (Leiden: Brill, 2012), 52–53.

other words, we should have commentaries that investigate the linguistic issues of the Greek text (I don't know of a commentary series devoted to such an approach), the historical and literary issues, or the theological issues; as well as commentaries that approach the text from a particular point of advocacy, such as an epistolary commentary, or a historical commentary, or a particular ideological commentary.[93]

I have elsewhere suggested something very similar. The key, in my opinion, is to keep the fundamental distinction between description and interpretation in mind.[94] I do think that interpretation remains a central task to exegesis. It thus needs to remain the goal of having high-quality and *succinct* sketches of the meaning of entire biblical books from the perspective of a specific interpretation theory. Neither is there any need for such commentaries to engage with all other possible interpretations, often presupposing entirely different norms, and, thus, conceptions of meanings, and, thus, methodologies. Nor is it realistic to expect these interpreters to leave no stone unturned in searching for information concerning all possible descriptive layers of the text. Scholars who specialize in establishing the meaning of a text might still have something to contribute to debates among experts of specific descriptive dimensions, such as the textual history. There still should be dialogue in both directions. I too, for example, have made observations about how my interpretations might influence text-critical decisions, having noticed that the reasoning in this area on a particular passage is driven in part by assumptions about the propositional structure of the text.[95] However, it cannot be my task as a nonexpert in textual criticism to determine how this might tip the balance in the end, in connection with the external evidence.

To make such determinations, we need specialized descriptive works that, in turn, are aware of interpretative options that might influence their respective decisions. Such an awareness will also be necessary in order to even select among the infinite number of possible descriptive operations.[96] This would not change, however, the very fundamental difference in orientation of such works. While interpretation has the objective of a methodologically controlled

93. Porter, "Linguistic Competence," 53.
94. Heilig, *Paulus als Erzähler?*, 1013–14. Cf. Heilig and Heilig, "Teaching Biblical Exegesis."
95. Heilig, *Paulus als Erzähler?*, 494–95, on Gal 1:11 in dialogue with Stephen C. Carlson, *The Text of Galatians and Its History*, WUNT 2/385 (Tübingen: Mohr Siebeck, 2015), 118–20, who in turn as a text-critic shows sensitivities for semantic and pragmatic properties of the text.
96. See Heilig and Heilig, "Teaching Biblical Exegesis."

understanding of texts, description aims at classifying them.[97] We thus desperately need whole commentary series that focus on one such descriptive dimension and adduce and *prepare* the relevant data for those scholars who are focused on the meaning of texts. There are some very early signs of developments along these lines, such as the *Papyrologische Kommentare zum Neuen Testament*, in which experts on papyrology present material to exegetes that is, in theory, accessible to all, but which requires a high degree of specialization in order to be assessed correctly.[98] At the same time, we need to be careful not to demand too much from such commentators. While interpreters of biblical texts need tools like these in order to navigate within the incredible mass of primary and secondary material, authors of more descriptively oriented works must not be expected to enter into each and every debate concerning the meaning of the text or even to take a specific overall position on them, especially when they have nothing to contribute to these passages from their specialized perspective.

97. Cf. Köppe and Kindt, *Erzähltheorie*, 35.
98. An *Epigraphic Commentary on the New Testament* (to be published by Mohr Siebeck) is also on the horizon.

CONCLUSION

We started this book by taking a close look at how Laura Robinson's article contributed to the debate that had emerged primarily between N. T. Wright and John M. G. Barclay. The latter had criticized the former's proposal of an anti-imperial subtext in Paul very effectively. If one analyzes Barclay's critique, one can see that he had identified a series of necessary conditions that all need to be true for Wright's proposal not to be falsified. Moreover, Barclay concluded with reference to ancient evidence that several of these conditions were not met. To begin with, he does not think that Paul's letters would have been affected by the rules of public discourse. Rather, they are assumed to give us direct insight into Paul's private thinking, the "hidden transcript" of the Pauline churches. Thus, there is no need for Paul to hide potential critical remarks between the lines. In addition, Barclay thinks that the shape of the "public transcript" would actually have allowed for a rather blunt critique of basic aspects of Roman ideology—so that the apparent lack of such comments should be taken as an indication that Paul had nothing of that sort to say. Lastly, Barclay does not think that the idea can be maintained that Paul would have shied away from speaking his mind simply because of potential sanctions.

In her recent article, Robinson now reinforces the first two lines of critique, arguing that, first, we do not have evidence for anything like the surveillance mechanisms known from modern suppressive regimes that are often adduced as potential analogies, and second, there are no clear legal grounds for Paul being particularly afraid of punishment for what he wrote. Like Barclay she thus concludes that the lack of obvious criticism of the Roman Empire means that Paul simply did not communicate such critical ideas in his letters.

In my judgment, Robinson's central thesis is not convincing. Her whole argument seems to suffer from not appreciating sufficiently the consequences that would come from the fact that early Christianity would have looked very problematic in its social context. In particular, Robinson's article does not provide an explanation for why we have very solid documented evidence from just a few decades later for intense social and governmental pressure on Christians in precisely the "liberal" Roman environment that she portrays. I thus conclude that it does seem plausible to maintain—against Barclay and with Wright—that many aspects of the Pauline "hidden transcript" would have been unacceptable and simply dangerous in the public sphere, especially for the fragile young congregations themselves.

In fact, against this backdrop, I reconsider the third of Barclay's critical lines of reasoning, emphasizing Paul's courage. Originally, in my 2015 book *Hidden Criticism?*, this last necessary condition caused me to conclude that Wright's hypothesis could only be maintained if the motivation for hiding the anti-imperial critique were modified. Rather than just referencing the risk of persecution and considering the subtext as a second-rate means of communication, necessitated by the external conditions, one would need to construe an argument for why a more subtle critique might actually be more conducive to Paul's communicative aims.

I still think that such allusions to Roman ideology are an important factor to be reckoned with in interpreting Paul's letters. However, it now seems more legitimate to me that Paul might indeed have decided not to write certain things explicitly that might have been on his mind for the simple reason that it was not worth the trouble such provocations might have caused for himself or his congregation. In the end, it is Robinson herself who forcefully makes this point by vividly portraying the extreme amount of pressure Paul and his converts would have been subjected to in their societal contexts. While she apparently thinks that in such a situation of intense confrontations Paul would not have cared that much about a bit more controversy caused by a rash comment in his letters, I think it is much more plausible that the apostle would have tried to minimize unnecessary conflicts.

Even though I vehemently disagree with Robinson's conclusion, it thus seems that she effectively pointed to the need for an additional necessary condition. For there to be a plausible expectation of some actively hidden criticism in Paul's letters, one would have to demonstrate for each individual set of circumstances of the writing in question that Paul would indeed have felt compelled to communicate some critical thoughts about his Roman environment. Where such an argument cannot be made, we might be forced to admit that the "hidden" criticism that we like to identify in these texts might actually be just "unexpressed." Paul might have cherished these angry thoughts about the emperors, but perhaps he did not see any acute occasion for why he would have to make that case—either explicitly or implicitly.

Besides vindicating Wright's original proposal and pointing to the possibility of an ultimately inaccessible Pauline "hidden transcript," Robinson's attack on the anti-imperial paradigm has made me reconsider yet another possibility. Robinson thinks that a big problem with the idea of concealed criticism is that if it were indeed so well concealed that it would become explicable why exegetes by and large have overlooked it for so long, it would also be irrelevant in its original context, because Paul's intended audience would also not have picked up on the critical vibes. Generally, this seems to be a valid argument. To be sure, there are many cases where the original audience is in a privileged position and we lack crucial background information. But it is true that a Rome-critical attitude would indeed have had always to negotiate between the two opposing poles of communicative clarity and potential sanctions. What Robinson misses, however, on a very fundamental level is that there seems to be a third option—between unintelligible and thus ineffective code on the one hand and being content with the apparent fact that Paul speaks about the Roman Empire at all only in Rom 13. The very fact that Wright thinks the hidden echoes of Rome can be heard so clearly and also Robinson's admission that Paul would have seemed very controversial to Roman eyes without any hidden layers point to the additional possibility that in Paul's letters we might find criticism of the Roman Empire that is not actively concealed by the apostle but rather quite blunt—with it simply having been overlooked systematically by exegetes.

One case of such an insight into Paul's "hidden transcript" is offered by 1 Cor 2:6, where Paul's formulation cannot be judged overly cautious at all. To be fair, it might be better not to call such verses "criticism" of the Roman Empire at all because they are not directed at the criticized party directly. It might be less misleading to speak of insights into Paul's "unease" with respect to certain aspects of Roman propaganda. In my perspective, we see dynamics at play in relation to these insights into Paul's hidden transcript that are similar to what we can see with respect to how Paul narrates stories in his letters. Often, the narratives that are present in Paul's mind find only fragmentary expression in the text. Paul can formulate in such a concise manner because he shares experiences and told stories with the addressees of his letters. Similarly, I suggest that very succinct formulations might be seen as provoking "dissonances" against the backdrop of the Roman public transcript, without there being any need for Paul to be more explicit. This dense style is not something that needs to be explained with reference to alleged elaborate coding strategies but is simply what our default expectation should be when we recognize the Pauline texts in their pragmatic contexts.

To be sure, even though Wright's hypothesis still seems valid in theory, every case of nonhidden, overlooked anti-imperial subtexts should lower our expectation of elaborate attempts of keeping formulations under a sanctionable threshold. Still, these options are not entirely exclusive. For in the end there is a great variety of potential reasons why Paul might at certain points have given us rather clear insights into the otherwise mostly "hidden transcript" of early Christian attitudes toward Rome. To be sure, one possibility is that we might not, in fact, be dealing with the hidden transcript itself but that—as Barclay suggested—certain elements of critique would be permissible as part of the public transcript. We must also be prepared for the fact that there is a certain grey area between public and hidden transcript—with the demarcation constantly being negotiated. Second Corinthians 2:14 might be a powerful illustration of this phenomenon of at least short-term disturbances of the boundaries around the public transcript that might have caused Paul to feel safer using his metaphor than he might have felt in other situations. But then there is naturally also the eventuality that the safety of certain statements is misjudged. A realistic perception of communication will cause us to reckon with unintentional confusions between the transcripts that apply in a certain situation, with misconceptions concerning what the public transcript may forbid, and even—and not the least—with affective violations of the rules that are in force in the public transcript.

Some readers might find this reasoning intuitively compelling but feel doubtful that New Testament scholarship might be simply overlooking such telling insights into Paul's critical perception of the Roman Empire. I have presented them with a detailed discussion of 2 Cor 2:14 in chapters 3 and 4 of the present book. To my knowledge, this verse has not been adduced by proponents of Wright's hypothesis as a case of "coded" criticism to any notable extent. Wright himself does not even see a specifically Roman reference here but thinks the metaphor is drawing on imagery from the military realm in a rather general way. Scholarship at times has tended toward weakening even this military connection, arguing that θριαμβεύω has some general meaning, comparable to the English phrases "making known" or "leading around."

The lexical evidence, however, is as clear as it could be and demonstrates that in Paul's time the verb referred to the ritual of the *triumphus*, the victory celebration carried out in Rome by the victorious general—more specifically, in the first century, by the emperor or other members of his family. By using the verb transitively, Paul paints himself and his coworkers as prisoners of war who are presented to the watching crowd in the triumphal procession in Rome.

To be sure, Paul's main intention here is not to criticize Rome. Rather, the critique contained in this metaphor is leveled against the Corinthians, who take offense at the rather chaotic travel movements that he had just recounted. Paul puts his critics in the shoes of the Roman crowd that watches the prisoners of war, who no doubt played a shameful role in the procession. At the same time, the Corinthians are forced to acknowledge that, whatever their problem with these people might be, their complaint would have to be directed to the one in charge, the triumphator. Plus, the longer they might look at the captives, the more they might recognize how they contribute to the triumphator's glory and thus, to some degree, actually partake in his splendor.

This inner-Christian dynamic notwithstanding, however, Paul's choice of words would have inevitably evoked contemporary discourses concerning Roman triumphal processions—in particular discourse on the one by Claudius that had been staged just a few years earlier, in 44 CE, the only triumphal procession by a Roman emperor during Paul's lifetime. This historical event is an obvious candidate as background for understanding Paul's metaphor, and yet it has still been missed by commentators—anti-imperial or not—almost without exception.

This is particularly astonishing because the historical evidence—including documented contact with potential eyewitnesses and concrete archaeological insights into a cult for Claudius's victory over Britannia in Corinth at exactly the timeframe we are interested in—is far better for this hypothesis than for any of its alternatives (e.g., the alternative claim that Paul is referring here to a Dionysus procession or that he has some encyclopedic knowledge about the Roman ritual).

When analyzed against this backdrop, it becomes clear that Paul here acts as a highly engaged observer of current political events. He is one of very few surviving contemporary voices that give us glimpses into how Claudius's triumph was perceived at the time. Interestingly, the quite obvious dissonances that Paul's metaphors would have created with respect to official Claudian propaganda are in line with some parts of the public transcript—or at least the hidden transcript of the elites—in the time after Claudius's death/assassination by Nero. This disturbance of the demarcations of what was permissible in public discourse might have brought us this beautifully complex metaphor that lets some of Paul's reservations toward Roman ideology shine through and hints at how he would have tried to interact with it in a way that would have been conducive to his own agenda.

The theory that Pauline scholarship might have overlooked rather obvious points of contention between Paul and the Roman Empire no longer looks speculative against that background. Rather, it shifts the focus from the question of whether it could be the case to why this phenomenon might exist. In an outlook, I thus identify a series of factors that in my opinion have blinded us in the past and that, if addressed properly, might sensitize us so that we might make more discoveries in the future. They are not meant to offer a comprehensive account but rather to highlight several loosely related factors that seem important to me.

First, I do think that the emphasis on "code" is counterproductive. It makes us overlook things that are not well-concealed. We should remain open to the possibility that seemingly vague statements in Paul's letters would sometimes have had very clear references to contemporary political events, figures, and ideas, but we must also be careful not to overlook the perhaps less spectacular but easier to establish cases of open interaction with Roman ideology. Even though I do not agree with Robinson's main conclusions, I think her article highlights once again that it is in the interest of the proponents of an anti-imperial reading of Paul to move on—or otherwise they will be forced to continue to debate about the same issues of the alleged safety of criticism in the Roman Empire, and so on. It is not that there is nothing more to be learned in that regard, but the problem is that it shifts attention away from the necessary interaction with actual texts.

Second, I think there is still a lot to be learned from people who have experienced oppressive regimes—as the Roman Empire for all its liberalism in *some* religious and administrative manners undoubtedly was. The danger of anachronisms is real, and Robinson has powerfully demonstrated that once again in her discussion of Wright's use of a Chinese playwright. However, there is also the equally real risk of missing important aspects of Pauline texts because of the limitations of our own experiences of life. The fact that Rom 13:1–7 is still adduced as a definitive proof that Paul cannot have said critical things about the Roman Empire elsewhere demonstrates this forcefully, in my opinion. Such a conclusion can only be reached if an extreme meaning of Rom 13:1–7 is assumed, which in turn can only be inferred if the background plausibility for such a reading is deemed to be very high (since the explanatory potential of this hypothesis clearly is not a hit). And this in turn requires us to ignore not only what we read in other Pauline passages—including 1 Cor 2:6—but also any empathetic understanding of Judaism under Roman rule. The passage will undoubtedly remain unclear to some extent even if we start from these latter insights as part of our background knowledge. But this does not mean that we can just discard all insights that were gained in postcolonial interpretation.

Third, I think a lot of the stagnation with respect to passages like 2 Cor 2:14 has to do with the fact that, to a large extent, New Testament scholarship refuses to reflect on its theoretical bases ("What are we after?") and the corresponding methodological consequences ("How do we get there?"). We do not teach students a systematic strategy for reconstructing past intentions and communicative effects. (I am speaking of scholars who work in contexts that are dominated by what has become known as the historical-critical method.) And "methods" like tradition-history are introduced without any obvious connection to semantics and pragmatics, hanging there somewhere between description and interpretation. This inhibits original insights about ancient texts. Where "background" is actually introduced into the discussion, it often happens in a way that for obvious epistemological reasons cannot produce solid results, namely by ignoring the explanatory potential of the hypothesis altogether, leaving the inference terribly incomplete.

There is one specific issue that needs to be better integrated into a methodology of interpretation within an intentionalist interpretation theory (which is a more precise way of saying "historical-critical method"), and I myself have not taken it into account yet sufficiently. This issue is the insights from cognitive linguistics, in particular as they pertain to lexical semantics. The idea that parallels between Paul's wording and texts of Roman propaganda can simply be swept aside by claiming that they constitute "different concepts" is extremely problematic from that perspective. Rather, in occurrences of words like κύριος we can see that the meaning of the word is constituted by a variety of cognitive domains, which are themselves deeply connected to the embodied experience of the members of the language community (like the political and the religious domain). Making such terminology apolitical by pointing to the separation of definitions—or, worse, glosses—in a dictionary is not at all convincing.

Fourth, the systematic methodology—the set of methods—for reconstructing authorial intent and textual effects will, if up to date, also contain a multitude of tools that have been developed as part of the emergence of the "digital humanities." Truly appreciating their revolutionary nature will go a long way in explaining why outdated interpretations of Pauline passages—like those of 2 Cor 2:14—still remain largely unchallenged. Even though some important aspects that dramatically influence background plausibility and explanatory potential seem rather obvious from today's perspective, uncovering them would have required an incredible amount of effort until very recently.

Fifth, biblical commentaries are to be blamed to a large extent for needlessly perpetuating interpretations of texts that do not take into account said new possibilities. Not only do many commentators lack these skills, and sometimes even a clearly formed methodology (or perhaps clearly defined theories of meaning) themselves, the genre of these works requires commentators to comment on issues they cannot possibly be qualified to address. Instead of resulting in lacunae in the commentary, the requirements of the format result in the handing down of assumptions that could easily be disproven by a quick search in, for example, the papyri. "Easily," that is, by the specialist, who in my opinion should be writing specialist commentaries, focused on one particular descriptive dimension of the text, and not being required to offer conclusive interpretations. It is with the help of such tools that commentators who want to offer concise interpretations of biblical books might be enabled to do so—without missing crucial bits of background knowledge.

I have mentioned before that Wright's subtext-hypothesis does not seem to have proven particularly heuristically fruitful in recent years. The supposedly muted "echoes of the empire" apparently remain difficult to be heard. However, if we take the above suggestions into account—and there are, no doubt, still many other factors that might be conducive to this effort—I am confident that we will be able to establish quite a robust picture of Paul's unease with respect to the Roman Empire.

Bibliography

Primary Sources

Appian. *Histoire romaine: Livre XII (La Guerre de Mithridate)*. Edited and translated by Paul Goukowsky. Collection des universités de France, publiée sous le patronage de l'Association Guillaume Budé. Paris: Les Belles Lettres, 2001.

———. *Historia Romana*. Edited by Paul Viereck and Anton G. Roos. First volume revised by Emilio Gabba. 2 vols. Leipzig: Teubner, 1905–1962.

———. *Roman History*. Translated by Horace White. 4 vols. LCL. Cambridge: Harvard University Press, 1912–1913.

———. *Römische Geschichte*. Translated by Otto Veh. Introduced and annotated by Kai Brodersen and Wolfgang Will. 2 vols. Bibliothek der griechischen Literatur 23 and 27. Stuttgart: Hiersemann, 1989.

Augustus. *Res Gestae Divi Augusti*. Translated and annotated by Alison E. Cooley. Cambridge: Cambridge University Press, 2009.

———. *Res Gestae Divi Augusti: Hauts faits du divin Auguste*. Edited by John Scheid. Collection des universités de France, publiée sous le patronage de l'Association Guillaume Budé. Paris: Les Belles Lettres, 2007.

Borzsák, István. "*Laus Caesaris*: Ein Epigrammzyklus auf Claudius' britannischen Triumphzug." Pages 342–56 in *Eine Handvoll: Ausgewählte kleine Schriften*. Budapest: Akadémiai Kiadó, 1999.

Cicero. *Orations: Pro Milone—In Pisonem—Pro Scauro—Pro Fonteio—Pro Rabirio Postumo—Pro Marcello—Pro Ligario—Pro Rege Deiotaro*. Translated by N. H. Watts. LCL. Cambridge: Harvard University Press, 1917.

Eusebius. *Ecclesiastical History*. Translated by Kirsopp Lake and John E. L. Oulton. 2 vols. LCL. London: Heinemann, 1926–1932.

———. *Histoire ecclésiastique*. Edited and translated by Gustave Bardy. 3 vols. Sources chrétiennes 31, 41, and 55. Paris: Cerf, 1952–1958.

Livy. *Livre XLV—Fragments*. Edited and translated by Paul Jal. Vol. 33 of *Histoire romaine*. Collection des universités de France, publiée sous le patronage de l'Association Guillaume Budé Paris: Les Belles Lettres, 1979.

Livy. Translated by Benjamin O. Foster, Frank G. Moore, Evan T. Sage, Alfred C. Schlesinger, and Russel M. Geer. 14 vols. LCL. Cambridge: Harvard University Press, 1919–1959.

Malloch, S. J. V. *The "Tabula Lugdunensis": A Critical Edition with Translation and Commentary*. Cambridge: Cambridge University Press, 2020.

Orosius. *Historiarum adversum paganos libri VII; Liber apologeticus contra Pelagianos*. Edited by Carl Zangemeister. Corpus scriptorum ecclesiasticorum latinorum 5. Vienna: Apud C. Geroldi Filium Bibliopolam Academiae, 1882.

Ovid. *Heroides—Amores*. Translated by Grant Showerman. Revised by G. P. Goold. LCL. Cambridge: Harvard University Press, 1914.

Philostratus. *Lives of the Sophists*. Pages ix–316 in *Philostratus und Eunapius*. LCL 134. Translated by Wilmer C. Wright. Cambridge: Harvard University Press, 1921.

Pliny the Elder. *Natural History*. Edited and translated by Harris Rackham, William H. S. Jones, and David E. Eichholz. 10 vols. LCL. Cambridge: Harvard University Press, 1938–1962.

Pliny the Younger. *Books 8–10—Panegyricus*. Vol. 2 of *Letters*. 2 vols. Translated by Betty Radice. LCL 59. Cambridge: Harvard University Press, 1969.

Plutarch. *Grosse Griechen und Römer*. Translated and annotated by Konrat Ziegler and Walter Wuhrmann. With an introduction by Konrat Ziegler and Hans Jürgen Hillen. 3rd ed. 6 vols. Zurich: Patmos, 2010.

———. *Lives*. Translated by Bernadotte Perrin. 11 vols. LCL. Cambridge: Harvard University Press, 1914–1926.

———. *Moralia*. Translated by Frank C. Babbitt, William C. Helmbold, Paul A. Clement, Herbert B. Hoffleit, Edwin L. Minar Jr., Francis H. Sandbach, Harold N. Fowler, Lionel Pearson, Harold Cherniss, Benedict Einarson, Phillip H. De Lacy, and Edward N. O'Neil (index). 16 vols. LCL. Cambridge: Harvard University Press, 1927–2004.

———. *Vies*. Edited and translated by Robert Flacelière, Émile Chambray, and Marcel Juneaux. 16 vols. Collection des universités de France, publiée sous le patronage de l'Association Guillaume Budé. Paris: Les Belles Lettres, 1957–1988.

———. *Vitae Parallelae*. Edited by Konrat Ziegler and Claes Lindskog. 3 vols. Leipzig: Teubner, 1964–1971.

Polybius. *Historiae*. Edited by Theodor Büttner-Wobst. 4 vols. Leipzig: Teubner, 1882–1905.

Pomponius Porphyrio. *Commentarius in Horatium Flaccum*. Edited by Wilhelm Meyer. Leipzig: Teubner, 1874.

Seneca. *Apocolocyntosis*. With Petronius, *Satyricon*. Translated by Michael Heseltine and W. H. D. Rouse. Revised by E. H. Warmington. LCL. Cambridge: Harvard University Press, 1913.

———. *Moral Essays*. Translated by John W. Basore. 3 vols. LCL. Cambridge: Harvard University Press, 1928–1935.

Smallwood, E. Mary. *Documents Illustrating the Principates of Gaius, Claudius, and Nero*. Cambridge: Cambridge University Press, 1967.

Solin, Heikki, and Marja Itkonen. *Paedagogium*. Vol. 1 of *Graffiti del Palatino*. Helsinki: Institutum Romanum Finlandise, 1966.

Suetonius. Translated by John C. Rolfe. 2 vols. LCL. Cambridge: Harvard University Press, 1913–1914.

Tacitus. *Dialogus, Agricola, Germania*. Translated by Sir William Peterson, Maurice Hutton. LCL. Cambridge: Harvard University Press, 1914.

———. *"The Histories" and "The Annals."* Translated by Cliffard H. Moore and John Jackson. 4 vols. LCL. Cambridge: Harvard University Press, 1937.

Tatian. *Oratio ad Graecos and Fragments*. Edited and translated by Molly Whittaker. OECT. Oxford: Clarendon, 1982.

Tertullian. *Tertullian—Minucius Felix*. Translated by T. R. Glover and Gerald H. Rendall. LCL 250. Cambridge: Harvard University Press, 1931.

———. *Opera I: Opera catholica. Adversus Marcionem*. Edited by Eligius Dekkers et al. CCSL 1. Turnhout: Brepols, 1954.

———. *Opera II: Opera montanistica*. Edited by Alois Gerlo et al. CCSL 2. Turnhout: Brepols, 1954.

Zwierlein, Otto. *Petrus in Rom: Die literarischen Zeugnisse: Mit einer kritischen Edition der Martyrien des Petrus und Paulus auf neuer handschriftlicher Grundlage*. 2nd ed. Untersuchungen zur antiken Literatur und Geschichte 96. Berlin: de Gruyter, 2010.

Zwierlein-Diehl, Erika, ed. *Magie der Steine: Die antiken Prunkkameen im Kunsthistorischen Museum*. Vienna: Brandstätter: 2008.

Secondary Sources

Allison, Dale C., Jr. "Exegetical Amnesia in James." *ETL* 86 (2000): 162–66.

Al-Otaibi, Fahad Mutlaq. *From Nabataea to Roman Arabia: Acquisition or Conquest?* BARIS 2212. Oxford: Archaeopress, 2011.

Aubrey, Michael G. "Linguistic Issues in Biblical Greek." Pages 161–89 in *Linguis-*

tic and Biblical Exegesis. Edited by Douglas Mangum and Josh Westbury. Lexham Methods Series 2. Bellingham: Lexham Press, 2017.

Aus, Roger David. *Imagery of Triumph and Rebellion in 2 Corinthians 2:14–17 and Elsewhere in the Epistle: An Example of the Combination of Greco-Roman and Judaic Traditions in the Apostle Paul*. Studies in Judaism. Lanham: University Press of America, 2005.

Bachmann, Philipp. *Der zweite Brief des Paulus an die Korinther*. 4th ed. Kommentar zum Neuen Testament 8. Leipzig: Deichert, 1922.

Barclay, John M. G. *Colossians and Philemon*. New Testament Guides. Sheffield: Sheffield Academic Press, 1997.

———. "Paul, Roman Religion and the Emperor: Mapping the Point of Conflict." Pages 345–62 in *Pauline Churches and Diaspora Jews*. Edited by John M. G. Barclay. WUNT 275. Tübingen: Mohr Siebeck, 2011.

———. Review of *Paul and the Faithfulness of God*, by N. T. Wright. *SJT* 68 (2015): 235–43.

———. "Why the Roman Empire Was Insignificant to Paul." Pages 363–87 in *Pauline Churches and Diaspora Jews*. Edited by John M. G. Barclay. WUNT 275. Tübingen: Mohr Siebeck, 2011.

Barr, James. *The Semantics of Biblical Language*. Oxford: Oxford University Press, 1961.

Barrett, Anthony A. "Claudius' British Victory Arch in Rome." *Britannia* 22 (1991): 1–19.

———. "The *Laus Caesaris*: Its History and Its Place in Latin Literature." *Latomus* 59 (2000): 596–606.

Bary, Corien, and Markus Egg. "Variety in Ancient Greek Aspect Interpretation." *Linguistics and Philosophy* 35 (2012): 111–34.

Beard, Mary. *The Roman Triumph*. Cambridge: Harvard University Press, 2007.

Binder, Gerhard, ed. *Apokolokyntosis*. By Seneca. Translated and annotated by Gerhard Binder. Sammlung Tusculum. Düsseldorf: Artemis & Winkler, 1999.

Bird, Michael F. *An Anomalous Jew: Paul among Jews, Greeks, and Romans*. Grand Rapids: Eerdmans, 2016.

Boardmann, John. *The Triumph of Dionysos: Convivial Processions, from Antiquity to the Present Day*. Oxford: Archaeopress, 2014.

Bormann, Lukas, and Hannah Kreß. "'Free from German "Schulmeinungen" and Other One-Sidedness': Die Entstehungsgeschichte der *New Testament Studies* (1936–1954)." *NTS* 66 (2020): 21–50.

Braund, David C. *Augustus to Nero: A Source Book on Roman History 31 BC–AD 68*. London: Croom Helm, 1986.

Brélaz, Cédric. "The Provincial Contexts of Paul's Imprisonments: Law Enforcement and Criminal Procedure in the Roman East." *JSNT* 43 (2021): 485–507.

Breytenbach, Cilliers. "Christologie, Nachfolge/Apostolat." *BTZ* 8 (1991): 183–98.

———. "Paul's Proclamation and God's 'Thriambos': Notes on 2 Corinthians 2:14–16b." *Neot* 24 (1990): 257–71.

Buraselis, Kostas. *Kos between Hellenism and Rome: Studies on the Political, Institutional and Social History of Kos from ca. the Middle Second Century B.C. until Late Antiquity.* TAPS 90. Philadelphia: American Philosophical Society, 2000.

Burk, Denny. "Is Paul's Gospel Counterimperial? Evaluating the Prospects of the 'Fresh Perspective' for Evangelical Theology." *JETS* 51 (2008): 309–37.

Burnett, Andrew. *Coinage in the Roman World.* London: Spink, 1987.

Burnett, Clint D. *Imperial Divine Honors and Paul's Churches in Greece.* Grand Rapids: Eerdmans, forthcoming.

———. *Studying the New Testament through Inscriptions: An Introduction.* Peabody: Hendrickson, 2020.

Calhoun, Crede H. "Panama Joyously Greets Lindbergh, after 4-Hour Flight from Costa Rica." *The New York Times.* January 10, 1928. https://www.nytimes .com/1928/01/10/archives/panama-joyously-greets-lindbergh-after-4hour -flight-from-costa-rica.html.

Campbell, Douglas A. *Framing Paul: An Epistolary Biography.* Grand Rapids: Eerdmans, 2014.

———. "The Provenance of Philippians: A Response to the Analyses of Michael Flexsenhar, Heike Omerzu, Angela Standhartinger and Cédric Brélaz." *JSNT* 43 (2021): 508–22.

Carlson, Stephen C. *The Text of Galatians and Its History.* WUNT 2/385. Tübingen: Mohr Siebeck, 2015.

Carter, T. L. "The Irony of Romans 13." *NovT* 46 (2004): 209–28.

Cohick, Lynn H. "Philippians and Empire: Paul's Engagement with Imperialism and the Imperial Cult." Pages 166–82 in *Jesus Is Lord, Caesar Is Not: Evaluating Empire in New Testament Studies.* Edited by Scot McKnight and Joseph B. Monica. Downers Grove, IL: IVP Academic, 2013.

Colbert, Stephen. "Drinking More? Having Less Sex? Throwing Tantrums in Public? Blame the Pandemic!" *The Late Show with Stephen Colbert.* October 2, 2021. https://www.youtube.com/watch?v=kjA2xu7idMc.

———. "Jeff Sessions Cites the Bible in Separating Children from Parents." *The Late Show with Stephen Colbert.* June 15, 2018. https://www.youtube.com /watch?v=j4KaLkYxMZ8.

Corke-Webster, James. "The Early Reception of Pliny the Younger in Tertullian of Carthage and Eusebius of Caesarea." *ClQ* 67 (2017): 247–62.

———. "Trouble in Pontus: The Pliny-Trajan Correspondence on the Christians Reconsidered." *TAPA* 147 (2017): 371–411.

Cullmann, Oscar. "Ist eine dritte neutestamentliche Zeitschrift notwendig?" *TLZ* 82 (1957): 73–76.

Danker, Frederick W., with Kathryn Krug. *The Concise Greek-English Lexicon of the New Testament*. Chicago: University of Chicago Press, 2009.

Danylak, Barry B. "Tiberius Claudius Dinippus and the Food Shortage in Corinth." *TynBul* 59 (2008): 231–70.

Dibelius, Martin. *An die Kolosser, Epheser, an Philemon*. 2nd ed. HNT 12. Tübingen: Mohr Siebeck, 1927.

Diehl, Judith A. "Empire and Epistles: Anti-Roman Rhetoric in the New Testament Epistles." *CBR* 10 (2012): 217–63.

Dodson, Joseph R. "The Convict's Gibbet and the Victor's Car: The Triumphal Death of Marcus Atilius Regulus and the Background of Col 2:15." *HTR* 114 (2021): 182–202.

Dorin, Alan, and Eva Anagnostou-Laoutides. "The Silver Triton: Suetonius *Claud.* 21.6.13–6." *Nuncius* 33 (2018): 1–24.

Du Mez, Kristin Kobes. *Jesus and John Wayne: How White Evangelicals Corrupted a Faith and Fractured a Nation*. New York: W. W. Norton, 2020.

Egan, Rory B. "Lexical Evidence on Two Pauline Passages." *NovT* 19 (1977): 34–62.

Elliott, Neil. "The Anti-Imperial Message of the Cross." Pages 167–83 in *Paul and Empire: Religion and Power in Roman Imperial Society*. Edited by Richard A. Horsley. Harrisburg: Trinity Press International, 1997.

———. "The Apostle Paul and Empire." Pages 97–116 in *In the Shadow of Empire: Reclaiming the Bible as a History of Faithful Resistance*. Edited by Richard A. Horsley. Louisville: Westminster John Knox, 2008.

———. *The Arrogance of Nations: Reading Romans in the Shadow of Empire*. Minneapolis: Fortress, 2008.

———. "'Blasphemed among the Nations': Pursuing an Anti-Imperial 'Intertextuality' in Romans." Pages 213–33 in *As It Is Written: Studying Paul's Use of Scripture*. Edited by Stanley E. Porter and Christopher D. Stanley. SymS 50. Atlanta: Scholars Press, 2008.

Fanning, Buist M. *Verbal Aspect in New Testament Greek*. Oxford Theology and Religion Monographs. Oxford: Oxford University Press, 1990.

Fee, Gordon D. *Paul's Letter to the Philippians*. NICNT. Grand Rapids: Eerdmans, 1995.

Findley, George G. "St. Paul's Use of ΘΡΙΑΜΒΕΥΩ." *Expositor* 10 (1879): 403–21.

Fink, Robert O. "*Victoria Parthica* and Kindred *Victoriae*." YCS 8 (1942): 81–101.

Fisher, Walter R. "Narration as a Human Communication Paradigm: The Case of Public Moral Argument." *Communication Monographs* 51 (1984): 1–22.

———. "The Narrative Paradigm: An Elaboration." *Communication Monographs* 52 (1985): 347–67.

Flexsenhar, Michael, III. "Paul the Trojan Horse: The Legacy of Triumph in Philippians." *JSNT* 43 (2021): 437–49.

Foy-Vaillant, Jean. *De Aureis et Argenteis.* 3rd ed. Vol. 2 of *Numismata imperatorum Romanorum.* Paris: Jombert, 1694.

Funke, Peter. "Rom und das Nabatäerreich bis zur Aufrichtung der Provinz Arabia." Pages 1–18 in *Migratio et Commutatio: Studien zur Alten Geschichte und deren Nachleben, Festschrift Th. Pekáry.* Edited by Hans-Jochaim Drexhage and Julia Sünskes. St. Katharinen: Scripta Mercaturae, 1989.

Garland, David E. *2 Corinthians.* NAC 29. Nashville: Broadman & Holman, 1999.

Gettyimages. "US-POLITICS-ELECTION-TRUMP." https://www.gettyimages.de /detail/nachrichtenfoto/supporters-of-us-president-donald-trump-wear -gas-masks-nachrichtenfoto/1230505388.

Gibson, Roy K. *Man of High Empire: The Life of Pliny the Younger.* Oxford: Oxford University Press, 2020.

Gilbert, Cathrin, and Martin Machowecz, with Bodo Ramelow. "Ich verstecke mich nicht mehr." DIE ZEIT 5/2021. January 28, 2021. https://www.zeit.de /2021/05/bodo-ramelow-thueringen-ministerpraesident-clubhouse-candy -crush.

Gooder, Paula. *Phoebe: A Story (with Notes): Pauline Christianity in Narrative Form.* London: Hodder & Stoughton, 2018.

Green, Emma. "A Christian Insurrection." *The Atlantic.* January 8, 2021. https:// www.theatlantic.com/politics/archive/2021/01/evangelicals-catholics -jericho-march-capitol/617591/.

Gruber, M. Margareta. *Herrlichkeit in Schwachheit: Eine Auslegung der Apologie des Zweiten Korintherbriefs 2 Kor 2,14–6,13.* FB 89. Würzburg: Echter, 1998.

Guthrie, George H. "Paul's Triumphal Procession Imagery (2 Cor 2.14–16a): Neglected Points of Background." *NTS* 61 (2015): 79–91.

———. *2 Corinthians.* BECNT. Grand Rapids: Baker Academic, 2015.

Haddad, Najeeb T. *Paul, Politics, and New Creation: Reconsidering Paul and Empire.* Washington, DC: Rowman & Littlefield: 2020.

Hafemann, Scott J. *2 Corinthians.* The NIV Application Commentary. Grand Rapids: Zondervan, 2000.

———. *Suffering and the Spirit: An Exegetical Study of 2 Cor 2:14–3:3 Within the Context of the Corinthian Correspondence.* WUNT 2/19. Tübingen: Mohr, 1986.

Halbertsma, Ruurd B. "*Nulli tam laeti triumphi*: Constantine's Victory on a Reworked Cameo in Leiden." *BABESCH* 90 (2015): 221–35.

Hardin, Justin K. "Decrees and Drachmas at Thessalonica: An Illegal Assembly in Jason's House (Acts 17.1–10a)." *NTS* 52 (2006): 29–49.

———. *Galatians and the Imperial Cult.* WUNT 2/237. Tübingen: Mohr Siebeck, 2008.

Harrill, J. Albert. *Paul the Apostle: His Life and Legacy in Their Roman Context.* Cambridge: Cambridge University Press, 2012.

Hays, Richard B. *Echoes of Scripture in the Letters of Paul.* New Haven: Yale University Press: 1989.

Heilig, Christoph. "Biblical Words and Their Meaning: An Introduction to Lexical Semantics in the NIDNTTE." *Reviews of Biblical and Early Christian Studies.* June 15, 2015. https://rbecs.org/2015/06/17/nidntte/.

———. "Caesar and Paul in the Roman Triumphal Procession: Reading Col 2:15 in Light of 2 Cor 2:14." Paper given as part of the program unit "Bible and Empire" at the International SBL meeting in Berlin. August 9, 2017.

———. "The First Christians' Responses to Emperor Worship." *Reviews of Biblical and Early Christian Studies.* November 30, 2016. https://rbecs.org/2016/11/30/fcrw/.

———. *Hidden Criticism? The Methodology and Plausibility of the Search for a Counter-Imperial Subtext in Paul.* WUNT 2/392. Tübingen: Mohr Siebeck, 2015.

———. *Hidden Criticism? The Methodology and Plausibility of the Search for a Counter-Imperial Subtext in Paul.* Minneapolis: Fortress, 2017.

———. "Introduction." Pages xi–xiv in *Hidden Criticism? The Methodology and Plausibility of the Search for a Counter-Imperial Subtext in Paul.* Minneapolis: Fortress, 2017.

———. "Lexical Semantics and Lexicography." *Zürich New Testament Blog.* March 26, 2020. https://www.uzh.ch/blog/theologie-nt/2020/03/26/lexical-semantics-and-lexicography/.

———. "Methodological Considerations for the Search of Counter-Imperial 'Echoes' in Pauline Literature." Pages 73–92 in *Reactions to Empire: Proceedings of Sacred Texts in Their Socio-Political Contexts.* Edited by John A. Dunne and Dan Batovici. WUNT 2/372. Tübingen: Mohr Siebeck, 2014.

———. "The New Perspective (on Paul) on Peter: How the Philosophy of Historiography Can Help in Understanding Earliest Christianity." Pages 459–595 in *Christian Origins and the Establishment of the Early Jesus Movement.* Christian Origins and Greco-Roman Culture 4. Edited by Stanley E. Porter and Andrew W. Pitts. Leiden: Brill, 2018.

———. *Paul's Triumph: Reassessing 2 Corinthians 2:14 in Its Literary and Historical Context.* Leuven: Peeters, 2017.

————. *Paulus als Erzähler? Eine narratologische Perspektive auf die Paulusbriefe.* Berlin: de Gruyter, 2020.

————. Review of *Divine Honours for the Caesars: The First Christians' Responses,* by Bruce Winter. *JTS* 67 (2016): 754–57.

————. "What Bayesian Reasoning Can and Can't Do for Biblical Research." *Zürich New Testament Blog.* March 27, 2019. https://www.uzh.ch/blog/theolo gie-nt/2019/03/27/what-bayesian-reasoning-can-and-cant-do-for-biblical -research/.

Heilig, Theresa, and Christoph Heilig. "Historical Methodology." Pages 115–50 in *God and the Faithfulness of Paul: A Critical Examination of the Pauline Theology of N. T. Wright.* Edited by Christoph Heilig, J. Thomas Hewitt, and Michael F. Bird. WUNT 2/413. Tübingen: Mohr Siebeck, 2016; Minneapolis: Fortress, 2017.

————. "Teaching Biblical Exegesis: The Distinction between Methods of Description and Interpretation." *Didaktikos* (forthcoming).

Hekster, Olivier. "The Roman Army and Propaganda." Pages 339–58 in *A Companion to the Roman Army.* Edited by Paul Erdkamp. Blackwell Companions to the Ancient World. Malden: Blackwell, 2007.

Hengel, Martin. *Paulus und Jakobus: Kleine Schriften III.* WUNT 141. Tübingen: Mohr Siebeck, 2002.

Hengel, Martin, and Anna Maria Schwermer. *Paulus zwischen Damaskus und Antiochien: Die unbekannten Jahre des Apostels.* With a contribution by Ernst Axel Knauf. WUNT 108. Tübingen: Mohr Siebeck, 1998.

Hock, Andreas. "Christ Is the Parade: A Comparative Study of the Triumphal Procession in 2 Cor 2,14 and Col 2,15." *Bib* 88 (2007): 110–19.

Holland, Tom. *Dominion: How the Christian Revolution Remade the World.* New York: Basic Books, 2019.

Horrell, David G. *Becoming Christian: Essays on 1 Peter and the Making of Christian Identity.* LNTS 394. London: Bloomsbury, 2013.

Horsley, Richard A. "Introduction: Jesus, Paul, and the 'Arts of Resistance': Leaves from the Notebook of James C. Scott." Pages 1–26 in *Hidden Transcripts and the Arts of Resistance: Applying the Work of James C. Scott to Jesus and Paul.* Edited by Richard A. Horsley. SemeiaSt 48. Atlanta: Scholars Press, 2004.

Huttunen, Niko. *Early Christians Adapting to the Roman Empire: Mutual Recognition.* NovTSup 179. Leiden: Brill, 2020.

Itgenshorst, Tanja. *Katalog der Triumphe von 340 bis 19 vor Christus.* Accompanying CD-ROM of *Tota illa pompa: Der Triumph in der römischen Republik.* Hypomnemata 161. Göttingen: Vandenhoeck & Ruprecht, 2005.

————. *Tota illa pompa: Der Triumph in der römischen Republik.* Hypomnemata 161. Göttingen: Vandenhoeck & Ruprecht, 2005.

Jakobsmeier, Heinz. *Die Gallier-Rede des Claudius aus dem Jahr 48 n. Chr.: Historisch-philologische Untersuchungen und Kommentar zur* tabula Claudiana *aus Lyon.* Quellen und Forschungen zur Antiken Welt 63. Munich: utzverlag, 2019.

Judge, Edwin A. "The Decrees of Caesar at Thessalonica." *RTR* 30 (1971): 71–78.

————. *The First Christians in the Roman World: Augustan and New Testament Essays.* WUNT 229. Tübingen: Mohr Siebeck, 2008.

Keown, Mark J. "Did Paul Plan to Escape from Prison? (Philippians 1:19–26)." *Journal for the Study of Paul and His Letters* 5 (2015): 89–108.

Kim, Seyoon. *Christ and Caesar: The Gospel and the Roman Empire in the Writings of Paul and Luke.* Grand Rapids: Eerdmans, 2008.

Kinzig, Wolfram. *Christian Persecution in Antiquity.* Translated by Markus Bockmuehl. Waco: Baylor University Press, 2021.

Koch, Dietrich-Alex. "Gottes Triumph und die Aufgabe des Apostels: Überlegungen zu 2Kor 2,14." *Sacra Scripta* 16 (2018): 7–20.

————. Review of *Paul's Triumph: Reassessing 2 Corinthians 2:14 in Its Literary and Historical Context,* by Christoph Heilig. *TLZ* 143 (2018): 622–24.

Köppe, Tilmann, and Tom Kindt. *Erzähltheorie: Eine Einführung.* Reclams Universal-Bibliothek 17683. Stuttgart: Reclam, 2014.

Kralidis, Apostolos F. "Evidence for the Imperial Cult in Thessalonica in the First Century C.E." *ΚΟΣΜΟΣ/COSMOS* 2 (2013): 87–102.

Krauter, Stefan. *Studien zu Röm 13,1–7: Paulus und der politische Diskurs der neronischen Zeit.* WUNT 243. Tübingen: Mohr Siebeck, 2009.

Kypke, Georg David. *Acta, Apostolorvm, Epistolas et Apocalypsin.* Vol. 2. of *Observationes sacrae in Novi Foederis libros ex ax avctoribvs potissimvm Graecis et antiqvitatibvs.* Wrocław: Korn, 1755.

Lee, John A. L. *A History of New Testament Lexicography.* Studies in Biblical Greek 8. New York: Peter Lang, 2003.

Leidl, Christoph. *Appians Darstellung des 2. Punischen Krieges in Spanien (Iberike c. 1–38 § 1–158a): Text und Kommentar.* Münchner Arbeiten zur Alten Geschichte 11. Munich: Editio Maris, 1996.

Leisi, Ernst. *Der Wortinhalt: Seine Struktur im Deutschen und Englischen.* 4th ed. Heidelberg: Quelle & Meyer, 1971.

Leithoff, Johanna. *Macht der Vergangenheit: Zur Erringung, Verstetigung und Ausgestaltung des Principats unter Vespasian, Titus und Domitian.* Schriften zur politischen Kommunikation 19. Göttingen: Vandenhoeck & Ruprecht, 2014.

Longenecker, Bruce W. "Socio-Economic Profiling of the First Urban Christians."

Pages 36–59 in *After the First Urban Christians: The Social-Scientific Study of Pauline Christianity Twenty-Five Years Later*. Edited by Todd D. Still and David G. Horrell. London: T&T Clark, 2009.

Manseau, Peter. "His Pastors Tried to Steer Him Away from Social Media Rage: He Stormed the Capitol Anyway." *The Washington Post*. February 19, 2021. https://www.washingtonpost.com/religion/2021/02/19/michael-sparks-capitol-siege-jan-6-christian/.

Marshall, Peter. "A Metaphor of Social Shame: ΘΡΙΑΜΒΕΥΕΙΝ in 2 Cor. 2:14." *NovT* 25 (1983): 302–17.

Metro D.C. Synod, Evangelical Lutheran Church in America. "From the Bishop's Desk: Addressing the Events of January 6, 2021." Facebook. January 6, 2021. https://www.facebook.com/metrodcelca/videos/827487214464232/.

Miller, Colin. "The Imperial Cult in the Pauline Cities of Asia Minor and Greece." *CBQ* 72 (2010): 314–32.

Miller, John F. "Reading Cupid's Triumph." *CJ* 90 (1995): 287–94.

Molthagen, Joachim. "'*Cognitionbus de Christianis interfui numquam*': Das Nicht-wissen des Plinius und die Anfänge der Christenprozesse." *Zeitschrift für Theologie und Gemeinde* 9 (2004): 112–40.

———. *Der römische Staat und die Christen im zweiten und dritten Jahrhundert*. 2nd ed. Hypomnemata 28. Göttingen: Vandenhoeck & Ruprecht, 1975.

———. "Die ersten Konflikte der Christen in der griechisch-römischen Welt." *Historia* 40 (1991): 42–76.

———. "Die Lage der Christen im römischen Reich nach dem 1. Petrusbrief: Zum Problem einer Domitianischen Verfolgung." *Historia* 44 (1995): 422–58.

Moss, Candida. *The Myth of Persecution: How Early Christians Invented a Story of Martyrdom*. New York: HarperCollins, 2013.

Mullen, Lincoln. "The Fight to Define Romans 13." *The Atlantic*. June 15, 2018. https://www.theatlantic.com/ideas/archive/2018/06/romans-13/562916/.

Naham, Matt. "Pizzeria Owner Charged for Jan. 6 Insists She Is 'Not a Person,' Gets into Bible Quoting Exchange with Trump-Appointed Judge before Being Brought Back to Jail." *Law and Crime*. September 24, 2021. https://lawandcrime.com/u-s-capitol-breach/pizzeria-owner-charged-for-jan-6-insists-she-is-not-a-person-gets-into-bible-quoting-exchange-with-trump-appointed-judge-before-being-ordered-back-to-jail/.

Nicholson, John. "The Delivery and Confidentiality of Cicero's Letters." *CJ* 90 (1994): 33–63.

Nida, Eugene A., and Johannes P. Louw. *Lexical Semantics of the Greek New Testament: A Supplement to the Greek-English Lexicon of the New Testament Based on Semantic Domains*. SBLRBS 25. Atlanta: Scholars Press, 1992.

Öhler, Markus. "Römisches Vereinsrecht und christliche Gemeinden." Pages 51–71 in *Zwischen den Reichen: Neues Testament und Römische Herrschaft*. Edited by Michael Labahn and Jürgen Zangenberg. Texte und Arbeiten zum neutestamentlichen Zeitalter 36. Tübingen: A. Francke, 2002.

Omerzu, Heike. "Paul, the Praetorium and the Saints from Caesar's Household: Philippians Revisited in Light of Migration Theory." *JSNT* 43 (2021): 450–67.

Otte, Johann Baptist. *Spicilegium, sive, Excerpta ex Flavio Josepho ad Novi Testamenti*. Leiden: Hasebroek, 1741.

Park, David M. "Interpretative Value of the Metaphorical Constructions in 2 Corinthians." PhD diss., Southwestern Baptist Theological Seminary, 1976.

———. "The Value of Biblical Metaphors (II Cor. 2:14–17)." Pages 253–68 in *Metaphor and Religion: Theolinguistics 2*. Edited by Jean-Pierre van Noppen. Study Series of the Vrije Universiteit Brussel: New Series 12. Brussels: Vrije Universiteit Brussel, 1983.

Porter, Stanley E. "The Linguistic Competence of New Testament Commentaries." Pages 33–56 in *On the Writing of New Testament Commentaries: Festschrift for Grant R. Osborne on the Occasion of His 70th Birthday*. Edited by Stanley E. Porter and Eckhard J. Schnabel. TENTS 8. Leiden: Brill, 2012.

Rabens, Volker. "Paul's Mission Strategy in the Urban Landscape of the First-Century Roman Empire." Pages 99–122 in *The Urban World and the First Christians*. Edited by Steve Walton, Paul Trebilco, and David Gill. Grand Rapids: Eerdmans, 2017.

Reichert, Angelika. "Durchdachte Konfusion: Plinius, Trajan und das Christentum." *ZNW* 93 (2002): 227–50.

Reichert, Angelika. "Gegensätzliche Wahrnehmungen einer ambivalenten Krisensituation: Das Plinius-Trajan-Konzept, der 1. Petrusbrief und die Johannesapokalypse." Pages 281–302 in *Bedrängnis und Identität: Studien zu Situation, Kommunikation und Theologie des 1. Petrusbriefes*. Edited by David S. du Toit, with the help of Torsten Jantsch. BZNW 200. Berlin: de Gruyter, 2013.

Richardson, John S. *Appian: Wars of the Romans in Iberia; With an Introduction, Translation and Commentary*. Warminster: Aris & Phillips, 2000.

Robbins, Jeffrey W., and Clayton Crockett, eds. *Doing Theology in the Age of Trump: A Critical Report on Christian Nationalism*. Eugene: Cascade, 2018.

———. "Introduction." Pages xi–xvii in *Doing Theology in the Age of Trump: A Critical Report on Christian Nationalism*. Edited by Jeffrey W. Robbins and Clayton Crockett. Eugene: Cascade, 2018.

Robinson, Laura. "Hidden Transcripts? The Supposedly Self-Censoring Paul and

Rome as Surveillance State in Modern Pauline Scholarship." *NTS* 67 (2021): 55–72.

Rordorf, Willy. "Die neronische Christenverfolgung im Spiegel der apokryphen Paulusakten." *NTS* 28 (1982): 365–74.

Rowell, Andy. "Tony Jones, N. T. Wright, Richard Bauckham, Scot McKnight, James K. A. Smith, Robert Bella and John Milbank: Audio from SBL and AAR." *Church Leadership Conversations*. November 21, 2007. andyrowell .net/andy_rowell/2007/11/audio-from-a-fe.html.

Sampley, J. Paul. "The Second Letter to the Corinthians." Pages 3–180 in vol. 11 of *NIB*. Edited by Leander E. Keck et al. Nashville: Abingdon, 2000.

Schmeller, Thomas. Review of *Paul's Triumph: Reassessing 2 Corinthians 2:14 in Its Literary and Historical Context*, by Christoph Heilig. *BZ* 63 (2019): 339–41.

Schmidt, Eckart David. Review of *Hidden Criticism? The Methodology and Plausibility of the Search for a Counter-Imperial Subtext in Paul*, by Christoph Heilig. SNTSU 42 (2017): 226–32.

Schnelle, Udo. *Die ersten 100 Jahre des Christentums: 30–130 n. Chr.* 3rd ed. Göttingen: Vandenhoeck & Ruprecht, 2019.

———. *Einleitung in das Neue Testament.* 8th ed. Göttingen: Vandenhoeck & Ruprecht, 2013.

Schollmeyer, Patrick. "Kleopatras Preziosen: Das hellenistische Schatzerbe der römischen Kaiser." *Antike Welt* 5 (2017): 8–12.

Scott, James C. *Domination and the Arts of Resistance: Hidden Transcripts*. New Haven: Yale University Press, 1990.

Sherwin-White, A. N. *Roman Society and Roman Law in the New Testament*. Oxford: Clarendon, 1963.

Smith, R. R. R. "*Maiestas Serena*: Roman Court Cameos and Early Imperial Poetry and Panegyric." *JRS* 111 (2021): 1–78.

———. *The Marble Reliefs from the Julio-Claudian Sebasteion at Aphrodisias*. Vol. 6 of *Aphrodisias*. Darmstadt: von Zabern, 2013.

Snyder, Glenn E. *Acts of Paul: The Formation of a Pauline Corpus*. WUNT 2/352. Tübingen: Mohr Siebeck, 2013.

———. "History of the Martyrdom of Paul." Pages 343–73 in *The Last Years of Paul: Essays from the Tarragona Conference, June 2013*. Edited by Armand Puig i Tàrrech, John M. G. Barclay, and Jörg Frey, with the assistance of Orrey McFarland. WUNT 352. Tübingen: Mohr Siebeck, 2015.

Spawforth, Antony J. S. "Corinth, Argos, and the Imperial Cult: Pseudo-Julian, *Letters* 198." *Hesperia* 63 (1994): 211–32.

Standhartinger, Angela. "Aus der Welt eines Gefangenen: Die Kommunikationsstruktur des Philipperbriefs im Spiegel seiner Abfassungssituation." *NovT* 55 (2013): 140–67.

———. "Die paulinische Theologie im Spannungsfeld römisch-imperialer Machtpolitik: Eine neue Perspektive auf Paulus, kritisch geprüft anhand des Philipperbriefs." Pages 364–82 in *Religion, Politik und Gewalt*. Edited by Friedrich Schweitzer. Veröffentlichungen der Wissenschaftlichen Gesellschaft für Theologie 29. Gütersloh: Gütersloher Verlagshaus, 2006.

———. "Greetings from Prison and Greetings from Caesar's House (Philippians 4.22): A Reconsideration of an Enigmatic Greek Expression in the Light of the Context and Setting of Philippians." *JSNT* 43 (2021): 468–84.

———. "Letter from Prison as Hidden Transcript: What It Tells Us about the People at Philippi." Pages 107–40 in *The People beside Paul: The Philippian Assembly and History from Below*. Edited by Joseph A. Marchal. ECL 17. Atlanta: SBL Press, 2015.

Standing, Giles. "The Claudian Invasion of Britain and the Cult of *Victoria Britannica*." *Britannia* 34 (2003): 281–88.

Stewart, P. N. C. "Inventing Britain: The Roman Creation and Adaptation of an Image." *Britannia* 26 (1995): 1–10.

Strecker, Christian. "Taktiken der Aneignung: Politische Implikationen der paulinischen Botschaft im Kontext der römischen imperialen Wirklichkeit." Pages 114–48 in *Das Neue Testament und politische Theorie: Interdisziplinäre Beiträge zur Zukunft des Politischen*. Edited by Eckart Reinmuth. Religions-Kulturen 9. Stuttgart: Kohlhammer, 2011.

Tajra, Harry W. *The Martyrdom of St. Paul: Historical and Judicial Context, Tradition and Legends*. WUNT 2/67. Tübingen: Mohr Siebeck, 1994.

Theißen, Gerd. "Respekt vor der Verfassung: Gegenlektüre eines staatstragenden Textes (Röm 13,1–7)." Pages 129–33 in *Erlösungsbilder: Predigten und Meditationen von Gerd Theißen*. Gütersloh: Kaiser, 2002.

Theophilos, Michael P. *Numismatics and Greek Lexicography*. London: T&T Clark, 2019.

Thompson, Jeremy, and Wendy Widder. "Major Approaches to Linguistics." Pages 87–133 in *Linguistic and Biblical Exegesis*. Edited by Douglas Mangum and Josh Westbury. Lexham Methods Series 2. Bellingham: Lexham Press, 2017.

Thraede, Klaus. "Noch einmal: Plinius d. J. und die Christen." *ZNW* 95 (2006): 102–28.

Turpin, William. *Ovid "Amores": Book 1*. Dickinson College Commentaries. Cambridge: Open Book, 2016.

Webb, William J. *Returning Home: New Covenant and Second Exodus as the Con-*

text for 2 Corinthians 6.14–7.1. JSNTSup 85. Sheffield: Sheffield Academic Press, 1993.

Weill, Kelly. "Pizzeria Owner Mounts Truly Bizarre Defense for Jan. 6 Riots." *Daily Beast.* July 11, 2021. Updated July 12, 2021. https://www.thedailybeast.com /pizzeria-owner-pauline-bauer-mounts-truly-bizarre-defense-for-jan-6 -riots.

Weinberg, Saul S. *The Southeast Building, the Twin Basilicas, the Mosaic House.* Vol 1.5 of *Corinth: Results of Excavations Conducted by the American School of Classical Studies at Athens.* Princeton: The American School of Classical Studies at Athens, 1960.

White, Joel R. "Anti-Imperial Subtexts in Paul: An Attempt at Building a Firmer Foundation." *Bib* 90 (2009): 305–33.

Wilckens, Ulrich. *Röm 12–16.* Vol. 3 of *Der Brief an die Römer.* 3 vols. EKKNT 6.3. Zurich: Benziger, 1982.

Winter, Bruce W. *Divine Honours for the Caesars: The First Christians' Responses.* Grand Rapids: Eerdmans, 2015.

Wintjes, Jorit. *Die Römische Armee auf dem* Oceanus: *Zur römischen Seekriegsge- schichte in Nordwesteuropa.* Mnemosyne Supplements: History and Archae- ology of Classical Antiquity 433. Leiden: Brill, 2019.

Winzenburg, Justin. *Ephesians and Empire: An Evaluation of the Epistle's Subversion of Roman Imperial Ideology.* WUNT 2/573. Tübingen: Mohr Siebeck, 2022.

Wischmeyer, Oda. "Staat und Christen nach Römer 13,1–7: Ein neuer herme- neutischer Zugang." Pages 149–62 in *Kirche und Volk Gottes: Festschrift für Jürgen Roloff zum 70. Geburtstag.* Edited by Martin Karrer, Wolfgang Kraus, and Otto Merk. Neukirchen-Vluyn: Neukirchener, 2000.

Witherington, Ben, III. *Conflict and Community in Corinth: A Socio-Rhetorical Commentary on 1 and 2 Corinthians.* Grand Rapids: Eerdmans, 1995.

Wolter, Michael. *Röm 9–16.* Vol. 2 of *Der Brief an die Römer.* 2 vols. EKKNT 6.2. Göttingen: Vandenhoeck & Ruprecht, 2019.

Woods, David. "Caligula's Seashells." *GR* 47 (2000): 80–87.

Wright, N. T. "America's Exceptionalist Justice." *The Guardian.* May 5, 2011. https:// www.theguardian.com/commentisfree/belief/2011/may/05/america-lone -ranger.

———. *Paul: In Fresh Perspective.* Minneapolis: Fortress, 2005.

———. *Paul and the Faithfulness of God.* Christian Origins and the Question of God 4. London: SPCK, 2013.

———. "Paul's Gospel and Caesar's Empire." Pages 160–83 in *Paul and Politics: Ek- klesia, Israel, Imperium, Interpretation: Essays in Honor of Krister Stendahl.* Edited by Richard A. Horsley. Harrisburg: Trinity Press International, 2000.

————. *2 Corinthians*. Paul for Everyone. London: SPCK, 2003.

Yoder, Joshua. *Representatives of Roman Rule: Roman Provincial Governors in Luke-Acts*. BZNW 209. Berlin: de Gruyter, 2014.

Zwierlein-Diehl, Erika, ed. *Magie der Steine: Die antiken Prunkkameen im Kunsthistorischen Museum*. Vienna: Brandstätter, 2008.

Index of Authors

Index of Subjects

Index of Scripture and Other Ancient Texts